The Legacy of German Jewry

The Legacy of German Jewry

Hermann Levin Goldschmidt
Translated by David Suchoff

FORDHAM UNIVERSITY PRESS

NEW YORK 2007

Library of Congress Cataloging-in-Publication Data

Goldschmidt, Hermann Levin, 1914–1998.
[Vermächtnis des deutschen Judentums. English]
The legacy of German Jewry / Hermann Levin Goldschmidt ; translated by David Suchoff.
   p.   cm.
Includes bibliographical references and index.
ISBN 978-0-8232-2826-3 (cloth : alk. paper)
1. Jews—Germany—History—1800–1933.   2. Judaism—Germany.   I. Title.
DS134.25.G6513   2007
943'.004924—dc22

                                              2007039171

Printed in the United States of America
09 08 07   5 4 3 2 1

Originally published as *Das Vermächtnis des deutschen Judentums* (Frankfurt am Main: Europäische Verlagsanstalt, 1957; Vienna: Passagen Verlag 1994).

CONTENTS

The Legacy of German Jewry

Willi Goetschel and David Suchoff

When *The Legacy of German Jewry* was first published in 1957, Hermann Levin Goldschmidt's book seemed a less than pressing concern to contemporary German and Jewish thought. Germany's "economic miracle" and resolve to "master the past" set its sights on an entirely new culture, as if the project of modernity were to be invented once more, this time in determined quest of a pristine renewal. At the time same, Jewish culture was in its postwar period of consolidation, responding to Cold War political pressures, moving resolutely forward to create new forms of national identification and expression. Germany's "zero-hour," however, as the phrase from the period had it, suggested a ring of bitter truth, audible amidst the din of efforts at reconstruction undertaken by the cultural left and right. The foundation of the state of Israel in 1948 gave Jewish life a new harbor for its hopes, international recognition, a burgeoning national center, and a feeling of renewed cultural pride, advocating a break with the diaspora that posed the problem in no uncertain terms. The future of

Jewish culture, it seemed, could be secured only through a painful separation from the past.

German Jewish culture, in this setting, suffered from a double sense of displacement. Postwar Germany seemed to view its surviving Jewish citizens with a sense of guilt at best, oblivious to the profound debt the German tradition owed to Jewish languages and culture. At the same time, the Jewish cultural renewal underway in Israel began to describe the history of German Jewry as a political and cultural dead end, and to view its achievements as anchored in illusion. According to Gershom Scholem, the Buber-Rosenzweig translation of the Hebrew Bible was "a kind of *Gast-Geschenk*," a present left by eager Jewish guests to their unwilling German hosts, which became their "tombstone," not the sign of a deep cultural exchange.[1] The German Jewish dialogue may indeed have taken place, Scholem noted acerbically, but only as wish-fulfillment: a self-deception indulged in by the Jews alone, who would ultimately be ignored, and worse, by the Germans they believed to be their partners.[2] While Scholem's writings eloquently captured the post-Holocaust sense that an "abyss" separated Germans and Jews, his role as a founder of modern Israeli scholarship led him to deny the obvious, intimate connections between a renascent Jewish culture and its roots in the German language and past.[3] German culture, meanwhile, continued to turn to its remaining Jews with a guilty but forgetful embrace. Scholem and many others faced what seemed to be a stark choice: between a Germany still steeped in denial, and newly independent, and assertive forms of Jewish life in Israel and beyond.

Hermann Levin Goldschmidt's biography placed him squarely between these competing currents of postwar German and Jewish culture. Born in Berlin in 1914, Goldschmidt was raised in a typically assimilated and successful family completely at home in the bourgeois form of the German classical tradition. Leaving Germany in 1938, Goldschmidt went to Zurich to study philosophy, completing his dissertation in 1941. Entitled "Nihilism in Light of a Critical Philosophy," this study was Goldschmidt's analysis of the bankruptcy of German philosophy, but it also signaled his rediscovery of the rich and powerful significance of his own Jewish sources.[4] In the midst of World War II, during one of humanity's darkest hours, Goldschmidt began what would eventually become one of the postwar period's major acts of Jewish cultural assertion. In Zurich, Goldschmidt set out to preserve the message of the Jewish tradition whose European existence, if one followed the news, seemed to have come to an end. As a refugee in Switzerland, Goldschmidt witnessed the murder and loss of Jewish life in Germany and the rest of Europe. Instead of relying on the notion of an abyss to describe the palpable break between German and Jewish culture, Goldschmidt faced the destruction, and saw the history of Jewish culture in Germany not as an end, but as part of a continuing, unfinished history. In Zurich, Goldschmidt developed his concepts of dialogue, the nature of modernity, and the continuing importance of Judaism and its message.[5]

Today, the boom of interest in the German Jewish experience has made its echoes heard everywhere. In Berlin the hypermodern design of the new Jewish Museum symbolizes this powerful attachment in startling architectural form. After the fall of the Berlin Wall, a new Germany has had to reimagine a new political and cultural identity, and the Jewish "past" has emerged as a history to be granted official, national recognition and institutionalization. German Jews resurfaced everywhere, or so it seemed. This obsession with history as well as memory sent a different but parallel message: both signaled a new recognition of the real loss that Germany, along with the rest of the world, had suffered in the almost complete destruction of its Jewish inheritance, and expressed a kind of longing for orientation in what Jürgen Habermas called the "postnational" constellation.[6] While there was thus something liberating in this turn toward the German Jewish past, history and the proliferation of the culture of memory were more a symptom than an answer. The irony was truly postcontemporary, in the sense of the future's signs being preserved in the past. German Jewish culture was being treated as archaic at the very moment it had an urgent contribution to make: not only to a new, "multicultural" German society, but also to an increasingly transnational world. The dynamic potential of the German Jewish contribution needs to be future-oriented in this context, not antiquarian, and Goldschmidt's life project—both in his work on German Jewry and beyond—laid the groundwork for this urgent and contemporary task. Goldschmidt teaches us how to rethink German Jewish culture as a site where the unfinished project of modernity depends on an encounter with the other. The path followed by German Jewry in this book leads to a postcontemporary threshold, where the importance of alterity to cultural creation comes into critical view.

Goldschmidt defines this Jewish achievement as its capacity to discover the linkages between German culture's most universal aspirations and

Jewish cultural particularity. German Jewish culture, he argues, must be regarded as one of the most forceful articulations of the modern project as a quest for the universal recognition of difference in all its cultural and philosophical forms. In its early stages, Goldschmidt's thought worked out this conception of modernity in his concept of the "dialogic," his notion that the mutual constitution of contending voices had transformed the traditional notion of a national culture as a seamless whole.[7] German Jewish writers and thinkers, he argues in this book, helped to create the modern notion of a liberated, modern culture, by connecting their inward quest to recover Jewish sources with humanity's aspirations to freedom. To understand this difference-centered interpretation of the German Jewish achievement, the inner and outer development expressed in its culture and way of life, and the legacy German Jews left to the post-Holocaust world, Goldschmidt himself turned to the biblical sources of the Jewish tradition. These efforts, undertaken during the war and after in Zurich, would bear fruit in a new interpretation of German Jewry as the bearer of a very modern, and very Jewish vision of liberation at the heart of *The Legacy of German Jewry*.

From Dialogue to Legacy: Philosophic and Literary Contexts

In working through traditional Jewish sources, Goldschmidt's philosophy casts the concept of modernity in a new and different light. After Nietzsche, Goldschmidt realized that philosophy's overreaching claim to a monopoly on truth, and privileged access to its determination, had finally run its course. Goldschmidt's early critique of philosophy in its grand, overreaching Western forms led him to recognize the emancipatory potential of the German Jewish tradition of thought. Thinkers like Hermann Cohen, Martin Buber, and Franz Rosenzweig had already challenged the universal title to reason that the philosophic tradition had so blithely claimed as its own. The "sources of Judaism," as Hermann Cohen so radically put it, though long ignored by the discourse of reason, were not historical relics, but a living voice with redemptive, critical force. In rediscovering this tradition, Goldschmidt had not hidden himself in the past, or turned away from the horrific concerns of the present, but moved forward, expanding the confines of modern philosophic practice. Where philosophy had seen the end of reason in existential, Marxist, or theological terms, Goldschmidt understood his return to Jewish sources as a new beginning. These sources, and the German Jewish commentary to which they gave rise, had already addressed the importance of historic particularity in the construction of reason. The claims of the particular, Goldschmidt understood, had yet to be granted their full importance by the tradition of philosophic thought.

Along with this work in philosophy proper, Goldschmidt began to read German Jewish writers such as Heine, Schnitzler, Wasserman, Kafka, Werfel, Zweig, and Wasserman as exemplary articulations of what seemed to be an insuperable divide between a universalizing German culture and its minority voices. These texts laid out the haunting dilemma of Jewish exclusion as a central theme of modern German literature.[8] Wasserman's *Mein Weg als Deutscher und als Jude* (My Path as German and Jew), for instance, exposed the false promise German culture had made to its Jewish citizens, and the tragedy of Jewish belief in universal reason as the royal road to acceptance. Goldschmidt's literary criticism—like his Kafka essay, published in the American journal *Commentary*—helped readers understand German Jewish fiction as an expression of the unbearable suffering of marginal existence.[9] While others began to conceive of German Jewish culture as a fatal error, Goldschmidt recognized a different, and sometimes hidden dialogue between German culture and its Jewish voices. This critical dialogue occurred in literature, as Heine reminds us, but just as deeply in the philosophic tradition of German Jewish thought. Reason, Cohen, Buber, and Rosenzweig maintained, could not be conceived of as a universal project. In their rethinking of Western philosophy, Judaism was no longer a particularistic leftover from the past, superseded by the Hegelian, that is to say, the Christian march of progress. Instead, Jewish tradition became a crucial and coequal partner in a long-standing, historic dialogue between the quest for universal freedom and respect for its particular forms. This dialogue was the expression of a modernity rediscovering its debts to the Jewish tradition: the "sources of Judaism," as German Jewish thinkers demonstrated, were central, not marginal for the modern reconception of a philosophy, and theology, that had never given Judaism its due.[10]

The liberating power of attending to the dialogue of reason with the Jewish tradition soon became apparent in Goldschmidt's work. Capturing the force of Hermann Cohen's conceptual breakthrough, Goldschmidt advanced a bold model of cultural interaction that traced the actual, historical give and take between German and Jewish, "universal" and "particular" cultures.[11] This dialogical relationship would become central to Goldschmidt's thought. While Cohen, Buber, and Rosenzweig developed their dialogical models in terms of contemporary philosophical language, Goldschmidt removed dialogue from this displaced, homeless status, and anchored it in the lived complexity of historical experience. Goldschmidt's dialogic model began to document the productive results of this exchange between diametrically opposed cultural positions, and to develop a new way of valuing the past. Previous historical and philosophical accounts had emphasized the fated, one-way march of historical progress. Instead, Goldschmidt stressed that history was not a collection of facts moving forward, but constituted by a back and forth of contending, opposed voices. While for Buber dialogue meant the event-bound aspect of the "dialogic principle," Goldschmidt developed the dialogic (Dialogik) as a critical concept, and used it to describe the continual reciprocity and conflict that defines culture, history, and tradition and the individual's understanding of them as well. In *Philosophie als Dialogik* (1948), Goldschmidt expanded his understanding of the dialogic as an insight into the open-ended nature of the historical process, and of the production of knowledge as well. Radical for its time, Goldschmidt's thought introduced a paradigm that spoke to his contemporaries' need for an emancipated view of both philosophy and history. Dialogic offered a challenging answer to the dead end of historical experience and contemporary philosophic thought.

After a fourteen-year stay in Switzerland as a refugee without Swiss citizenship or the legal right to reside there, Goldschmidt was finally granted Swiss residency in 1951. Soon thereafter, he founded the Jüdisches Lehrhaus Zürich outside the university and its constraints. If Franz Rosenzweig's Jüdisches Lehrhaus in Frankfurt addressed the predicament of Jewish identity in a Weimar Germany alienated by its confrontation with modernity, Goldschmidt and his contemporaries confronted a radically different and deeper dilemma. At this postwar moment, Judaism had been called into question in the most existential way. The depth of this challenge gave all questions regarding Judaism, Jewish history, and identity a new and sharper sense of urgency. The guiding insight of Goldschmidt's work at the Jüdisches Lehrhaus was postcontemporary: that Judaism's present depends on the past, and a working-through of the Jewish tradition that would rediscover its meaning for the future. The Lehrhaus did not look to "master the past," as the German phrase had it, a term with negative connotations that gained wide currency in Germany but that could also imply a desire for repression (*Vergangenheitsbewältigung*). Opposed to any attempt to draw an historical divide between a lost world of the past and the present, Goldschmidt's Lehrhaus instead emphasized the continuing importance and contribution of Jewish life in Germany.[12] Founded and directed by Goldschmidt from 1951 until it closed its doors in 1962, the Lehrhaus began a project whose results were gathered in the publication in 1957 of *The Legacy of German Jewry*.

In the year of his death, Leo Baeck recommended that the Europäische Verlagsanstalt publish *The Legacy of German Jewry*, and its first edition appeared in 1957. The third edition in 1965 contained substantial new additions, all included in the final German edition issued under Goldschmidt's supervision in 1994. In one sense, Goldschmidt continued the line of thought that Baeck had pioneered at the beginning of the twentieth century in his work *The Essence of Judaism* (1905).[13] Both reject the normative conventions of historiography, which separate cultural and intellectual history from political events. As a result, both Baeck and Goldschmidt produced wide-ranging, unconventional histories in the strict sense of the word, writing innovative works that reclaimed Judaism's history as a powerful presence in twentieth-century thought. The different historical points of departure were more than apparent to Goldschmidt. Where Baeck looked confidently forward with liberal hope to Judaism's eventual inclusion as a co-equal partner in culture and society, Goldschmidt was forced to look backward after the Holocaust, and recover the tradition that German Jewish culture had bequeathed. The backward glance of *The Legacy of German Jewry*, in other words, became its way of looking to the future, a redemptive notion of the cultural past that Adorno's *Negative Dialectics* (1966) would express in philosophic terms: "Philosophy, which once seemed obsolete, lives on, because the moment to realize it was missed."[14]

The Origins of the Modern

Grounding his book in a critical reappraisal of the Jewish role in "the breakthrough to modernity," Goldschmidt uses section 1 of *The Legacy of German Jewry* to change the terms commonly used to describe the process known in historiography as Jewish emancipation. Here, Goldschmidt describes a historical trajectory that differs from standard narratives of the "Origins of the Modern," the title of his first section of part 1. In Goldschmidt's account, Jews were not idly sitting by, waiting for an emancipation and inclusion that would liberate them from the ghetto and its political and social constraints. On the contrary, *The Legacy of German Jewry* begins with the reminder that Jewish society and culture is one of humanity's oldest messengers of a radical vision of universal liberation. This comprehensive view of Jewish history as a tradition of progress argues for the importance of figures as diverse as the Baal Shem Tov, the founder of the Hasidic movement, Baruch de Spinoza, and Moses Mendelssohn. Jewish tradition for Goldschmidt was not simply religious backwardness to be overcome. As the pairing of the Baal Shem Tov and Spinoza already suggests, Goldschmidt saw their transformative views of biblical thought and Jewish religiosity as harbingers of modernity's push for emancipation from the limits of tradition. With these predecessors as his foundation, Mendelssohn could be understood by Goldschmidt as a thinker who accomplished a "breakthrough to modernity," building on cornerstones already laid by Jewish civilization in the past.

In this account, Mendelssohn assumes the status of an exemplary figure. His publication of *Jerusalem, or On Religious Power and Judaism* in 1783 was a signal event and, as Goldschmidt calls it, Mendelssohn's "declaration of independence." Mendelssohn defined the Jewish breakthrough to modernity as neither a particular event of significance to the Jews alone, nor a transcendent achievement that would require Jews to leave their traditions behind. "Mendelssohn," according to Goldschmidt, "instead . . . views the particular freedom he demands on behalf of the Jews and the universal freedom to which all peoples are entitled as one and the same." For Goldschmidt, the Jewish breakthrough to modernity found liberating expression in Hasidism, which broke a narrow religious framework for tradition and validated individualism, albeit within a new religious form. Spinoza's philosophic project, by contrast, broke with religious presuppositions altogether, and created a modern, critical view of culture and society in which Jews could realize their full individuality and potential. For the first time, a Jew and philosopher had come to see tradition as a fundamental source of modernity. On a practical level, Goldschmidt points out, Mendelssohn took up both of these strands, and grasped modernity as the creative contest between these dialogically contending secular and religious voices. As a leading spokesperson for the rights of Jews to join modernity as full partners, Mendelssohn argued for "Equal Rights, not Assimilation." Decades of advocacy on behalf of Jewish equality led Mendelssohn to write *Jerusalem* in 1783, a work that rethinks both Jewish tradition and the obligations of modernity to particular cultures. "Mendelssohn's efforts," Goldschmidt argues, "made it possible for the Jews to enter the modern world, while at the same time introducing the world to the universal truth that a living Judaism would continue to exist."

German Jewry's Outer Development

Goldschmidt understands Mendelssohn's biography and career as a harbinger of the outer and inner development that German Jewish modernity would undertake. Subsequent sections of *The Legacy of German Jewry* reread German Jewish cultural and political history as a two-sided process, reaching outward toward a universal modern culture and inward toward the consolidation of Judaism's particular strengths. "Outer Development" interprets movements as diverse as the Wissenschaft des Judentums, the creation of the modern discipline of Jewish history, the quest for equal rights, Gabriel Riesser's self-conscious reassertion of the name "Jew," Martin Buber's rediscovery of traditional Jewish culture as world literature and philosophy, Herzl's Zionism, and the Jewish battle against anti-Semitism, its "greatest foe," as part of the same modern project. Goldschmidt defines the outward cultural reach of German Jewry as part and parcel of the project of Jewish emancipation itself. As a result, Goldschmidt understands political efforts that might at first glance seem at odds as partners in the same emancipatory quest to establish Judaism's universal right to particularity. "Outer Development," for Goldschmidt, means finding the legal and political venues to assert Jewish cultural particularity as essential to the universal claims of modernity.

Herzl's project of establishing a Jewish state, with all the trappings of a modern nation, was thus for Goldschmidt a keen response to the predicament Jewry confronted when, in the era of imperial crisis, European nationalism took on new urgency. Every particular form of human existence, or so it seemed, required a universal outlet to remain part of the modern world, and minority nations were no exception. Herzl's greatness consisted of his bold response to the exigency of this historic moment, and the statesmanlike skill and wisdom he displayed in tirelessly advocating the Jewish cause to the world. In an era of heightened nationalism, Jewry would be able to renew its creative powers only if it could discover its own form of cultural expression. In keeping with Goldschmidt's dialogic perspective, Herzl's Zionism was a "dual legacy," both particular and universal in its effects. First, the quest to establish a home for the Jewish people was an attempt to guarantee the political existence of the Jews in a world in which statehood alone could legitimate a people's continuing existence. The liberatory power of Herzl's dream, however, was at the same time a legacy for all nations: politics, in his vision, was the sphere of human activity in which the particular aspirations of all peoples could find a legitimate form of self-determination. In this spirit, Goldschmidt interprets Herzl's rejection of *Homeward* as the name for the official organ of the Zionist movement as symbolic of the universal reach of his thought. Instead of a narrow, nationalistic slogan, Herzl chose a name that expressed mankind's common longing for freedom, recognition, and peace: *The World*.

Martin Buber's life work, in Goldschmidt's presentation, offers a different version of the dual force of German Jewry's outward reach. As a philosopher and cultural leader, Buber, as Goldschmidt points out, gave Jewish religiosity a modern form, both in his translations of Hasidic tales into German and his assertion of Jewish nationhood as part of the Zionist movement. "Outer Development," in Buber's case, meant taking the particular and traditional sources of Eastern European, Yiddish-speaking Jewish culture, as well as Hebrew, and asserting their modern philosophical and political forms. In his work, traditional Jewish culture was set in dialogue with cutting-edge developments in twentieth-century thought. The discovery of the I-Thou relationship recovers the innovative, open-ended force of Jewish tradition, and makes it possible to grasp the creative potential of its modern impulses. Buber's constant commitment to "stand up responsibly to the world," however, set him in opposition to modernity and political convenience. As a nationalist, Buber would oppose Herzl, and argue for the importance of cultural work, "consistent in his oppositional stance." Buber's "life work" created modern forms for traditional Jewish culture, while insisting that this outward reach would be meaningless unless it preserved the particular, "face-to-face" forms, ethical norms, and biblical message that had helped to set the modern project in motion.

Assimilation, in other words, was only half of the story. The dialectic of outer development, for Goldschmidt, pushed German Jewry into world culture as the only possible arena in which Jewish culture could realize its full potential. That consolidation and renewal, at the same time, turned its most profound thinkers back to their own sources, bringing thinkers like Rozenzweig, Baeck, and Cohen to rethink the most particular and specific aspects of the Jewish cultural tradition. This "Inner Development," as Goldschmidt calls it, was the inevitable, dialectical result of the push forward into modernity. The modern world that might guarantee the continuity of Jewish life and the fullest expression of its message would be meaningless unless it carried with it the depths of the tradition that German Jewish thinkers explored with a unique and penetrating vision.

Inner Development: Recovery and Renewal

The German Jewish move outward, as Goldschmidt describes it, was also a contest and struggle with assimilation. But as the phrase "dual legacy" suggested in the book's previous section, this assertion of Jewish culture in the German cultural sphere was far from a one-sided process. As German Jews became part of German society, this consolidation came under increasing attack. Jewish emancipation came to be seen as a no-win affair: either a loss of Jewish tradition and identity, or an unseemly arrogation of cultural privileges and political rights reserved for "Germans only." While German Jewish writers had to wrestle with this predicament, Goldschmidt sees the encounter with the pressures of assimilation as a productive spur to the deepest and most creative impulses of Jewish thought. Instead of viewing the entry into German culture as a dead end or fatally one-sided process, Goldschmidt redefines assimilation and the Jewish quest for acceptance as the challenge that enabled the project of German Jewish inner development to bear fruit.

The move outward, Goldschmidt argues, motivated the work of Hermann Cohen, Leo Baeck, Martin Buber, Franz Rosenzweig, and Simon Dubnow, who shaped the critical force of this inner growth. For these and other prominent Jewish historians and thinkers, addressing the mainstream intellectual establishment meant challenging its bias against Jews and Jewish tradition. Responding to the distorting dictates of assimilation and the dominant interpretation of Judaism, these writers engaged German claims of cultural superiority directly. They self-consciously created new forms of Jewish cultural expression, historiography, and theology that revised those claims and gave Jewish perspectives an equal voice. Assimilation and its pressures, Goldschmidt argues, provoked German Jewish thinkers to reexamine their own tradition and its sources. The result was the response of Jewish inner development: a rethinking of Jewish tradition that was able to assert its powerfully modern, critical force.

Leo Baeck exemplifies this self-conscious pride in Judaism that characterized German Jewry's inner development. As one of the most significant champions of liberal Judaism, Baeck became a leading spokesman for Jewish culture in Germany. And to many critics in his period and after, Baeck's theology and history of Judaism seemed an overly, if not exclusively, German reading of Jewish tradition and its sources. In fact, the title of Baeck's signal work, *The Essence of Judaism*, carries a quintessentially German ring that seems to proclaim a desire to define Judaism as a definitively German kind of essence. For Goldschmidt, however, Baeck did anything but posit Judaism as a separate, metaphysical absolute. The conception and publication of *The Essence of Judaism* was one of the fiercest moments in the struggle for Jewish cultural autonomy, a struggle that "ultimately produced one of the most crucial intellectual breakthroughs and victories of Judaism in modernity." Harnack's popular and influential series of lectures, "The Essence of Christianity," had gained wide currency and acclaim when published in book form: its claim for the superiority of Christianity seemed to have demonstrated Judaism's cultural inferiority once and for all. In response, Baeck's book offered a bold and self-conscious articulation of Judaism as a living and vital tradition. The cultural significance of Judaism, he argued, had to be recognized as a crucial and equal contributor to a modern concept of religion. Baeck's work takes Jewish emancipation to a new and assertive stage, reclaiming full cultural and religious equality for a Judaism he would later define as a "world religion."

Hermann Cohen made an equally assertive claim for Judaism's significance for philosophy, as he set about the task of rethinking philosophy "out of the sources of Judaism." Unlike Steinheim, Formstecher, Hirsch, Moritz

Lazarus, and the historian of Jewish philosophy, Julius Guttmann, representative of Jewish philosophy of the nineteenth and early twentieth century and beyond, Cohen went beyond the narrow disciplinary bounds of the philosophy of religion. Instead, he argued for the significance of the Jewish sources for the conception of reason itself. Like Baeck, Goldschmidt argues, Cohen showed that a universal idea of reason was not only fully compatible with Jewish tradition but grounded in religion's legacy of prophetic thought. Critics of Cohen questioned whether his posthumous *Religion of Reason out of the Sources of Judaism* signified a break with the neo-Kantian school Cohen had been so instrumental in creating. Others saw this turn to Jewish sources as fully consistent with the overall trajectory of Cohen's work. In making this dialogue between philosophy and its Jewish sources possible, Goldschmidt shows, Cohen had advanced a paradigm for critical philosophy. Neither reason and its claims, nor religion, could be given primacy: each, in his model, had to acknowledge the other's rightful voice. Cohen's breakthrough to a new philosophy assigned reason and Jewish sources an equal place, in an "unmediated testament, seized by the force of revelation."

Goldschmidt understands the tradition of German Jewish biblical translation in similar, dialogic terms. Every great Jewish civilization, he notes, consolidated its inner development only by turning outward, and translating the Hebrew Bible into the language of the land in which it lived. "The Jewish Quest for a German Bible," as Goldschmidt aptly calls it, followed in the footsteps of all great Jewish communities of the past, where life in a non-Jewish language deepened, rather than narrowed, the richness of Jewish experience. "Only when a foreign language could be fused with Judaism's own religious message," as Goldschmidt puts it, "could a Jewish community be said to have struck roots, enabling its message to blossom and ripen to fruition." In this respect, Bible translation for the German Jews represents an assertion of particular Jewish identity, but also a critique of the Christianization of Jewish scripture. Goldschmidt carefully follows the history of Jewish biblical translation into German from its beginnings with Jekutiel ben Issak Blitz and Josel Wittzenausen of 1676 and 1679 to Moses Mendelssohn's German translation, printed in Hebrew letters; the work of the founder of the Wissenschaft des Judentums, Leopold Zunz, and his collaborators Heymann Arnheim, Julius Fürst, and Michaels Sachs; Ludwig Phillipson's *Israelitische Bibel*, completed between 1839 and 1853; Samson

Raphael Hirsch's efforts of 1867 and 1882; and on to the Buber-Rosenzweig translation that Buber completed in Israel after World War II. In the culminating example of this translation, Buber and Rosenzweig sought to capture the alliterative texture of spoken Hebrew in a German voice, correcting the false universalism of Luther's classic and forgetful text. Their modern version instead found the voice of Hebrew in German, bringing German Jewry's inner development to a close as a legacy, an act "no less significant for the fact that their final translation arrived too late in the day for German Jewry itself."

Goldschmidt charts the many different ways this inner development of German Jewry flourished and redeemed Jewish tradition. Chapters on German Jewish literature, Franz Rosenzweig's re-creation of Jewish education in the Lehrhaus in Frankfurt, and Jewish theology's claim to equal stature, portray the powerful and deepening expression of Jewish culture that German Jewry achieved. At the same time, "Inner Renewal" is the section of *The Legacy of German Jewry* in which Goldschmidt describes the barriers that would bring this development to a premature end. Phenomena such as "Jewish Self-Hatred," to which he devotes a chapter, anti-Semitism, which Goldschmidt had described in "Outer Development," and the Holocaust, which he treats in "End, Sorrow, and Continuity," are analyzed as external limits. In Goldschmidt's analysis, this opposition had little if anything to do with Jewish culture itself. Instead, hostility toward the Jews was driven by a fear of modernity, expressed by those worried that the modern age would leave them behind. A full understanding of anti-Semitism's invidious force, Goldschmidt argues, can be gained only by realizing that this phenomenon has nothing to do with the Jews themselves. This view of anti-Semitism as an external barrier to Judaism's inner development distinguishes his approach, and it enriches our understanding of German Jewish culture by freeing its message of liberation from a belated, post-hoc determinism:

> Let it be said as clearly and directly as possible: anti-Semitism as an historical phenomenon is a byproduct of modernity, an unjust blaming of the Jews that falsely looks for its logic within Judaism itself. . . . As a result, nothing the Jews have ever done to stem the anti-Semitic surge has ever had any effect: trying not to step on too many toes, keeping a low profile, submissiveness, public protest, and reasoned argument in refutation of anti-Semitic premises have all been tried in vain. Judaism's actual behavior plays no role whatsoever in anti-Semitic reactions . . . for no matter what Judaism does, anti-Semites will construe Judaism as a threat.

For Goldschmidt, anti-Semitism and the Holocaust were a foreclosure of the unfinished dialogue between particular peoples and modernity that German Jews had worked to achieve. Jews could be scapegoated as archaic throwbacks, or repressive agents of modernity, but this dual fear could never cancel the deeper and redemptive message that became the lasting legacy of German Jewry: the right of all peoples to both a particular, and universal significance. Persecuted as a primitive threat, or as the witting or unwitting agents of a fearsome modern world, German Jewish culture in fact carried a message of liberation, the hope and promise of a modernity they sacrificed their lives to help German culture achieve. This future-oriented contribution of German Jewry becomes apparent in the next and in some ways darkest section of Goldschmidt's unique work.

German Jewry: End, Sorrow, and Continuity

Unlike other historians and critics of German Jewish culture, Goldschmidt approaches the end of German Jewry without the sense of final rupture that often inflects interpretations of the Holocaust. This disastrous sense of finality, of course, was powerfully present in the crucial documents of the era. Leo Baeck, as Goldschmidt recalls, declared that on April 1, 1933, "the thousand-year history of Germany's Jews" had "come to an end." Goldschmidt places this sense of closure in its particular historical context. His account describes the faults in the German Jewish response with unflinching, unforgiving historical accuracy. Both a blind faith in the universal values of German culture, and an "unacceptably submissive" posture often characterized the Jewish response to the unfolding disaster. Looking beneath the traumatic surface, however, Goldschmidt reads the anxiety and despair voiced by German Jews as signs of the underlying process of recovery that was already underway. "The German Jewish history that had already come to an 'end' in 1933," as he points out, "nevertheless continued to move forward until 1943, under the passionate leadership of no less a figure than Leo Baeck himself." In examining the continuous frenzy of German Jewish creativity after 1933, *The Legacy of German Jewry* discovers something more than destruction. As Michael Brenner would later argue, Jewish culture in Germany underwent a "renaissance" that continued up and through the Nazi period.[15] Social welfare efforts, presses, magazines, and a host of other activities sought to preserve Jewish life. The fatal last decade of German Jewry's existence, Goldschmidt demonstrates, was the crucial historical moment for rethinking German Jewry's demise. This end was also a beginning: the start of German Jewry's transformation of its unfulfilled achievements into a legacy for the postwar world.

This account of the end of German Jewry is followed by Goldschmidt's direct confrontation with the Holocaust's unspeakable sorrow. Like Job, German Jewry seemed to have lost everything, and was tempted to curse God's name. With Margarete Susman's pioneering response of 1946, *Das Buch Hiob und das Schicksal des Jüdischen Volkes* (The Book of Job and the Fate of the Jewish People), Job became a symbolic focus for addressing the disaster that brought the Jewish people to the brink of destruction.[16] In *The Legacy of German Jewry*, Job's temptation takes center stage, as Job becomes Goldschmidt's figure for the Jews as they confronted the challenge to their very existence and cultural continuity. Like the inexplicable suffering inflicted upon the Jews, symbolized for Goldschmidt in the murder of millions of innocent children and adults, Job's afflictions have neither reason nor cause; his torments represent "the sacrifice of Jewish innocence." And like the Holocaust, Job's subjection to loss after unbelievable loss cannot be explained as part of any divine plan. By evoking the sorrow of Holocaust as event, Goldschmidt's reading of the biblical text enables him to critique religious interpretations of the Holocaust's meaning and their "empty theological pronouncements." In *The Legacy of German Jewry*, the Holocaust must first be confronted as the failure of such universal dreams. Goldschmidt's turn to Job recognizes this despair and utter abjection—the sense of a final break—which characterizes so many accounts of the Shoah. At the same time, keeping Job in mind envisions sorrow as necessary point of transition, not an end in itself. In connecting the biblical tradition to the darkest hour of Jewish modernity, Goldschmidt reads Job as a parable of Jewish existence which, despite the most unjustifiable of blows, retained its connection to its own biblical legacy, and hence the will to carry Jewish life into the future.

Job's endurance, then, becomes Goldschmidt's parable for the Jewish encounter with the meaning of the Holocaust. He refuses, however, to separate the utter negativity of destruction from the will to carry on after the war. The idea of "Continuity," the next section of *The Legacy of German Jewry*, is firmly grounded in Job's disaster, because the confrontation with the failure of modernity and the will to carry on afterward were for Goldschmidt deeply linked. The legacy of loss and sorrow, in this reading, is transformed into the energy of critique. Job's friends, in Goldschmidt's account, resemble facile explicators of the Holocaust, who in the end blame Jewish particularity itself, symbolized by Job's stubborn clinging to his faith, for the suffering the Jews were forced to bear. On the other hand, Job also confronts "friends who make an unbearable situation worse" by looking for redemptive, theological meaning in his suffering. In this evocative parable of theology and cultural criticism, Goldschmidt uses Job to critique two different post-Auschwitz views. God-is-dead theology, with its ties to existentialism, and the attempt to discern some shadow of divinity in the Holocaust both pale in the face of the suffering Job undergoes. Goldschmidt discovers inspiration, however, and the will to move forward in Job's refusal to acknowledge any higher reason for his sorrow: Job is strengthened by his insight that no ultimate revelation is at hand. Those who found the will to go on living and creating after the Holocaust followed in Job's footsteps in this regard, refusing to renounce the idea of justice despite unjustifiable sorrow. At the same time, Job's experience of abject misery only reconfirms his identity and connection to the world, a will to carry on symbolized in the new family he founds. Like the Jewish world after Auschwitz, Job receives no answer, but undertakes the hopeful work of continuity in the face of unspeakable sorrow and loss.

The problem of German Jewish continuity after the war, however, was not a simple one, as Goldschmidt's next section shows. Historically, *The Legacy of German Jewry* gives an historical accounting of the dispersal of Jewish survivors worldwide, and the small group who chose to stay on in Germany, or return from the varied sites of refuge to which they had fled. The number of German Jews who returned was small, and Goldschmidt honors the loyalty of their attempt to continue a culture that had been destroyed. The post-1945 situation in Germany, however, required a different kind of response. Whereas German Jews sought to re-establish the tradition of Jewish life in Germany, German culture imagined itself as making a clean break with the past, and leaving its burden behind. The welcome Germany extended to Jewish refugees, as Goldschmidt notes, was therefore partial and conditional. For the Jews in Germany, life after Auschwitz meant keeping a low profile, and thus a cruel erasure of the tenuous link they strove to sustain with their cultural heritage. The culture that German Jews hoped to reclaim was rejected a second time, now by the eager will to reconstruction. Finding no voice or cultural space in Germany, German Jewish culture found itself forced into exile. And as German Jews took root throughout the world, in the United States, Israel, and elsewhere, they brought the German Jewish tradition with them. Unable to flourish in Germany, their legacy remained alive and bore fruit in the postwar world, in the work of figures as diverse as Martin Buber, Gershom Scholem, Erich Fromm, Hannah Arendt, Theodor Adorno, and Emmanuel Levinas and the intellectual movements that followed in their wake.

The Remnant That Remains: The Legacy of German Jewry

The legacy of German Jewry lives on in the dream of liberating the particular in its broadest sense, a vision of modernity grounded in the respect for the other. This ultimately biblical message, as Goldschmidt points out, depended on German Jewish culture's creative reappropriation of its most traditional and ancient sources. The concluding plea of *The Legacy of German Jewry* for the universal meaning of difference is based on the book's presentation of cultural history, but also on its notion of the past as promise, a radical view of the tradition's urgent significance for modernity that Goldschmidt once cast in biblical terms: "The Jewish millennia:—the most contemporary form of the present."[17] "Legacy" became Goldschmidt's modern term for the radical, future-oriented meaning of tradition, a concept crucial to understanding the central impulse of his work. By calling this book the "legacy" rather than the "history" of "German Jewry," Goldschmidt refuses to regard their achievements through the lens of apocalyptic disaster. Instead, this book's eloquent conclusion describes the German Jewish thinkers, writers, and ordinary Jews—those who were lost, and who survived—as transmitters of their message of universal respect for difference as a legacy to postwar culture.

A legacy, we might say, is history that concerns us in the present— something from the past that remains, as a remnant—but a past whose meaning is not fully present to us, because its task has yet to be fulfilled. The past remains alive, in this sense, not because it has taken place, but because it has *not yet fully occurred*, like a liberation that awaits completion, and therefore must be preserved as a living tradition if it is ever to reach fruition. As history's remnant, the German Jewish tradition became a legacy because its quest for a universal culture that would preserve Jewish difference has been forgotten, to a certain extent, but also preserved as the larger goal of post-Auschwitz culture:

> The right to their own particularity fought for by German Jewry would achieve a universal legitimacy after them, applicable to all groups throughout the world. Indeed, it is this right that constitutes the outstanding legacy of German Jewry, for it came to be recognized by the world only through them, though it has indeed yet to be realized in practice.

Such universal, recognized acceptance for the Jews, and all peoples—in 1957, as today—is still far from having been achieved, and as a legacy that awaits its fulfillment, cannot therefore be regarded in strictly historical terms. As "the remnant that remains," to borrow from Isaiah, German Jewry preserved the idea of the "universal legitimacy" of cultural difference, and of the particular strivings of "all groups throughout the world," and thus helped set the intellectual and political agenda for modern thought as a whole. Though now part of the cultural past, the German Jewish recognition of cultural difference as the emancipatory impulse of modernity remains alive: a reminder that the right to participate in a universal culture is just as powerful as the need to express human particularity in all its forms. After giving voice to Judaism's age-old vision of emancipation, German Jewry's message of liberation became a legacy—a dream yet to be realized in practice—and hence a task that still awaits its completion.[18]

In this vision of a human liberation not yet achieved, German Jewry remains postcontemporary in its significance for a globalized world. As Goldschmidt argues in his concluding section, the contribution of Moses Mendelssohn, Martin Buber, Franz Rosenzweig, Franz Kafka, and everyday German Jews extends beyond the measure of cultural treasures and intellectual work. The message carried by German Jewry was expressed just as powerfully in their simple, everyday efforts to live a full life as both Germans and Jews. The success German Jews achieved in becoming "German," we know in hindsight, was a costly one, given their ultimate rejection by the Germany that needed them most. The German Jewish re-creation and transmission of Jewish tradition, however, was just as expansive and significant, even if the trauma of the Holocaust has at times made it difficult to appreciate the depth of their enrichment to Jewish life and thought. The continuing importance of German Jewry rests not on its German contribution, nor its Jewish one, but on the depth of cultural and human exchange that it strove to establish between the two. German Jewry did anything but compromise its identity. Instead, German Jews asserted a challenging paradigm of cultural identity that envisioned difference as the crucial moment in cultural creation. The historical significance of this German Jewish contribution, as Goldschmidt so forcefully argues, still awaits its recognition.

PART ONE

ONE

Origins of the Modern

Modernity has for centuries been on its way to a peak that it is far from having been scaled. The Middle Ages, to be sure, and their hierarchy and predominant sense of isolation, were explored long ago: but the project of a modernity that faces the obligations of its responsibility, independence, and freedom remains restless and unfulfilled. Today's earth has been fully charted, and though humanity—as never before in human affairs—unites itself before our eyes, we have not yet begun to come to terms with the opportunities and demands this new situation has disclosed. Yet we dare not hesitate, nor to shrink from the task. Those who fail to take part will have no one but themselves to blame for their decline. The Jews, along with all other peoples sharing this historical moment, have joined the quest to gain full entry to modernity. But the Jews find themselves in a situation different on two accounts: first and foremost, because Judaism has already lived through four thousand years of world history as an active and self-aware contributor to the Middle Ages, and the world of antiquity before that. This singular fact confers a power all its own. Judaism's antiquity, whose message encompasses all mankind, from the creation to the redemption of the world as a whole, provides a certain sense of equanimity during history's twists and turns. Yet a people as old as this also becomes fixed in its ways. When Judaism suddenly faced modernity's wholly new set of challenges, it was difficult to shed the hold of the Middle Ages in an instant and re-conceive itself from the ground up. Jochanan ben Sakkai had faced the same difficulty two thousand years ago. When faced with the destruction of the Second Temple in the year 70 CE, he overcame Judaism's previously inviolable tie to the ritual site with his famous words: "A form of atonement remains for us: acts of loving kindness."[1]

A second situation specific to Judaism subjected its entry into modernity to repeated interruptions from without: against their will, this people was time and again thrown back centuries into the past. The year 1492, when Columbus discovered the Americas, bringing the Middle Ages to an irrevocable close—a Columbus motivated in no small part by an awareness of his Jewish ancestry—marked the final expulsion of the Jews from Spain during the Inquisition. This meant nothing less than the destruction of Judaism's most advanced sector, the Jewish community most capable of modernization at the crucial historical juncture that Spanish Jewry had itself helped to create. A similar fate befell the resurgent Jews of the Ukraine roughly 150 years later, when Ukrainian Jewry suffered its own "Spanish catastrophe" and was decimated by the Cossacks in 1648–49, as a larger Polish kingdom succumbed to its foes. And it was during these same years that Spinoza set out on his own Columbus-like journey into modernity.

The expulsion of Spanish Jewry occurred at the very historical moment that other Western nations were entering the modern world, just as the Renaissance, humanism, the Reformation, and the Counter-reformation began to make their influence felt. To make matters worse, the Jews of the Ukraine, the core settlement of what was later to become Polish and Russian Jewry, were destroyed just as the Jews of Western Europe had recovered enough for one of their own to launch his own modern quest. Spinoza was a descendant of Spanish Jews who had converted in order to escape the Inquisition and fled to Portugal, France, and eventually Holland, where they were to follow the faith of their fathers once more. But while this Spanish Jew entered a modernity from which his forebears had been excluded—a Spinoza who remained steadfastly Jewish, despite the ban the

Jewish community of Amsterdam placed on him and his works—the Jewish masses then moving eastward, who should have been inspired by the modern spark of his work, suffered a devastating blow.

At the same time, the Jews were still a people in motion, actively chafing at the limits of the ghetto and its isolation. The Jewish predicament, to be sure, was only part of the subjugation suffered by all groups during the medieval period. Yet the Jews bore an added burden: the ghetto's isolation, despite the ties the Jewish community sustained with the surrounding world, deprived the Jews of a full feeling for the surrounding culture. Despite such obstacles, traditional patterns began to fade, and modern impulses began to make themselves felt, struggling to break through to full expression. This gradualist description, however, does not begin to suggest the powerful, messianic drive in Jewish society that fought to realize itself historically during those turbulent years. One illustration can be found in the work of Manasse ben Israel, Spinoza's teacher and Rembrandt's friend. Sabbatai Z'vi, a false messiah only six years older than Spinoza and who died at almost the same time, provides another case in point. The modern breakthrough and turning point Spinoza signifies in intellectual history marks one end of the medieval world-picture. That same ending and modern beginning finds parallel but different expression in the messianic hopes expressed by Manasse ben Israel and Sabbatai Z'vi. Both figures felt that the arrival of the messianic age was imminent, establishing an historical break and advent of a new era that would cancel the validity of all that had come before. Both, in other words, helped bring the Middle Ages to an end.

Sabbatai Z'vi claimed he was the Messiah. Then, in the nick of time, he converted to Islam in order to save his own skin. This act of betrayal threw Jewish believers into a despair and disappointment so deep that it could no longer be concealed. Having believed Z'vi to be the Messiah incarnate, a figure come to life from the messianic legends that were a staple of medieval culture, his followers were betrayed and made fools of in the worst possible way. Manasse ben Israel, on the other hand, helped bring the Middle Ages to their intellectual conclusion. Though he discussed the modern impulse as consonant with medieval aims and objectives in the groundbreaking *Vindication of the Jews*, ben Israel at the same time envisioned a process that was bound to shatter the medieval worldview. First published in London in 1656, and then reissued by Moses Mendelssohn in 1782, *The Vindication of the Jews* announced that according to Daniel 12:7 and Deuteronomy 28:64, the arrival of the messianic age depended on the Jewish diaspora's being extended until it reached the ends of the earth. The Jewish people were certainly not free, ben Israel conceded, in their contemporary homelands: the Jews, he pointed out, had been banished from England. But with the arrival of the God's kingdom on earth—as Manasse ben Israel put it in his letter to Cromwell—that banishment would have to end, along with every other form of Jewish persecution and exclusion, for this was a people destined to spread throughout the world.

At roughly the same time, England lifted its ban on the Jews, in force since 1290. Soon after Manasse's premature death in 1657, Spinoza himself would announce his belief that a national renaissance for his people remained a distinct possibility. In his *Theological-Political Treatise* of 1670, the work that set him at odds with the contemporary Jewish world, Spinoza declared, "Indeed, I would absolutely believe that, unless the foundations of their religion were to make their spirits effeminate, they will someday, given the occasion—as human affairs are changeable—erect their imperium once more."[2]

But the determining event of these years was the fearful blow the Cossacks dealt to East European Jewry, a wound compounded by the devastating sense of disappointment Sabbatai Z'vi had caused. The consequences would make Menasse ben Israel's hope for his people's acceptance throughout the earth nothing but a distant dream. Spinoza, barred from participation in his people's affairs, would be unable to exert any direct influence whatsoever. Decades would elapse before modernity's threshold would be approached again. The ground of Podolia and Wolhynia would have to be soaked with the blood of Ukrainian Jewry before one young person—the Baal Shem Tov, founder of the Hasidic movement—would achieve the self-consciousness and maturity needed to express a joyous and unabashed love of Judaism in its midst. Before we describe the entry to modernity proper in the West, we must first take the contemporary Hasidic into account as the final precursor to Judaism's inner renewal, even if Hasidism was unable to bring to fruition the splendid seeds of the modern which blossomed at its start.

The motivating impulse behind the Hasidic movement was also aimed at discovering modernity, a New Land. Here the question was whether that territory could be gained by deploying a medieval vocabulary and its everyday perspectives, or whether the modern would be grasped through the age-old watchword, "Hear, O Israel" (Deuteronomy 6:4) of Moses, given biblical expression in medieval or ancient form. The Hasidic quest was to find new ways of expressing the modern impulse as it emerged, and the process, not coincidentally, would be reminiscent of Spinoza's core teachings, independently discovered and given a wholly different expression. The Hasidic insight was that religious feeling had a right to its own form of expression as compelling, gripping emotion and boundless devotion. This earthly and human inwardness was to become the Hasidic sensibility that fused absolute religious commitment with joyous love. In Hasidism, joy is the moving force of the world, a joy entwined with equanimity. Sorrow—or evil—excludes joy, but joy encompasses both the ineluctability of sorrow and an unacceptable evil just as strong, for true joy retains its equanimity in the face of whatever it encounters. That is why coincidences are meaningless: it is a denial of the blessed plenitude at work in creation to see anything as unnecessary. The world as a whole finds expression just as fully in the material realm as it does in the spiritual. Like Spinoza, the Hasidic movement takes earthly existence as its starting point, bypassing the upside-down view of man in late Talmudic thought and leaving it far behind. Man himself can be a Torah! Earthly existence can become an image for what was once called the full, lived body and soul of blessed creation, so long as man does not transform, repress or degrade earthly life into nothing but means to an end. In medieval times, only the soul and the spirit were seen as capable of this task. The Hasidic path toward individual fulfillment is therefore a process of authenticating oneself before one's neighbor: for the Hasidic movement, love of one's neighbor becomes an expression of love for God as well. Everything centers again and again on "HIM," who demands to be loved "with all your soul, with all your heart, and with all your might" (Deuteronomy 6:5), and who offers nothing in return! "Happiness is not virtue's reward," says Spinoza, "rather, virtue is its own reward." And what says the Baal Shem Tov? "If I love God, what need do I have of the world to come?"

Israel ben Eliezer, known as the Baal Shem Tov, entered the world around 1700, twenty-three years after Spinoza's death and twenty-nine years before Moses Mendelssohn's birth. He died in 1760, before his disciples had brought his movement to the peak of its influence in the same decades when Jews were granted citizenship in North America and France and German Jews registered their equality in the intellectual domain. Modernity had begun its move forward in the West, despite the many obstacles and painful setbacks progress faced. The eastern Hassidic world, meanwhile, fell under the spell of a second Middle Ages, when the influence of the Baal Shem's two chief opponents—the scholarly rabbis and the kabba-listic magicians and miracle workers—began to make itself felt. The western Jews made their modern breakthroughs, and their repercussions began to make themselves felt in the east. The second Hasidic wave stood ready to squelch any kind of movement for change, and to lend its support to the enemies of progress.

The molten energy of the piety released by the Baal Shem Tov was never successfully forged into a single, religious community. It was yet more dif-ficult for his doctrine to gain a firm foothold at such a turning point in history. The gap between rich and poor that had opened up in the late Middle Ages, shameful and anti-Jewish as it was, still remained. The poor, uneducated Jewish masses stood on one side, and the narrow rabbinical elite, throwing their influence on the side of the rich, stood on the other. The divide was a dangerous one, and the resultant social pressures produced distortion and inversion. For the masses, the only way out seemed to place one's hopes in the miraculous. One way this flight from reality expressed itself was belief in Sabbatai Z'vi, the self-proclaimed Messiah, a contempo-rary of Manasse ben Israel and Spinoza, later succeeded by the Baal Shem Tov's false Messiah, Jacob Frank. The Jewish community of Amsterdam went so far as to ban Spinoza for un-Jewish activities in 1656, and eventually fell under Sabbatai Z'vi's sphere of influence in 1666, the year believed to inaugurate the messianic age—the same year Z'vi himself converted to Islam. Podolia and Wolhynia would succumb to the Frankist abyss. Both Jewish communities had experienced a renewal of Jewish life under the Baal Shem Tov, but were soon entranced by Jacob Frank, a messiah no less false than Z'vi himself.

The Baal Shem Tov had been spreading his message to the world since roughly 1740, as Frederick the Great ascended the Prussian throne, and Moses Mendelssohn moved to Berlin. A year before the Baal Shem Tov's death in 1760, Jakob Frank converted to Christianity, after Poland's ruler, King August III, exerted personal pressure to force Frank to accept baptism. Afterward, the common folk began to speculate about the legend of Frank that quickly arose. A rumor spread that the Baal Shem Tov's departure from this world had been hastened by his sorrow over Frank's downfall, and out of sorrow that the Master had failed to prevent it and the loss of Frank's followers that ensued. Frank's disciples, however, were able to reconcile his enthusiastic, magical practices with the scholarly tradition, and the Hassidim who rose in stature to become the ghetto's new elite, the community's new leaders, and finally its exploiters, took on the guise of wise men, Zaddikim. Instead of leading a life of holiness, embodying the traces of living Judaism tended to through the ages by their community of fellow Jews, these Zaddikim claimed to represent salvation itself, and believed they could bring salvation through the sheer force of their piety. Heaping riches on the Zaddik became the Hassidim's most important task. In a final, distorted form of the heights of greatness the Middle Ages achieved, a greatness never to be regained, the past had triumphed once more. But the days of this form of medieval life, and all others, were numbered.

The Breakthrough to Modernity

By 1783, modernity could be said to have begun for Judaism, thanks to one external event and two achievements of Judaism's own. The victory of the United States in its revolutionary war confirmed its proclamation of 1776, that all men were created equal, and that the creator had endowed all men, without exception, with inalienable rights, among them the rights to life, liberty, and the pursuit of happiness. The two achievements of the Jewish people that brought them into modernity proper were Moses Mendelssohn's crowning effort in his quest for Jewish renewal, his translation of the Hebrew Bible into German, published in 1783, and his treatise *Jerusalem, or on the Religious Power of Judaism*, a declaration of independence in its own right.

This work calls for something more than the liberation of the Jewish people from their shackles: instead, Mendelssohn views the particular freedom he demands on behalf of the Jews and the universal freedom to which all peoples are entitled as one and the same. Judaism is conceived of as an active participant in world history, closely connected with the most pressing issue that confronted the humanity of Mendelssohn's age. The treatise raises Jewish demands and those advanced by Jewish supporters, bringing them to the forefront of current discussion, refusing to ground those claims in the dim historical past, or to treat the Jewish case as a vast historical exception. Instead, Mendelssohn addresses the battle for Jewish emancipation as the most urgent question of his age's quest for progress, as part of the universal struggle for the freedom, to be waged by all and for all of humanity.

For, unlike Spinoza, Mendelssohn did not write as an isolated pioneer entering modernity on his own, but as an individual who laid claim to modernity on behalf of the Jewish people, making him the first "conscious Jew" on modernity's ground. Both Spinoza and the Baal Shem Tov had shaped their innovative thought within the closed confines of a ghetto, offering them a stark choice between the modern world and the Middle Ages. Spinoza chose modernity and left the ghetto behind, while the Baal Shem Tov and his followers chose the ghetto, only to be engulfed by the medieval world once more. Mendelssohn developed his thought without the ghetto as his reference point, within the intellectual context of "Bildung" or enlightened education that characterized his age. Yet by following the Baal Shem Tov on Spinoza's path, Mendelssohn remained loyal to his own Jewish community, whose worldview remained distinctly medieval in many respects.

In the midst of his transformation into a German sage and man of letters, Mendelssohn was startled by Johann Caspar Lavater's demand that he convert to Christianity. Suddenly made aware that he could either continue his progressive course, merging himself completely with the Christian Occident, or take his people along with him on his journey westward if he wished to remain a Jew, Mendelssohn made his choice: he returned to Judaism. In 1769, at the peak of his career, the forty-year-old Mendelssohn—winner of the Berlin Academy Prize, famed for his contributions to the *Bibliothek der schönen Wissenschaften* and *Briefe, die neueste Literatur betreffend*, an author celebrated for his *Briefe über die Empfindungen*, and above all for his *Phaedon*—henceforth devoted his efforts to Jewish matters alone, to his "nation," as he called it. Only when all Jews had been led forth from the Middle Ages could modernity as such be said to have begun for Judaism; only then could each individual Jew remain a Jew on modernity's ground.

Mendelssohn's bold venture met with success. While marking the start of a project that remains incomplete almost two hundred years after Mendelssohn's "return to Judaism," it was Mendelssohn and Mendelssohn alone who set this course of events in motion. Though perhaps lacking Spinoza's intellectual power and rigor, and falling short of the Baal Shem Tov's feel for the sacredness of all things, Mendelssohn managed to shape the subsequent development of Jewish culture in such a clear and marked fashion that every Jewish movement would represent some variant of his pathbreaking thought. Liberal as well as orthodox Jewish movements, the cosmopolitan Judaism of the "citizen" as well as the Zionist "Jewish-staters," supporters of the "Science of Judaism" as well as the drive to revive Hebrew as a living language, all stood in his debt. Mendelssohn was the watershed figure whose emergence made it impossible for all subsequent positions and programs to retreat from modern ground. Even the Orthodox who fought Mendelssohn's liberal followers by tenaciously clinging to the vestiges of medieval thought in work could never avoid the debt their existence owed to Mendelssohn's modernity.

Mendelssohn's efforts made it possible for the Jews to enter the modern world, while at the same time introducing the world to the universal truth that a living Judaism would continue to exist. After Mendelssohn, Judaism's movements would take many forms. But all were concerned to secure the place of Jewish life and culture within a modern framework Mendelssohn helped to define, despite the significant weaknesses that hamstrung his concept of Jewish emancipation. These movements will be presented in more detail, when the conflict between emancipation and assimilation is discussed in chapter 5. Here it may suffice to note that Mendelssohn did not seek to replace the Jewish Middle Ages with an equally all-encompassing modernity, but demanded civil rights for the Jews simply because the Jews were human beings. Judaism, for Mendelssohn, was a purely private and personal matter, something to be preserved but that did not necessarily have to be renewed, and that renewal never became part of his vision of emancipation. Certain ideas would always remain foreign to this man of the Enlightenment.

Mendelssohn could not conceive of the fact that Judaism still had an historical role to play, remaining crucially necessary in the modern world. The idea that the Jewish people could keep pace with the revolutionary changes of their era only by becoming agents of their own historical destiny also escaped him. And the notion that the Enlightened Jew, for all the splendor of his intellect, stood in need of a Jewish people active in contemporary affairs for his most basic support: this too stood beyond the explicit scope of his thought. For Mendelssohn, Jewish cultural associations and ties played themselves out in private, beyond the public sphere, a consequence of Jewish political exclusion since the late Middle Ages. For him, Jewish cultural bonds were no longer national—unlike the role of culture in the nation state—and thus no longer connected Jewish culture to Jewish or the universal march of history. All this meant, for Mendelssohn, that absolutely nothing in Jewish tradition needed to be transformed. As if this people had not more than once in their history sought radically new forms to transmit a message whose core was immutably valid, new expressions of a message as legitimate in the present as it was in days of yore.

Here Mendelssohn's traditionalist Jewish opponents showed great insight in sensing the revolutionary potential of his thought. They pronounced a ban on his works, just as they banned Spinoza and the followers of the Baal Shem Tov before. Mendelssohn's foes correctly grasped the fact that any measure that sought to accommodate the modern world, whether modest or not, would inevitably lead to a breakdown of the medieval synthesis. Mendelssohn's modern distinction between the citizen's public obligations and the right to religious fulfillment in the private sphere went against the grain of Jewish culture and its traditions, just as it runs counter to a human nature whose expressions make themselves felt all across the broad expanse of human life. The public and private divide contradicted the full existence that Judaism and all humanity demands, which brooks no half-measures. And many Jews, just beginning to hold their own alongside their cultural contemporaries, soon felt the need to cast aside medieval practices and their underpinnings altogether, no matter how much discretion or private reserve they practiced as they entered the modern world. Even when a Jew believed himself to be keeping faith with his tradition in every meaningful respect, any little foothold granted modernity announced the fact that the Middle Ages had indeed come to an end.

Fully intending to remain observant and keep faith with Jewish religious practice supposedly unchanged from time immemorial, Mendelssohn was finally unable to concede to what a medieval Jew would doubtlessly have felt obliged: he refused to obey the ban levied against his work by his community's official transmitters of tradition. In the decisive year of 1783, Mendelssohn's unflinching independence produced his landmark new German translation of the Hebrew Bible, a work that, along with his *Jerusalem*, gained worldwide attention and announced that the inner ghetto had been shattered once and for all. Despite being banned in 1779 by the rabbis of Fürth, Frankfurt, Hamburg, and Prague and book-burnings in Posen, Lissa, and Vilna, Pentateuch and the Psalms were published in 1783.

In the process Mendelssohn's translation brought new life to a petrified Hebrew vernacular. His achievement was consolidated with the help of followers who founded the Union of the Friends of the Hebrew Language in 1783, published the first edition of *Hameasef* (The Collector), the first Hebrew periodical to spring from the soil of modernity. They also issued a commentary, *Biur*, on his German Bible, which Mendelssohn composed in Hebrew. In the process of renewing the Hebrew language, Mendelssohn had at the same time acquired a new German idiom for the Hebrew Bible. This was a revolutionary event, comparable only to those few and distinctive peaks of achievement in the four-thousand-year world history of the Jewish people of similar consequence in different linguistic realms. Mendelssohn's translation bears comparison with the Septuagint, the work of Egyptian Jews who translated the Hebrew Bible into Greek, with the Targumim, its translation into Aramaic, or to Saadia's translation of the Bible into Arabic, presaging the golden era when Judaism flourished amidst the Islamic world and Spain.

Since the Babylonian exile, no full Jewish life has existed without translating the Bible into the language of the land in which that life was bound to develop. Only when a foreign language could be fused with Judaism's own religious message, when that message itself was able to merge with the intellectual and spiritual depths of another linguistic world, could a Jewish community be said to have struck roots, enabling its message to blossom and ripen to fruition. Then, and only then, when life's variety and plenitude feels itself immediately addressed by the biblical call, in a mother tongue that was no longer Hebrew, could a Jewish community, whatever its vernacular, experience itself as the fully authentic successor of the biblical calling in every respect, feeling its life preserved and validated anew. Only then would Jeremiah's prophecy ring true, confirming once more the vision first proclaimed to the Babylonian exiles, when Jews feared it would be impossible to remain Jewish without their traditional roots in the Land of Israel. Jeremiah evoked the prophetic possibility of remaining Jewish anywhere in the world:

Build houses and live in them, plant gardens and eat their fruit. Take wives and beget sons and daughters; and take wives for your sons, and give your daughters to husbands, that they may bear sons and daughters. Multiply there, do not decrease. And seek the welfare of the city to which I have exiled you and pray to the LORD on its behalf; for in its prosperity you shall prosper. (Jeremiah 29:5–7)

The consequences of this synthesis of the Hebrew Bible with the German language would be remarkably productive indeed, and the stimulus that the Jewish translation gave to the reexamination of Christianity and its history then underway would be among its most important results. This critical spirit is typified in a letter Karl Lessing wrote upon receiving several pages of the so-called Old Testament in Mendelssohn's new Jewish and German translation. Lessing addressed his letter to his famous brother, Mendelssohn's comrade-in-arms, and its note of distress is palpable: "What will people say when they read Mendelssohn's interpretation of the Psalms, a part of the Bible that we Christians have always read as prophesying the coming of Christ?"

The liberation of the Jews was not only basic to the struggle for the liberation of all men and all nations, but represented a fulcrum of the progressive movement as a whole. Freedom for the Jews was first and foremost a signpost marking the way of the future, but forward-looking in this universal sense precisely because the Bible had long ago become part of an inheritance in which all humanity held a share. Could any individual or group belonging to the human family, any group with historical ties to the Jewish covenant, remain unmoved when considering the destiny of the Jews in the modern world? Could anyone remain indifferent while waiting to see whether the Jews would ossify, wither, and succumb, or instead arise, renew their culture, and progress?

Though Mendelssohn's translation of the Hebrew Bible into German became an important event for Christianity as well, its most important consequence was the fact that the notion of "German Jewry" had been created. Mendelssohn, of course, had only come up with a name for a community that had long been in existence. In a certain sense, there had always been a group of Jews in Germany who shared a common set of responses to their surrounding world and its influences, quite a number, in fact, going all the way back to the days of the Romans on the Rhine. German Jews as a group had striven resolutely both to become part of the surrounding culture and to realize themselves as a distinct Jewish community. Mendelssohn's translation was a continuation of that effort, though his work included only the Psalms and the Five Books of Moses. Others who followed carried his mighty venture to its conclusion by producing an unusually large number of outstanding translations. The last translation was to be completed by Martin Buber and Franz Rosenzweig, whose consummate linguistic mastery kept faith with both the Jewish and German demands levied by their task. In the end, their efforts came to represent a kind of intellectual summit of German Jewish culture. (Chapter 22 will give a more detailed account of their work.) The German Jewish Bible remained such a living and existentially important project that Buber finished it despite the horrific and brutal interruption of all German Jewish coexistence and the Second World War. Not even the bitter fruits rained upon Jewish devotion to Germany in 1933, exactly 150 years after Mendelssohn's magisterial leap forward, could keep the promise of his achievement from being fulfilled. Begun by Rosenzweig in 1924, the Buber-Rosenzweig translation of the Bible that the former joined, interrupted by Rosenzweig's untimely death in 1929, would be continued by Buber alone and completed by him in 1962.

Mendelssohn's groundbreaking work may have sparked the Jewish push to modernity, but in 1783, when the Jewish advance was being overshadowed by the American victory in the revolutionary war, its most important practical consequence was yet to come. In a vote taken as the French National Assembly convened in Paris on September 28, 1791, French Jews were granted full legal and civil equality, and the years that followed would promise full emancipation to all nations who fell under the French flag as it advanced during the Napoleonic Wars. But Mendelssohn's unforeseen boon of seeing anchored in statute what his own program had proposed a mere eight years before were not the fruits of his efforts alone. The most important German landmarks on the road to Jewish emancipation were deeply influenced by Mendelssohn's stature as a public figure, and inspired by contact with him and belief in what he came to represent, including Gotthold Ephraim Lessing's drama *Nathan the Wise* of 1779 and Christian Wilhelm Dohm's essay *Über die bürgerliche Verbesserung der Juden* (On the civil improvement of the Jews) of 1781. The most forceful French argument for Jewish emancipation also stood in his debt, as its title already suggests: *Sur Moses Mendelssohn, sur la réforme politique des Juifs: Et en particulier, sur la révolution tentée en leur faveur en 1753 dans la grande Bretagne* (On Moses

Mendelssohn, on the political reform of the Jews: and in particular, on the revolution on their behalf of 1753 in Great Britain). Written by Count Mirabeau and published in London in 1787, this impassioned tract called for nothing less than a revolution in Jewish affairs and demanded that the principle behind Jewish emancipation be applied to the European continent as a whole. Mirabeau came to Berlin for the first time on January 20, 1786, sixteen days after Mendelssohn's premature death, but it was Mendelssohn's importance and depth as a representative figure for his era that motivated the crucial advocacy on behalf of the Jewish people that Mirabeau would undertake.

THREE

The Role of German Jewry

With the ghetto shattered by North America and France from without and by its own intellectual activity and vital energy from within, the diversity of Jewish modernity began to replace the uniform cast of Jewish life in the late Middle Ages. This variety resulted from the specific way Jewish freedoms were gained: not in a single stroke, but as individuals, or at best in small groups of people who won their freedom one step at a time. The move forward took place not as a single leap, but piecemeal, a natural course of events that unfolded as Jews freed from the ghetto's isolation once again got their bearings in the world and were stamped by its changing character. Jews immersed themselves in the language of one nation after another, becoming citizens of a different state in each. Occurring amidst the depths of what were still deadly and lurking dangers, their transformation still followed a time-honored Jewish route, the path, as it were, by the twelve tribes who embodied the single people of biblical Israel, "both houses of Israel" who, as Isaiah put it (8:14), had established two states but still comprised the one and only Israel. Modern Jewry thus followed the same path taken by many other Jewish communities at the end of antiquity—whether Babylonian, Palestinian, or Egyptian—who continued to count themselves as part of a single Jewish nation.

Israel had arisen not in a land of its own but under a covenant joined in the desert, a pact founded on revelation alone, after its people had made their conscious break with Babylonia in the east, Egypt in the west, Midian in the south, and Canaan in the north. Israel was from the start, and evermore so afterward, connected with the world as a whole. From its beginning, moving forward to its ultimate goal—from its origin in the desert, to its contemporary presence in all regions of the world—Israel had always felt itself called to the path that Judaism resolutely pursued after its breakthrough to modernity had been achieved. Israel had understood from its very inception that Mendelssohn's one Jewish "nation" was in fact made up of many different Jewries and Jewish groups, and that new Jewish communities would be founded in the future, just as our one and only earth provides for the existence of many different languages, states, and cultures.

Yet decades laden with deep disappointment were to pass before Judaism's mission throughout history, well adapted to modernity but unchanged in its core, would make itself felt as a distinct presence amidst the divergent forms Jewish life would take during years of decline, fragmentation, and disintegration. Decades would elapse before it was clear that this very diversity and cultural variety was Judaism's guarantor and signpost of the future, before the deeper and more authentic relation between Judaism's present and past would make itself felt in the bond linking modern Judaism with its biblical and postbiblical tradition of antiquity and the Middle Ages.

The overriding emphasis on German Jewry in what follows can therefore be said to characterize the course taken by Israel as a whole. Rather than give equal treatment to all Jewish communities, our discussion instead selects one for examination, since Israel's course can be understood only by looking closely at one of its several distinct manifestations. This focus on German Jewry is also justified by the leading role that fell to German Jews during the first half-century of Jewish modernity. That centrality was due in part to the decisive role Germany itself played during the years when the middle of Europe became the hinge on which world events turned. But the extent of that influence was also due in no small part to the German Jews themselves—to their fervent efforts and the battle they themselves had won for complete self-determination. Their struggle had been waged on behalf of Judaism's larger message and of all Jewish groups and communities without exception, giving German Jewry an exemplary and inspiring status at the forefront of world Jewry. In addition, the bell of history tolled the arrival of the kind of era that occurs but once in many centuries: an hour when a revolution in basic social circumstances offering countless opportunities finally allowed the abilities of German Jews to determine the extent of their advancement. Their talents had stored within them the kind of potential productive of the kind of harvest one sees but once every thousand years. Other factors contributing to the special preconditions of this success were the unusually long duration of the Jewish presence in Germany, and another fact as well: that this kind of full Jewish participation in every aspect of German life had never previously occurred. Energies long dammed could now burst forth onto the ground of modernity. Opportunities were seized with the full confidence, fervent devotion, and inner assurance that the deepest and fullest kind of belonging had been achieved.

Jews had come to Germany with the Romans, possibly even before the year 1 according to the Christian calendar, and had certainly arrived centuries before the earliest beginnings of Christianity among the Germans. Constantine's decree of 321 has been preserved, revoking the privilege previously granted the Jews of not holding city offices. This privilege was less an honor than a burden in times when it meant the disadvantage of having to pay a burdensome tax in all but a few cases. The evidence of this legislation suggests that a considerable number of Cologne Jews had property at their disposal, for without owning land, city offices could not be held. Constantine's decree, as the beginning of a new era, marked a change that brought the previous period to a close. At this moment before Christianity's elevation to the official status of state religion, Jewish contributions had been part of a productive life that had been honored and secure for decades and centuries on end.

German Jewry achieved the prominent profile it would sustain without interruption until the rise of Charlemagne when the imperial court permitted German Jews to become active in all spheres of public life. Jews became an estate like all others; and the not inconsiderable number of Jews in German lands of the time may have even been the result of frequent conversions to Judaism. The first three centuries of the early Middle Ages saw close

mutual ties forged between Jews and Germans, and a broad-based efflores-
cence of Jewish culture that continued until the beginning of the First Cru-
sade in 1096. That event, which marked the beginning of a process of
gradual decay that would eventually end the Middle Ages, while claiming
many social strata, peoples, and many noble cultural achievements among
its victims, soon transformed itself into a series of anti-Jewish campaigns
that would last for horrible centuries on end. Then as now, Jews were never
the only ones to suffer when anti-Jewish attacks were mounted. But the Jews
persisted in self-consciously preserving the group awareness characteristic
of the Jewish way of life. The almost unavoidable exclusivity of cultural
memory therefore recalls the period in a somewhat misleading and partial
fashion, remembering only the Crusaders' attacks against the Jews, a trauma
that haunts the Jewish people to this day.

The Jews were eventually banished from England in 1290; from France
in 1306 and 1394; from several Swiss cantons even earlier, leading to an
almost complete expulsion from Switzerland; from Spain and Portugal in
1492; from the Mark of Brandenburg in 1577; and from Vienna in 1670.
Even so, Jews were never banished from German soil. The explanation is
wholly instrumental: no such thing as a unified Germany existed at the time.
Another "state," usually only a few miles away, was always nearby where
one could seek refuge and a new domicile. Many tens of thousands of Jews
nonetheless perished in an unforgettably noble martyrdom, Jews who might
have saved themselves by agreeing to a baptism that was repeatedly offered
to them, whether during torture, immolation at the stake, or even while
suffering robbery and murder at the hands of the Crusaders. Untold thousands of others were expelled to the east, hungering in foreign lands for any
news of their homeland's exploits, as true pioneers in Eastern Europe. Only
a very few thousand survived the persecution suffered on ground they had
regarded as their own from time immemorial, an unbroken bond that would
leave its stamp on them for all time.

No deeper forms of common life developed in this early period because
the German language had not fully become the instrument of intellectual
exchange, which still took place in Latin. That the Jews had rooted themselves in the German language meant little for their inclusion in higher
German intellectual life. The fact that their own philosopher, the great
Maimonides, had been taken up by Albertus Magnus, Thomas Aquinas,
Meister Eckhart, Nikolaus von Kues, and Paracelsus, never drew the Jews

into the culture's larger intellectual discussion. Only the elite class of the literate granted "Rabbi Moses" recognition, and knowledge of his achievement remained a phenomenon restricted to the Latin-speaking strata. That intellectual elite at the same time remained unaware of or simply failed to see any worth in the fact that in Süsskind von Trimberg, Jewish culture had produced a German troubadour. Nor was any mention made of what Jews in the East had accomplished. The pioneering opening of Eastern Europe by Western Europeans had been a success in the most productive sense of the term, and that development had itself been made possible to a significant degree by Jews whose efforts are still underappreciated by historians. Jews who went east from Germany in the late Middle Ages remained passionately and powerfully attached to the medieval German they spoke, so devoted, in fact, that their linguistic affections kept that Middle High German alive in the Yiddish that Jews speak today.

Mendelssohn consciously sought to close the gap between Judaism and the modern German language. His efforts aimed at closing the divide between Jews who, because of "the Spanish catastrophe," had been unable to join in a modernity already underway for centuries in other European nations, and the modern German tongue. By the time Mendelssohn succeeded, a person who spoke German was no longer forced to remain on the margins of intellectual life. On the contrary: speaking German gave the individual the chance to dive into the wellspring of cultural renewal and be carried by its sources at the proud moment when its current was about to crest in German's intellectual rise. This linguistic meeting between Jews and the German language was another underpinning of German Jewry's central role, for this kind of synthesis between Jews and a resurgent language had occurred only once before, in the Arab world where its effect had been felt for centuries in many lands. Judaism's own rise in Central Europe, complete within a few decades, coincided with the mighty upsurge of the European linguistic domain. The culmination of German Jewry and Germany's classical period supported, heightened, and forwarded each other, presaging that singular cultural moment when the European occident would become the center of the world. Germany's prominence gave every step forward by the German Jews a historic significance hardly lavished on even greater accomplishments that have occurred before or since, or are that are likely to be seen again.

Three other preconditions had to be in place for this special role to be possible. German Jewry's breakthrough to modernity could count on the support of its own advance troops, its own reserve units, and an absolutely inexhaustible supply of replacements. "Court Jews" and "privileged Jews" had already risen to occupy high positions for two or three centuries, especially in the period spanning the eight decades between the outbreak of the Thirty Years War and Mendelssohn's birth. These were Jews who had advanced side by side with those Spanish Jews who had never fully settled in the ghetto. Several hundred of their families had been able to save themselves by escaping to Germany. In addition to these urban Jews, a long-established group of landowning Jews had lived amidst the peasants and villages for centuries. And there were also the Eastern European Jews, whose core consisted of what had once been the Jews of medieval Germany. Backed by his people's lengthy and uninterrupted settlement on German soil, and by their unparalleled skill in working together, dammed up and suppressed time and time again, Mendelssohn was far from alone when Germany's individual development and Europe's reached their peak. Mendelssohn had forerunners, traveling companions, and a troop of successors stretching to the horizon along with him on the road to modernity.

The forerunners of what could only later be called German Jewry in the full and final meaning of the phrase were families of Spanish Jews who arrived at the courts of various German principalities, following predecessors of their own, in order to save themselves just after the Thirty Years War. They were admitted to Germany's major city, as the Letter of Entry issued in 1671 by the Electors of Prussia and Brandenburg put it, "to further both trade and commerce." Like the Huguenots, well-to-do and industrious Jews were welcomed by countries devastated and laid to waste in the long, brutal war and were freed from most of the restrictions their suffering ghetto brethren still faced. Court Jews were expected to be agents of credit, administer the minting of money, introduce new industries, supply armies, and foster economic growth.

And so when Mendelssohn left Dessau, the city of his birth, at the age of fourteen in 1743 to stay close to David Fränkel, his teacher called to Berlin to become its chief rabbi—Mendelssohn dragged himself, hungry and exhausted, around half of Berlin trying to find the one gate that permitted Jews to enter, but then only after they paid the tax levied on them like animals. Then and only then did Mendelssohn discover a class of Jews who were already educated, freethinkers who were in contact with the city's leading intellectuals. There he met a medical student, Aaron Gumpertz—the great-grandson of Elias Gumperts, who had once been named a "court agent" by the Grand Elector Friedrich Wilhelm—who soon taught him French and English, directed him toward the philosophy of Leibniz and Wolff, and introduced him to Maupertuis, the president of the Berlin Academy of Sciences, and to Lessing.

While Mendelssohn was now able to rise, in a fashion, he could not keep his offspring from apostasy. Like most families of the first privileged Jews, Mendelssohn's descendants succumbed to conversion, since complete emancipation for the Jews of Prussia in 1812 could hardly be taken for granted. The remaining Jewish community that followed Mendelssohn, however, was spared such dissolution. The strong group of landholding Jews in existence at the time was enough to serve as counterforce to the social solvent represented by the newly powerful cities, even when these landed Jews moved to the cities themselves in accord with the general trend. And then there were the Eastern European Jews. The broad mass of the Jewish people stood just to the rear of the German Jews, flowing westward in an unbroken stream as they left the ghetto in Mendelssohn's footsteps. Instead of becoming easier, it became more and more difficult for the modern Jew to break off ties with the Jewish community, and all but impossible to shed all evidence of that one was indeed a Jew, without leaving a trace. Mendelssohn's breakthrough to modernity, far from leaving Jewishness behind, became a lasting achievement of the Jewish people as a whole.

For the Eastern European Jews walked side by side with the German Jews who had gradually risen to full citizenship in the decades before the French revolution, an achievement won through hard struggles and bitter defeats soon to be discussed. A majority of the eastern Jews had themselves resided in Germany several centuries before, and all spoke Yiddish. A bridge between Yiddish and modern German was quickly and easily constructed. The first partition of Poland, moreover, transformed many eastern Jews into Germans, and others into Austrians, especially during the last few decades of Mendelssohn's life. And as if to spite all those who were directing the course of history, two fiercely anti-Jewish monarchs, Frederick the Great, the king of Prussia, and Maria Theresa, the empress of Austria—along with Catherine the Great, empress of Russia—in an unthinking lust for spoils, began to carve up Poland in 1772. By pocketing Posen here and

Galicia there, these rulers not only disrupted the center of medieval Jewry but also multiplied their own number of Jewish subjects many times over.

The Jewish masses belonging to Prussia and Austria after the second and third partitions of Poland in 1793 and 1795 now had to face the challenge of becoming modern citizens whether they wished to or not, and regardless of whether their rulers sought just the opposite. Even those Jews clinging to the medieval past were spurred on to join the fight for a fully modern right to self-determination. Meanwhile, their rulers plotted ways to deny them full emancipation even after other sectors of the Jewish population had been emancipated: even when, as in the Prussia of the Napoleonic Wars, civil rights had been explicitly guaranteed to the Jews. Elsewhere, this unjustifiable delay in granting full Jewish freedom prevented Jews already enjoying full emancipation, who considered themselves to be wholly German Jews, from enjoying any equally strong sense of security in their new status. Alliances with their as yet unemancipated Jewish brethren had to be established in many different situations as the years went on, and led to a deeper and ever more wrenching reflection on who they in fact were as Jews, and what their Judaism meant.

PART TWO

Historical Stages

The final section of the first work of Jewish history composed on modernity's ground, Isaak Markus Jost's *History of the Israelites, from the Time of
the Maccabees to Our Own Times, According to the Original Sources*, published
between 1820 and 1828 in nine volumes, concerns *The Recent History of the
Jews in Christian Europe*, covering the period "from Frederick the Great's
ascension to the throne to the end of foreign rule (1740–1815)." The crucial
and immediately pressing decades of Jost's own historical epoch were
thereby treated as a constituent element of Prussian history as a whole.

But what is permitted a writer at the height of mature self-awareness, as
in the case of Dubnow, which we are about to examine, turns into a dead
end when that consciousness turns exclusively inward. To avoid this, Jost
divides his material into different historical stages when publishing the final
three volumes of his work between 1857 and 1859 as *The History of Judaism
and Its Sects*, summing up and concluding his life's work by continuing the
series begun in two previous volumes. The first volume was his *World

History of the Israelite People (1831–33), whose title was the strongest assertion of Jewish nationhood scholarship would see before Dubnow. Jost himself, to be sure, acknowledged the Jews to be a nation only during two brief
periods when ancient Israel managed to become a full-fledged state, but not
during the period of "scattered polities and sects" that followed. Jost thus
titled the second volume of his work *The More Recent History of the Israelites*
(1845–47). Three decades after finishing his history's initial volume, Jost's
title for its final volume would summon its legitimacy from his people's
character alone. *The History of the Jews in Modernity, from the Middle of the
Eighteenth Through the Beginnings of the Nineteenth Century* closes by defining
the high point of the era as a strictly Jewish event, whose significance is
almost impossible to overstate: the founding of the first modern Jewish university, the Breslau Seminary, on August 10, 1854.

Meanwhile, Jost's greatest successor, Heinrich Graetz, having started his
career as a teacher at the seminary, begins publishing his *History of the Jews
from the Most Ancient Times to the Present*. The first of its eleven volumes
appears in 1853, the last in 1875. Yet despite his passionate commitment to
Judaism, better scholarly training and finer mastery of the writer's craft,
Graetz, like the younger Jost before him, allows his work to be submerged
within the larger current of Prussian and German history. Having shared in
the dreams of the revolution of 1848, undaunted by the failure of its struggle
for freedom and refusing to abandon those hopes, Graetz decides to end his
History of the Jews in the year 1848 by broadening his focus to include history.
He describes Judaism as having contributed to the universal good of having
brought the "foreign domination" of German lands to an end, very much in
the spirit of Jost. Yet Graetz also views this most recent period through a
Jewish lens alone, deploying the fitting term he would use in his concluding
volume already published in 1870 by referring to his era as an "age of increasing self-awareness." Graetz, unlike Jost, begins his history with the "era of
Mendelssohn" in 1750, unlike Jost several decades earlier, who began his
historical narrative with Frederick the Great's taking the throne in 1740. For
Graetz, the bellwether of his own century is not the accession of Frederick
the Great to sovereignty, but the emergence of Moses Mendelssohn.

How does Simon Dubnow divide Jewish history into periods in his consummate fulfillment of Jewish historiography, *World History of the Jewish
People, from its Earliest Origins to the Present*? Dubnow's ten volumes, composed in Russian and first issued in a magisterial German translation by

Aaron Steinberg, can truly be said not only to have recounted but also to have made history. A full assessment of the significance of Dubnow's achievement must await our subsequent discussion of German Jewry's inner renewal. As far as the organizational emphases of his history go, Dubnow puts sociological and political processes in the foreground, never losing sight of nor failing to take full measure of religion's significance, Judaism's core content, which transcends the framework of the nation-state. While Graetz had placed his emphasis on "Juden," like Salo Wittmeyer Baron's "Jews" in his *Social and Religious History of the Jews*, who looked to Graetz rather than Dubnow for his terms, Dubnow sees the Jewish people and their culture as the steady and powerful determining constant of Jewish history. Thanks to his mature and sovereign Jewish self-awareness, Dubnow was able to make use of the usual historical break points to organize his historical narrative: 1789, 1815, 1848, and 1914. Yet between those dates and throughout them, Dubnow's account portrays the Jewish people determining and pursuing a path of their own.

"The first era of emancipation," according to Dubnow, began in 1789 and ended in 1815, marked by the achievement of equality in France that spread throughout Europe. The "first era of reaction" followed from 1815 to 1848, beginning with Napoleon's downfall. At that point, a new period of reaction ensued, resulting widespread efforts to crush the freedoms Napoleon had introduced—except in France and Holland—and culminated in the wholesale revocation of emancipatory measures that had been achieved or promised. This conservative pullback collided with the Jewish people's assertion of its own right to exist, a movement that had in the meantime become all the more deep and passionate. "The second era of emancipation" followed hard on this period's heels, characterized by the upsurge of emancipatory energy and outward development unleashed by the revolutions of 1848. Constitutional guarantees of full civil equality that the various peoples of Europe wrested from their governments also contained provisions stipulating full integration for Europe's various Jewish populations. But for reasons to be discussed more fully, a "second era of reaction" took hold after 1881, ushering in an era of new attempts to reinstate repressive measures from the past and to introduce new forms of persecution. The fact that Jews responded to these efforts with new and creative forms of resistance signifies before all else the powerful commitment to Jewish self-development characteristic of the period.

In charting these events, Dubnow always keeps his eye on the larger goal toward which Jewish and world history are striving, a history that promises to fulfill itself in redemption, a process first envisioned at biblical Jewry's joining of the covenant. In Dubnow's "Epilogue" of 1929, concluding his final volume spanning the years 1914–28 (a period he might have been able to celebrate as "the era of the third emancipation"), the phrase Dubnow uses to look out upon this lofty goal is "the era of peace on earth." With the advent of such an epoch, the Jewish people, "history's veteran," would rest assured that its struggle for brotherly love, peace, and justice had not been in vain. "If only the people of Israel might be permitted to partake in the pleasures of such a joyful epoch!" Dubnow's "Epilogue" reads to us today as if a presentiment of what was to come had fallen, like a shadow, over his faith in his people's promised future.

But even the "era of the third reaction" that was about to befall Dubnow in 1929, those devastating events of 1933, and all that resulted from and continues to be shaped by them—the unfathomable annihilation that is still scarcely conceivable, and the unspeakably horrible and scandalous destruction that those events unleashed—even those events failed to remove "history's veteran" from the course of history.

For before all else, German Jewry, the Jewish communities of Europe, and indeed the West as a whole, had handed down a legacy made up of a body of modern scholarship and religious insights that were being actively produced and shaped well into the 1930s. And just as today's Europe remains the guarantor of its own legacy, alive to its own powers and their creative depths, yet indebted to the legacy of German Jewry, indispensable in a world in which all corners of the earth are responsible for one another, and just as Germany is now, despite the recent past, in the process of recovering its historical legacy as a land that was once and is now again inhabited by Jews—so too Dubnow's "world history of the Jewish people" moves forward, and the legacy German Jewry with it, in Europe and beyond, lives on as an exemplary messenger whose achievements will bear fruit in the Israel of today and in days to come.

One of the more recent histories of German Jewry, already offering us an account of the events that took place between 1933 and 1945, divides German Jewish history into valuable and thought-provoking stages, though different divisions of the subject matter will be shown to be necessary in the following discussion. Adolf Leschnitzer's *Saul and David*, published in 1954, part of his larger study, *The Problematics of German-Jewish Life and Community*, suggests two basic categories: one that encompasses non-Jewish events, and the other that restricts itself to the Jewish community's own development. The period between 1648, beginning with the rebuilding of Germany after the Thirty Years War, and the year 1933, marked by Germany's eruption into self-destruction, spans two hundred or so years that include the life of Goethe (1749–1832) and eighty-three years of a balance of power that held all tensions at bay. The history of German Jewry's rise and dissolution could also be accounted for in this scheme were it not for the fact that this singular Jewish community—true to the laws of its own inner nature—defies such a non-Jewish framework. Leschnitzer's second set of historical stages are more productive and insightful, according with the laws of German Jewry's inner development by dividing this history up into four sixty-year periods, the first two running from 1690 to roughly 1754, and then on to 1812, and the second two from 1812 to roughly 1871, and then forward to 1933.

The first 120 years (1690–1812) include the rise of several hundred influential Jewish families, those "predecessors" of Mendelssohn already described. The second 120-year period (1812–1933) witnesses the inclusion into this ascent of the entire German Jewish population of the time, approximately 200,000, as they gradually acquire full citizenship and the rights to pursue unrestricted economic and intellectual development. A first turning point occurs in 1754, marking a change for the good: the beginning of the friendship between Lessing and Mendelssohn. The second occurs in 1871 and marks a turn for the worse: deadly threats begin to be made against the Jews. The full fury of German nationalism erupted three different times in the period between 1812 and 1933, each time suddenly venting its wrath against the Jews. During these militant outbreaks against "foreign domination," when the defeat of German nationalist movements unleashed their emotional charge in the decades after 1812, nationalism saw the Jewish community as a victim that seemed to willingly hand itself over, helpless each time to become anything but prey. Growing nationalist sentiment led to the first actual outbreak of anti-Semitism in the first two decades after 1871, then to attacks that became more virulent after the recent victory over France, and finally to the post-1933 period that Leschnitzer calls "the horrible fifth act of an historical drama ending, like a classical tragedy, in catastrophe."

Yet what seems to resemble the final act of a drama in the history of the "the German Jewish community of experience" is in fact nothing but an interlude in the much more extensive drama that the "world history of the Jewish people" represents. Nor was the "fifth and final act" of German Jewry in the sense of its final and concluding appearance on the historical stage, neither in Germany—though this was potentially the case—nor by any means in the world as a whole. This "fifth act" was not the climax of a tragedy, but the conclusion of a criminal act. For while periods of reaction never lacked in the departments of destructive energy and intent, they remain devoid of any larger historical significance, even while the constant alternation between emancipation and reaction Dubnow describes was underway. In these circumstances, emancipation alone determines the course history will take, while the best reaction can do is to heap obstacles in progress's path. It is even clearer that anti-Semitism, as we will see in the next chapter, possesses no determining power whatsoever to direct the course of history, and indeed, lacks any fundamentally "Jewish" significance whatsoever, or any deep and lasting significance of its own. The decisive historical force more influential than any external setbacks or obstacles was the rise the Jews themselves accomplished, a push forward impelled by Jewish culture's own inner necessity and supported by all the cultural authority Judaism's four-thousand-year history could provide. The Jewish reawakening and renewal during the first stages of Jewish modernity were regarded by early historiography as a result of the largesse granted by the majority culture, and nothing more. But external support in reality did little to advance the Jewish cause, other than repair some of the immeasurable damage anti-Jewish repression had done in keeping Judaism behind the times. In fact, the modern flowering of the Jewish people springs from Judaism's own age-old tradition. The central achievement of German Jewry—and indeed, the message that became its legacy—was that it sparked this Jewish renaissance, and above all, that its vigorous outward reach moved forward until it became a movement for inner Jewish renewal as well.

Historically, Judaism's invigorated reach outward to the surrounding culture, and the inner renewal that eventually achieved fruition, provide us with a far more significant narrative than charting "reactions" to the Jews, however "reactionary" they might be. This dual focus avoids the snare of reading Jewish history through the lens of anti-Semitism, regardless of the serious consequences that anti-Semitism's idiocy and criminality would produce. Following the tension between outer development and inner renewal is also more important and incomparably more effective than following the twists and turns of the road to emancipation, whose measures—now generously, now sparingly put into force—determined the parameters within which the Jewish push forward into the surrounding culture, which we are about to sketch, took place. The terms "outer development" and "inner renewal" used here, and the link they establish between external and internal development in recent Jewish history, represent new categories for dividing the history of German Jewry into stages. Taking their cue from the "World History of the Jewish People" developed by Jost, Graetz, and Dubnow, these categories give serious consideration to the intellectual and religious upheavals and contemporary challenges that Jewish antiquity and the Jewish Middle Ages had confronted and overcome. The loyal creativity of Jewish modernity now faced similar challenges, and it was likewise equal to the task in every respect.

Around 1900, the fact that the Jews shared the rights of all men to citizenship and its obligations had gained wide acceptance, even though this recognition had not been realized in practice. It was also widely taken for granted that the Jews—though marked by the same variety, in their own way, as their fellow citizens were—comprised a people and community dispersed throughout a number of states, a community whose rights also carried the obligation to fulfill certain civic duties. But what had not been widely grasped, much less greeted with enthusiasm, was the right of each and every individual Jew, and the right of the Jewish people as a whole, to their own Judaism. The Jewish people and their culture had a right to their own independent tradition. The recognition had not yet taken hold that the Jews were human beings who constituted a developing social group, following its own path, and possessing the self-awareness and historically forceful personality of an authentic people. Such is the path every people must follow if they are to heed the call obliging them to continue their collective existence. And such was the path that the Jewish people had always followed, from the joining of the covenant sworn in the Bible and kept ever after. The Jewish path was a universal one, representing a beacon others might follow. It could not be left off halfway, by settling for one form of self-fulfillment or another. But the universality of that path was possible through Judaism's particularity alone, a particular path that in the end ceases to belong to this people, and unites itself with the paths of all peoples to create a single humanity.

FIVE

Equal Rights, Not Assimilation!

Emancipation is a word basic to the emergence of modernity, a word shaped by the concept in Roman law that defines emancipation as freedom from the power of life and death of the *paterfamilias* over the household. The modernity of an earth whose reaches have been fully explored—a modernity described in philosophical terms, in my own work, as "dialogic" (from 1944 forward)—requires such emancipation, and demands maturity from every human being, and from all humanity, and on their behalf as well. And so the hour of freedom tolls. Whatever form the relations between people, regions of the earth, between tribes, age groups, or occupational groups may take in the future, each is now, in its own way, equal in status to the other. Before such a universe can reestablish forms of mutual differentiation, all must first be addressed, treated, and recognized as mature equals, entitled to the same rights. This holds true—to mention but a few of those who have marched under the banner of emancipation in the last few centuries—for peasants, for workers, for women, for blacks, for slaves, for all the so-called colonized peoples, for the Catholics in Protestant lands, the Protestants in Catholic lands, for the Jews in all the lands of the earth into which they have been dispersed, for all those who make up the brimming tide of a movement that manifests itself in the hour of equality: a cresting wave of unity, breaking everywhere at once.

Emancipation demands freedom for each and every person in order to replace the self-alienation felt by all. Yet the full and equal rights needed to realize such freedom carry a double meaning that is not completely benign. For the seductive demand for equality—leading to a submerging of one's identity—insinuates itself all too eagerly into the emancipatory assertion of the right to difference and into the push to enfranchise the diverse. For the tempting, secondary claim to be found within the push for equal rights for all is that a mutual erasure of difference might be the path toward equality for all. This secondary meaning of equality seeks an end to all forms of difference, from race all the way to the peculiar particularity of a Judaism that explodes every framework imposed upon it. Such a smoothing out of all difference, the goal of assimilation and its conformity, represses those disparities and inequalities visible from both sides of the process while the achievement of equal rights and "emancipation" is underway. The pretense is that—with equality supposedly having been achieved—difference no longer has any claim to persist. But the fact that the right to the same freedom as others implies the freedom to become like others, that the seductions of becoming like others are to be found on every path leading to equal rights, cannot and therefore ought not be held against the project of emancipation. The seductions of equality indict neither the significance, nor the necessity of emancipation, which must, under all circumstances, be fought for and won.

Like every other group called to modernity's world-historical moment, which they shared in common, the Jews made the struggle for equal rights their own, and thus were entangled in the most serious difficulties that an excessive adaptation can produce. Jews had from the very start been split into two camps: those who fought for emancipation and equal rights on behalf of each and every citizen, and those who took up the fight against assimilation, so that Jews granted equal rights would not cease being Jews once equal rights had been won. In this sense, both camps waged a double battle: against the outside world, but also within the Jewish community, fighting not just against Judaism's enemies, but also against its friends. Heinrich von Treitschke and his slogan represented only one of the enemy's faces: "The Jews are our misfortune." This was the same von Treitschke who had announced his support for assimilation in no uncertain terms: "What we demand of our fellow Israelite citizens is simple: to become German." Yet Count von Clermont-Tonnerre, a man free of all anti-Jewish animus, declared much the same thing when he spoke as a friend and enthusiastic supporter of Jewish emancipation in the Parisian National Assembly on December 23, 1789: "To the Jews as a nation, nothing, to the Jews as individuals, everything!"

The temptation announced was to become exclusively French instead of remaining French Jews, or to become exclusively German instead of remaining German Jews. Emancipation could be achieved, not as supporters of Judaism, but as men. And this, of course, was to gain equal rights at the cost of one's identity, and thus meant the opposite of true emancipation, amounting to assimilation and nothing more. The model of assimilation did not further the Jewish people's entry to modernity, but the opposite: the right of the Jews to enter the modern world was guaranteed, providing they met the simple condition of ceasing to remain Jews. Two quite different factors—one in force since biblical times, the other strictly modern—explain why Jewish modernity succumbed to the blandishments of exaggerated adaptation and loss of identity so often. The first was the special circumstances created by Judaism's peculiar kind of particularity, and the second, the specific historical context and circumstances in which Mendelssohn's breakthrough to modernity occurred.

In what does this already biblical particularity of Judaism consist, a particularity that consistently explodes every confining and external framework? It lies in this people's unique fusion of a decided particularity with the most decisive kind of universality, a particularity expressing itself as an ineluctable belief-centeredness that goes hand in hand with an equally irrevocable commitment to history. In the distant past, the covenant Moses joined in the desert of Sinai under this message not only founded the existence of his own people but also originated the idea of humanity's ultimate fulfillment; that same covenant obligated the Jews to carry that message forward into the present, thus inaugurating the demand for the unconditional Jewish devotion to history, a commitment that requires their continued existence as a nation as well as a religious community. This is a people, moreover, who must claim equality among the nations as a religion, while the equality with other religions it demands must be sought as a people. The peculiar particularity of Judaism—seemingly granted equality only when the Jewish people accept a conformity bent on erasing the very particularity emancipation sought to preserve, an emancipation sought in the first place in order to ensure their enduring existence as a people—is a specificity inseparable from the universality of the path laid down and held fast to from the biblical covenant forward, a specificity constantly pointing beyond its own particular path. This is a path whose particularity ceases only with the achievement of humanity's ultimate goal: the kingdom of God, or as the Bible puts it more simply, the kingdom, when Judaism's singular road merges with the ways of all humanity, who will then beat their swords into ploughshares and their spears into pruning hooks (Isaiah 2:4).

But had not this goal—that no nation would lift its sword against another, and that they would "learn war no more"—already been achieved, as Jewish progressives hopefully saw it, or was it not at least close at hand, thanks to modernity and its advances? Assimilation seemed the only sensible course left in the modern world, far preferable to standing at the historical margins in religious expectation, saving one's strength for the messiah who was yet to come. With this new line of argument, modernity was able to drive Judaism into yet another corner, demanding that Jews become like everyone else, refusing to consider full Jewish emancipation, or being prepared to grant it only in return for their complete assimilation. For had not modernity initiated a process that left the covenant far behind, and superseded it: the covenant that originated the idea of a kingdom of freedom and profound peace, begun the joining of the covenant at Sinai, then handed down through a biblical succession that each generation renewed, with every renewal of that covenant only affirming what was already implicit in the original Jewish bond? Did not the modern age, by contrast, signify a new origin, placing all of mankind at the very threshold of a freedom and liberation for all, and peace among men? Why was a particular messenger like the Jews, the herald carrying the universal message and its promise to the world as a whole, still necessary in revolutionary times such as these? Was not the more legitimate path now to merge as fully and quickly as possible with that universal dream? Jewish advocates of progress, enthusiastic to the brink of fanaticism, rushed forward to greet modernity, passing through the breach Mendelssohn had opened. Mistakenly imagining that a secular messianic age was already at hand, Jewish progressives saw a new world being created before their eyes, but they never considered the fact that the surrounding world as well as the Jews themselves still inhabited an age whose redemption required that Jews remain Jews, trailblazers of the path that would lead to a humanity in which all would have a share. Jewish worshipers of progress struggled to prove they were members of universal "mankind," and nothing more, with spirits all too blithe, instead of continuing to build a "nation" of their own: for humanity, they knew in their hearts, would soon merge all peoples, states, and religions into one.

Mendelssohn himself had led the way in this development; given the extent of his reputation, his thought should have long since made its influence felt far and wide. But behind him stood a Jewish people with its cultural traditions intact, cut off from the wider world, a culture that remained vital throughout the First World War and beyond, lending its support to Mendelssohn's successors. If the balance of power in the Jewish world lay anywhere, it was not in a future well beyond any realistic horizon, but in the hands of the traditional Jewish world. And stretching from Russia and Poland, to North Africa and Yemen, tradition still did not wish to let its children go. The ghetto wasn't fearful about preserving its way of life—the fight to preserve tradition had been waged successfully for many, many years—but concerned with the consequences and prospects that would result from the imminent and long-delayed lifting of restrictions now at hand. This sense of a secure background of support helps explain why Jewish advocates of freedom left their Jewishness behind with so little hesitation when offered the chance to enter the modern world, left it behind, like a reliable possession that could be reclaimed and put back into use when the need arose.

This attitude toward tradition also accounts for a certain tension built into Mendelssohn's foundational and magnificent tract of 1783, his "declaration of independence," as it were: *Jerusalem, or, On Religious Power and Judaism*. While arguing its thesis with consistent intensity, Mendelssohn's plea for freedom of religion nonetheless falsely conceives its solution to its specifically Jewish concerns. Mendelssohn passionately demands freedom for the Jews in fiery tones, standing up for religious liberty and defending it against any kind of "religious authority" or state coercion. Yet Mendelssohn does not carry that freedom forward to its logical conclusion within Judaism itself. Judaism's "religious power" is still granted a sovereign power akin to that of the state. This self-limitation subsequently raises the question: "What are the laws of Moses but a system of religious government, of the power and right of religion? . . . '. . . How then, can you, my dear Mr. Mendelssohn, remain an adherent of the faith of your fathers . . . , when you contest the ecclesiastical law that has been given through Moses and purports to be founded on divine revelation?'"[1]

"This objection," Mendelssohn replies, "hits at the heart," though he does not hesitate to meet it. Both the Bible's universal moral strictures, governing the Jews and all of mankind, and the biblical commandments levied upon the Jews alone, were for Mendelssohn valid without exception as a guide to Jewish action, and represented no infringement whatsoever on Jewish liberty. For Judaism prescribes no fundamental articles of belief and sets no bounds whatsoever on the use of human reason. As a Jew, the individual was obliged to observe and sustain only those Jewish practices that preserve his particularity—just as every individual sustains those practices that preserve his or her particularity amidst the universal, differences that make possible the common work of building human community. But the individual Jew, while bound to his particularity, for his own part possessed the same liberty as all men, or the same liberty that they ought to possess: to believe and to think whatever the truth demands.

Mendelssohn's gaze, however, remained fixed on the future, on the guarantee of freedom for all. The full range of human possibility to be realized stretched out before his eyes, possibilities that would now be accessible to the Jewish people, giving them the chance at complete self-development by taking part in every sort of worldly and spiritual endeavor the world has to offer. In the process, Mendelssohn falsely identifies the continued existence of his people—a fact he took for granted—with sustaining the restrictiveness of his people's medieval forms of religious observance, a ritual practice whose renewal played no part in his program. Instead of demanding civil rights explicitly in the name of Jews who had been transformed by modernity, Mendelssohn demanded those rights for them only in the name of their humanity, without seeking a fundamental renewal of their Judaism. Such a universal humanity, of course, cannot exist without striking firm roots in its own forms of particularity. Only this prior form of emancipation can prevent the individual from conforming to a particular culture that is not his own, that is, keep him from blindly accepting the larger culture instead of seeking emancipation from within.

The decisive fact for Jews who lived during the century and a half after Mendelssohn's *Jerusalem*—the central period for German Jewry, from 1783 to 1933—was that their full emancipation as members of humanity was possible before their emancipation as Jews, a situation that produced various and exaggerated forms of mimicry, whether of the contemporary culture that surrounded them or its imagined future. Jews were dazzled by the prospect of an emancipation that would liberate each and every member of Jewish society, indeed, all of mankind, before those freedoms were close to being practically realized. As Jews continued to struggle against an exaggerated urge to become like others, which seemed the quickest path to freedom, the limits that still existed to full Jewish equality, achieved in fits and starts, and sometimes only hesitantly challenged by the Jews themselves, began to be overcome. When all was said and done, the Jews would achieve a profound and lasting insight into their own particularity as a people, the kind of vision that Jewish awareness had seldom possessed in the past.

But the full realization of that vision and all it entailed—an insight into their own particularity as a mission, and task for the future—was cut short when annihilation rained down on German Jewry midway on their journey, forcing them to a halt and imposing shattering reverses. No other Jewish community, moreover, was truly able to carry the German Jewish mantle forward by continuing their work at the same level, for by the second half of the nineteenth century and the first half of the twentieth, a significant outmigration from Europe to all corners of the earth had taken place, a population shift that included a significant new diaspora of the Jewish people that will be discussed shortly. Settling in North and South America, Palestine, South Africa and other lands, these Jews had first to transform—as they continue to change and modify—the path that German Jewry had already hewn before them. For without coming to terms with that legacy, their communities could not move forward into the future and continue where their predecessors, and indeed the West as a whole, had been forced to a premature halt.

We will shortly give a detailed account of German Jewry's exemplary path as a forerunner of modernity, highlighting both its progress toward equal rights as well the detours that consisted of its excessive and defensive mimicry of the surrounding culture. We will also present the accomplishments this same course allowed them to achieve. For the right to their own particularity fought for by German Jewry would acquire a universal legitimacy in their wake, a right that came to be seen as part of the heritage of all groups throughout the world. Indeed, it is this right to difference that constitutes the outstanding legacy of German Jewry, for it came to be recognized by the world only through them, though it has indeed yet to be realized in practice. When we examine the German Jewish path, both applauding their struggle for equal rights and criticizing their confused desire to fit in at any cost, we must always recall that emancipation and assimilation worked on both an individual and collective level. Emancipation would at times affect individual Jews rather than the Jewish people as a whole, and at other times it would affect the Jewish people as such rather than individual Jews. In light of the breakthrough signified by the founding of the state of Israel in 1948, a new beginning without parallel—yet nothing so fundamentally new that would cast a shadow on the legacy of German Jewry—it should be unambiguously clear to all that the initial tension between equal rights and conformity is not some historical relic now behind us, but a battle still underway in the present, and a challenge to our future.

Acting as kind of lone wolf, it was possible for a person—and indeed still is—to enter modernity by dint of individual initiative alone, as a "privileged Jew," or even in small groups, as the French, English, and Italian Jews did, while the broad masses of Jews remained in the Middle Ages. In these cases, the people as such were not involved in the process of renewal. Emancipation was instead accomplished individually, by Jews who harbored the most authentic feeling for and commitment to their Jewish heritage. But this version of the process of emancipation bore with it what was finally the unavoidable consequence of individual assimilation: the exaggerated effort of individual Jews or Jewish groups to fit into the surrounding community and society that had granted them equal rights. The Jewish people provided such individuals no support, because their emancipation had not been won as part of a common struggle.

But the opposite course was also possible, and still is. Jews could enter modernity as a people, but without at the same time renewing each of Judaism's underlying cultural supports. This version of the process is already evident in the first Book of Samuel, when the desire of the Jews to be "like all other nations" (1 Samuel 8:5, 20) finds its first biblical expression with the anointment of Israel's first king and is duly castigated. But collective emancipation, carried out on behalf of the people as such, when a Jewish community settles for the state's version of emancipation rather than its own, is really nothing more than collective assimilation, another exaggerated and excessive attempt to fit in. This time assimilation is not the desire of an individual Jew who wishes to merge with the crowd, but the wish of a people to merge itself with the world of nations. When an individual Jew steps forward into a modernity that remains closed to the distinct difference of his people, conformity, not equality, has been achieved. Individual equality can be said to have been achieved only when, thanks to the equally vital and indispensable achievement of equality for the Jewish people as such, each and every individual can remain loyal to a Judaism whose personal validity no foreign state, nor his own, can deny.

SIX

Steps Toward Emancipation

While the Jewish achievement of full civil equality took its course, despite severe setbacks and bitter delays, and as modernity began to include more and more Jewish communities within its scope—communities fighting against excessive adaptation to the ways of their fellow citizens and nations—the battle to grant equal stature and rights to Judaism itself had begun. Judaism had continued to retain its hold and influence in the early stages of this process, even when Jews who had made social advances and claimed citizenship strove to play down their Jewishness. Judaism's influence began to wane only when their children and grandchildren, no longer regarding it as a stay and support, soon lost all memory of a Judaism that had been the wellspring and center of an entire way of life. Without a fully enfranchised Judaism with a firm foothold on modernity's ground, and without a vibrant Jewish community able to announce in no uncertain terms that Judaism's message had become part of every area of human endeavor— for such an assertive, public Jewish presence did not yet exist—the desire to turn away from all things Jewish and disappear into a world where "equal rights" had been achieved was unavoidable. All the while, however, the visibility of explicitly Jewish participation in public affairs was on the increase, signaling the beginning of the fight for the emancipation of the Jews as Jews.

This fight for Jewish emancipation found an unlikely ally and comrade-in-arms in what was otherwise an absolutely poisonous, superfluous, wholly undesirable, yet timely and helpful opponent. Rising from the abyss, help of a sort arrived from none other than the chief enemy of Jewish equality: from so-called anti-Semitism, whose greed, delusion and murderous lust reached far enough to lay a finger even on Jews who were hardly identifiable as such, aside from Jewish origins they had long since cast aside. These non-Jewish Jews were persecuted as Jews as well. Suddenly reminded of the Judaism their fathers had left behind, the assimilated strata faced anti-Semitism, and tried to shunt it aside as well, if only to reject the caricature proffered by Judaism's enemies. Still, these nominal Jews were forced to confront Jewish identity anew: a Judaism that was not some historical fossil, but a past of their own of decisive importance, indeed, a past that would today, in the present, decide whether they would live or die. Judaism's own slumbering but nonetheless powerful resources, when roused to action, would help ward off the threat of Jewish disappearance that assimilation posed. These Jewish strengths hardly needed any "assistance" from anti-Semitism; such stimulus to Jewish self-awareness became a significant factor only once Judaism's own independent renewal of its unbroken, living tradition and its enduring significance had already begun. But anti-Semitism's delusion and criminality dramatize time and time again the utter futility of the exaggerated and determined efforts Jews made to fit in. Anti-Semitism thus fanned the flames of the fight to gain equality for Jewish particularity.

Jewish religiosity was the first realm of Jewish culture to achieve wide-ranging emancipation and recognition, and as a result, Judaism as a religion soon ran the risk of becoming just like any other "confession" or set of "religious beliefs." In mounting its defense against this prospect, Judaism's religious perspective was able to make important advances, and in the process to rediscover its deepest and most authentic roots. This religious development took place at the same time that Jews successfully entered the sciences and humanities in significant numbers, and these successes were the work of individuals fully aware of the symbolic as well as intellectual importance their actions carried for their era. Some would succumb to the lures of conformity along the way, whether from careerism or by adopting an apologetic stance. But in the end their efforts would achieve a full scholarly enfranchisement for Judaism, culminating in the first modern movement for the scholarly study of Judaism, the Wissenschaft des Judentums. Theirs was an achievement that transcended any attacks, or countering defense. For when all was said and done, the Wissenschaft des Judentums succeeded in providing us with a scholarship fully as rich and full of significance as its Jewish subject matter deserved.

The development of scholarly discipline of Jewish history, the cutting edge of the Wissenschaft des Judentums, provided the argument for complete Jewish emancipation with its most pronounced academic support. The achievements of Jost, Graetz, and Dubnow and the historic milestones they represent in this regard have already been touched on in our discussion of the historical stages of modern Jewish history, and will be considered more fully when we attend to the turning point that Dubnow's *World History of the Jewish People* signified in German Jewry's process of inner renewal. At the very same moment, however, Protestant biblical scholarship was winnowing through its own historic sources, and suddenly stumbled upon the fact that Judaism possessed an independent historical existence of its own. With exemplary honesty, Protestant biblical scholars publicized their recovery of Jewish historical sources, shedding new light on Jewish history. Judaism, they showed, was indeed responsible for the advent of Christianity and inseparable from the origins of Christianity. Protestant scholarship remained convinced, of course, that ancient as well as contemporary Judaism had long since been superseded by the new Christian dispensation. Scholarly exchange between Christians and Jews took place despite the fact that Judaism's continuing existence was itself a blatant affront to Christianity's original and guiding self-conception as the new order. And this Christian-Jewish discourse would continue until the combatants rediscovered an historical truth marginalized during the peculiar circumstances of the Jewish entry to modernity: the historical fact that the Jews were a people and nation, and had remained one until the present day. Only this recognition would make the "final step toward emancipation" possible, a movement whose outlines we are about to sketch.

Judaism is religiosity, and achieved its initial modern recognition as a religion, though from the time of Bible forward, Judaism's religious origin and vision had belonged to all peoples who, like Judaism, struggled for an emancipation and freedom of their own. What the rest of the world questioned was the rationale for Judaism's continuity: Jewish culture was now, in the full light of public day, claiming the right to reclaim every one of its religious and national traditions in modern form. This effort was questioned on theological as well as political grounds: the demand for freedom of religion laid out its vision of a new historical era with uncompromising clarity for all the world to see, and necessarily drew opposition from all those forces who had prospered under the old regime, and whom modernity had left behind.

Judaism is religiosity—that is, a living, changing religious way of life, and thus both orthodox and liberal: orthodox insofar as its message and messengers testify to a timeless, transcendent Jewish continuity, and liberal insofar as those same witnesses are obliged to testify to this enduring existence in historical era after era, and to carry out Judaism's own renewal as well. The transhistorical core of Jewish teaching leads to orthodoxy, while its historicity leads to liberalism. The former meets the challenge of history's changing, demanding winds with steadfast loyalty, while the latter faces those same challenges by bringing about and furthering historical change, until history fulfills itself in the kingdom of God and a peace that transcends the historical. Both directions blossomed in the period that followed 1818, when contemporary liturgical innovations, including the introduction of the organ into services conducted at the Temple at Hamburg became a focus of heated debate: for the liberals, such adaptation symbolized Judaism's ability to change with the times, while for conservatives, such deviations represented the symbolic final straw that joined them together in common cause to resist any further falling away from the past. This "battle of the Temple" provoked representatives of every shade of opinion to enter the fray and voice their positions pro and contra, from the extreme right to the extreme left: their debate paralleled with precision the factional division that the seating order in the French Assembly had defined in the same period.

On the far right stood Samson Raphael Hirsch (1808–88), the instigator of the Orthodox withdrawal and their break with the rest of the Jewish community over whether the strictest observance and faith in the ritual law would be maintained. Closer to the moderate middle, but with the same belief in the law as the key to sustaining the Jewish community, as long as others left him room for his own mode of expressing his piety, stood the rabbi of Würzburg, Seligmann Bär Bamberger (1807–78), later the founder of Germany's Orthodox Jewish community. Conservative resistance, of course, provoked opposition of its own, led on the extreme left by Samuel Holdheim (1806–60), who championed a break with the Jewish community's traditional self-conception and "Jewish" notion of the future to allow a full engagement with the contemporary world. On the right, Abraham Geiger (1810–74), the most important leader of liberal Judaism, which unlike the Orthodox, owes its origin to a number of leading figures, established enough space between himself and the left to stake out a middle ground, allowing him to continue with traditional observance while vigorously endorsing the possibilities of the present. Zacharias Frankel (1801–75), who by comparison seems a somewhat dull figure, was nonetheless strikingly successful in arguing for this middle way, eventually becoming the father of conservative Judaism. Frankel rejected out of hand the presumptuous suggestion that a tradition handed down and preserved throughout history could in any way be considered obsolete. Jewish tradition, Frankel argued, represented a path which, while connected to the past, at the same time led forward to a future that would be fundamentally transformed.

Religiosity, in other words, had achieved its own victorious breakthrough and emancipation: but not without a kind of imitative adaptation that was far too extreme, an adaptive adjustment that would henceforth define all Judaism, whether right, left, and center as simply another religious "confession" or "confession of faith" whose obligations extended to only part of life's expanse. Regarded as one of life's peripheral phenomena, Judaism as mere "confession" was stripped of its deeper influence on Jews now swamped with far more encompassing social obligations, those countless duties of citizenship that were part of the everyday life amidst the peoples and states that had become their homes. Religious life was now merely a persuasion, and increasingly amounted to nothing more than the domestic, personal concern of each individual believer. The historical reality of the Jewish covenant—the framework that took individual Jews and forged them into a single Judaism, for the obligation to bear witness to the covenant had preserved the Jews as both a spiritual force and national culture—began to fade away. The idea of religious confession alone sufficed—and does not suffice—to sustain them as Jews in perpetuity.

But one form of Jewish emancipation moved far beyond the scope of religious confession. The recognition achieved by the Wissenschaft des Judentums, representing this people's full acceptance by the intellectual world, staked out a bold position in the intellectual landscape. The vibrant activity of Jewish scholars contradicted Hegel's doctrine—then at the peak of its influence—that every world-historical people could be called to lead or share leadership in the march of world history but a single time. Hegel's system implied that modern Jews had no choice but to become Germans, and thereby merge with the German tide of history if they were ever to amount to anything at all. At the same time, German governments intoxicated by their victory over France reimposed repressive and irksome restrictions on their Jewish communities, reintroducing legal barriers which at the very least delayed and where possible sought to undo their transition to modernity. This reactionary legislation culminated in the Prussian Ordinance of August 18, 1822, with its particularly ominous consequences for intellectual endeavors. The Prussian statute banned Jews who had achieved citizenship by March 11, 1812, along with Jews enfranchised during the wars of liberation of 1813–15, from holding teaching positions at the universities and secondary schools unless they consented to baptism.

But as Judaism is religiosity, so it is also scholarship—and Jewish research into and exploration of Judaism cannot be done without it! And so in 1818, at the very moment that liberalism and orthodoxy were flowering, set off by the "Temple Battle"—and simultaneous with Hegel's arrival in Berlin— Leopold Zunz had already produced his groundbreaking, programmatic tract "On Rabbinic Literature." Zunz's work opened the door to an immensely promising deepening of Jewish modernity, requiring only a change in external circumstances before powerful cultural forces who were ready and willing would carry on his work. In 1818, Zunz, Eduard Gans, and Isaak Markus Jost, together with the first modern historian of Judaism, Ludwig Marcus, Moses Moser, and three other friends, founded the Society for the Culture and Science of the Jews (Verein für Kultur und Wissenschaft der Juden). Heinrich Heine would join the group in 1822. Each of these figures was born in the last decade of the eighteenth century, and all were gifted with the full bloom of youth and its energy. Yet their journal, *Zeitschrift für die Wissenschaft des Judentums*, had been in print for barely two years, from 1822 through 1823, when the dissolution of the society was at hand. In 1825 its president, Gans, agreed to be baptized in order to continue his work as Hegel's colleague, that is, in order to become a professor, though he was, to be sure, not the first apostate from the society. On June 28, 1825—almost half a year before Gans took the identical step, which he completed on

December 12—Heine acquired his baptismal certificate in order to obtain, as his famous phrase has it, his "entrée-billet [ticket] to European culture."

Yet in spite of this, the entrée of the Wissenschaft des Judentums had been won. And with each succeeding decade of the nineteenth century, it became more and more clear that antiquity, the Middle Ages, and the West's stature as a world power all drew part of their strength and inspiration from the spirit of Judaism, until the fact finally became impossible to overlook. "Entrée" to European culture, and all of modernity's crucial innovations, of course, had not originated from Jewish sources alone, but neither had they passed Judaism by, but had moved ahead together with Jewish culture: modernity's push toward the future had always taken place in partnership with the Jews. This insight, of course, came too late for many and indeed for almost all the best of those "emancipated" Jews who grew up in the nineteenth and early twentieth centuries. The corresponding institutional realization followed even later—and in Germany itself only piecemeal and always inadequately—with the specific integration and inclusion of Jewish subject matter into the university curriculum through the establishment of chairs in Jewish studies.

Yet when ninety-two-year-old Leopold Zunz closed his weary eyes for the last time on March 17, 1886, having kept faith with the project begun in his youth along with comrades from his same generation, Zunz himself obviously grasped the intellectual significance of the fact that Judaism was now a living presence at the university and within scholarship, despite casual as well as explicit attempts to see it eclipsed. This subject will be entered into more fully in a later discussion of German Jewry's inner development and the process of establishing chairs of Jewish studies in Germany, which remains piecemeal and inadequate. Here it is worth noting that even crucial progress that the success the Wissenschaft des Judentums represented was constantly threatened by attempts to imitate and assimilate into the surrounding culture, sometimes finding expression in political gestures and other times as apologetics. Assimilation remained a constant threat to authentic equality, though it brought fewer and fewer advantages to the individual Jew who pursued its course. The assimilated Jew was less and less able to return to the haven of his people after defeats, and reminded in ever-more shrilly voiced demands that his efforts serve the German nation and state alone. Only this way, he was told, would his cultural efforts be of any use.

The Wissenschaft des Judentums, meanwhile, unearthed a trove of Jewish knowledge and history. The intellectual measure of their efforts, of course, must be taken using scholarly criteria alone. Yet those same treasures lent support and continue to aid the battle of the Jewish community, within its own confines and beyond them, for the prestige and authority its people deserve. The cultural and historical material rediscovered by Jewish historians refuted charges holding the Jews responsible for every conceivable sin. Jewish scholarship was also a refutation of slurs that have taken almost every conceivable form, ranging from straightforward objection and doubts to derision, suspicion and defamation, though anti-Jewish charges rarely had anything to do with evidence, and were hardly susceptible to rational disproof. But in the end, the difficulty the Wissenschaft des Judentums faced time and time again, constantly sidetracking its own best efforts, was its apologetic stance—that is, its defensiveness—an attitude still in evidence today, both in the United States as well as Israel.

Yet a scholarship seduced into cultural weakness can also achieve self-consciousness, when its subject matter is authentic, as in the case of Judaism, and eventually cast its crutch aside and stand on its own. The resulting scholarship remains objective through and through, and is in the end no longer distracted by politics. Apologetics, on the contrary, soon dissipates its own energy, until it becomes dependent on the very opponents whom it is crucial to resist. Before long, apologetic scholarship can neither remain objective nor attain the kind of confident, self-conscious angle of vision that allows the most productive scholarship to succeed. The irony was that the mounting anxiety of Jewish scholars over whether Jewish culture should exist in the future was stoked by well-meaning philo-Semites, possessing little if any knowledge of the Jewish tradition. Meanwhile, the actual magnitude and depth of Judaism's cultural resources should have nipped any such worries in the bud. Extramural pressure of this sort nonetheless had the effect of marginalizing research into Jewish subject matter precisely when its topics were the most compelling and legitimate. But even this apologetic suppression of scholarly objectivity was soon to pass.

Sooner or later the truth wins out, so long as its foundation has been laid, and the fact that Judaism's intellectual values represent the most distinguished kind of cultural achievement—and thus deserve public recognition—is such a foundational truth. The many blandishments of conformity had their effect, encouraging scholars to exaggerate Jewish difference for political effect or to minimize it with apologetic ends in mind, instead of trusting that the truth would gradually emerge on its own. But the process that began when the Jewish right to equality was recognized could not be stopped, and the truth gradually reveals itself to the researcher precisely because it is the truth, waiting to be found. The Wissenschaft des Juden-tums set about its work with a powerful constancy commitment that served as a shield against withering attacks launched from outside the university's walls, allowing Jewish scholars to confront their opponents with a steadily increasing sense of independence well suited to its object of study:

> Gird your sword upon your thigh, O hero,
> in your splendor and glory;
> —in your glory, win success;
> ride on in the cause of truth and meekness and right. (Psalms 45:4–5)

SEVEN

Gabriel Riesser's Greatest Deed

Gabriel Riesser died in Hamburg on April 22, 1863, at the age of fifty-seven. This was eight decades after Mendelssohn's decisive breakthrough of 1783 opened up the prospect of full cultural participation for German Jewry on the ground it had settled some two thousand years before, and eight decades before the police-ordered closing of the last office of the Reichs-vereinigung der Juden in Deutschland (Reich Association of German Jews) in 1943, cutting German Jewry off from the ground it had settled for two thousand years. At the moment of his death, the achievement of full civil emancipation for the Jews in Germany was so complete that Riesser, the movement's leader and pioneer, scarcely left any loose ends that would allow others to carry on with his life's work. It seemed impossible to imagine—incomprehensible, in fact—that Riesser, who in 1860 became the first German Jew who retained his membership in the Jewish community to be selected as judge, had actually been unconditionally banned from holding any office thirty and forty years earlier in that same Hamburg, city of his birth, and subject to other forms of discrimination as well. The era of equality was now in full bloom, thanks to Riesser, and such "individual emancipation" was now, for a larger reason, a matter of course, thanks to Riesser as well.

Riesser never waged his battle with only the Jews in mind, nor to gain, where possible, exclusive benefits on their behalf. It is thus all too easy to forget that Riesser had waged his battle as a very Jewish one, and that it had become necessary to fight in precisely those terms. Riesser conducted his campaign as a Jewish struggle, but one to be joined in by all, a fight that was to be celebrated as a battle for freedom and justice for all. The terms in which he cast his actions thus defined him as a Jew after Judaism's own heart, as he took the point position in the struggle for freedom and justice in his fatherland, and for humanity as a whole. As a member of the provisional Frankfurt parliament of 1848, then a member of the German National Assembly, convened in the Paulskirche (Church of St. Paul), one of its finest speakers, and eventually its vice president, as one of the major framers of the German constitution to be completed some seventy years later by Hugo Preuss, another German Jew, and as one of the thirty-three representatives who offered the imperial crown to the king of Prussia on April 3, 1849, Riesser stands out as a major figure not only in German history, but also in the history of German Jewry, and—by virtue of his great deed—in the history of modern Jewry as a whole.

We owe thanks to Riesser as well for another achievement: all Jews today stand as its beneficiaries, unaware of the courageous venture this bold champion of their interests undertook on their behalf. Why is it, for example, that Jews in France are known not as "Jews" but as "Israelites," or that the leading representatives of Swiss Jewry are known as the "Israelite" community, or as heading "Israelite" organizations? And why did Riesser himself name his first pamphlet, the bold production of a twenty-four-year-old, *On the Position of Those Confessing the Mosaic Faith in Germany*? Because the word "Jew" had carried only negative connotations since the late Middle Ages! To Riesser's contemporaries, the word "Jew" was almost exclusively a pejorative term—an insult, and nothing more. To a certain extent, it carries that charge to this very day; the word "Jew" was painful to Jews themselves who, as citizens of modernity, sought to leave the shame and humiliation the ghetto had attached to their Jewishness behind. In response, Riesser gave

his *Blätter für Religion und Gewissensfreiheit* (Journal for Religion and Freedom of Conscience), first published on April 2, 1832, this name: *Der Jude*
(The Jew)! What follows is Riesser's defense against charges that he had
damaged the Jewish cause by reintroducing the word "Jew"; it was printed
as the introduction to his journal's second volume and published on April
2, 1833. Riesser's opponents had argued that living "Jews" no longer had
anything in common with the nonsense and unsavory connotations the
word had carried for centuries. Instead, they wanted to be called "Confes-
sors of the Mosaic Faith," or "Israelites," something absolutely new, fundamentally different and better than mere "Jews." Riesser's reply was eloquent
and blunt:

> You claim that so much that is hateful and despicable has attached itself to this
> name that it must be avoided, so that unpleasant connections and memories are
> not aroused. But does not the hate that seems to attach itself to the name derive
> more fundamentally from the state of affairs, and men, and must not men fight
> against that hate and cast it away, if it is to end? If unjustifiable hatred clings to
> our name, should we then disavow it, instead of setting all of our energies to the
> task of bringing it honor? And what if this very name is a historical one, which
> can never be forgotten, not the name of some unknown, whose name can disap-
> pear along with the person? And if it is the same name with which we have
> designated our manner of worshipping the divine, and with which we have taught
> our children to designate it, a name we thus owe respect and love—should we
> disavow it to please those who hate it and those they remember under that name?
> Should love hide itself in the face of hate? Should the goddess veil her counte-
> nance, in cowardly fear, before the Fury? Should not love bestow its most tender
> care, its warmest blessings precisely where hate has struck its most painful
> wounds? We laugh at the childlike custom our ancestors had of changing the
> name of the mortally ill, as if the Angel of Death would then not know where to
> find him. Are we not just as foolish with our modern, rewritten designations?
> Believe me, hate knows where to look just as well as the Angel of Death, and as
> long as he's looking, he will recognize the right name amidst thousands of pacify-
> ing expressions.

Thanks in large part to Riesser, who had the courage to stand up for his
name despite the hatefulness and spite encrusted upon it, and despite the
fact that this choice might arouse "unpleasant connections and memories,"
the German Jewish achievement of full civil equality became one of the
greatest accomplishments of the modern era, equal in its import to the

greatest achievements of Jewish antiquity and the Jewish Middle Ages, and a worthy addition to the ongoing saga of Judaism's four-thousand-year-old inheritance. "If unjustifiable hatred clings to our name, should we disavow it?"—the unjustifiably despised name of 'Jew'—instead of "setting all of our energies to the task of bringing it honor? And especially when this name is an historical one?" Judaism's new hour tolled not just for Jews alive at the current historical moment, but also for Judaism's historical existence as such. In trying to shed the burden of their past, Jewish descendants of antiquity and the Middle Ages had also sacrificed its depths. Jettisoning the past might—perhaps—allow them to succeed in the contemporary world, but such a break would leave them bereft of a past that provided the crucial basis for setting out and seizing the future, and leave them shorn of the fundamental ground of their continuing existence as Jews. Standing up and reveling in the bright chapters of one's history is not enough. Only by including history's dark chapters makes those who dare into bearers of history's promise, for history's light can free itself of those darkening shadows only by applying the most tender care and love's warmest blessing precisely there, "where hate has struck the deepest wounds."

Riesser, to be sure, had in mind only that small group of Jews for whom he demanded full civil rights when he named his journal *Der Jude* in 1832. Martin Buber correctly observed as much eighty-four years later, when he reclaimed Riesser's watchword and used it for the title of his own journal. "We give our journal this same name," Buber wrote in its inaugural issue, "but we take that name not to signify the individual, but the Jews as bearers of their nationhood and its task. We demand freedom of religion not for members of a faith, but the freedom to live and work for a national community that has been held back, and demand that those who today are for the most part treated as objects, subject to the course of events, instead become the free and shaping subjects of their own fate and work, developing a potential enabling their fulfillment of the offices they owe humanity as a whole." This extension of the meaning inherent in the watchword "Der Jude" was fully justified, offered as it was by the leader at the forefront of the battle for the "national emancipation" of the Jewish people, and so were other extensions of its original meaning offered since. Such notions were not yet available to Riesser, the champion of "individual emancipation" for the Jews. That such breakthroughs were and still are possible remains a consequence of Riesser's achievement, thanks to his courage and boldness. This was Riesser's greatest deed.

EIGHT

Emancipation's Greatest Foe

Anti-Semitism demands consideration at this point in our presentation, for without it, the Jewish entry to modernity would have taken a far different course. Had anti-Semitism not arisen—or had its disastrous criminality been promptly recognized for what it was and decisively stopped—German Jewry would not have been decimated and cast to the winds. European Jewry, and in fact Europe itself, would not present us with the heaping ruins and field of death we see before us today. While the force of that event and the anti-Semitism still with us both demand analysis, the discussion that follows will treat these matters with simple abhorrence and only with the greatest regret. Anti-Semitism owes its place in the following discussion to its crimes and nothing more. Were we not to mention these shameful acts and their context—acts otherwise unworthy of discussion—the fact that the term "legacy" is now required to discuss the achievements of German Jewry would be incomprehensible. Yet we still cannot and never will be able to say enough about the six million wounds suffered by a bloodied Jewish people, robbed of a full third of its number. We will never find sufficient words to describe this martyrdom of Jewish innocence, an event of world-historic significance despite the base nullity of the anti-Semitism that carried the blame.

Judaism's original awakening to the meaning of divinity was a call to arms against idol worship, paganism, the thrall of nature, the delusion of power and the arrogance of reason, as well as tyranny. It is thus little wonder that Judaism has and time again confronted and continues to find itself opposed by a special form of animosity, a hostility that proves itself to be simply Jew-hatred when all is said and done. Such hostility was a reaction to the particular form Judaism had to assume in order to go on bearing witness to its message long after its demise as a state. Hasn't anti-Christian hatred flared up as well whenever and wherever Christians have dared to resist the regnant idols of the day? How could hatred not have been enflamed against a Judaism scattered to the four winds, a defenseless minority settled in foreign states, proclaiming the existence of a court in which all people, and the earth as a whole, have already been preliminarily judged, and will one day face final judgment?

> He is the LORD our God;
> His judgments are throughout the earth.
> He is ever mindful of His covenant,
> the promise He gave for a thousand generations. (Psalm 105:7–8)

Hatred of the Jews, the delusion that sprang from modernity, is unambiguously distinct from anti-Semitism. It remains, however, an equally unjustifiable hatred, an animosity that flared up and lashed out against an existence that defeats every limit set by itself, or others, a Jewish existence that not only demands complete tolerance but also allows us to glimpse the prospect of ultimate victory, in the form of the inclusion of all peoples in the biblical promise of redemption and judgment for all.

Another factor in the equation—never, of course justifying Jew-hatred, but prevalent and thus requiring our consideration—was Judaism's unqualified affirmation of the meaning of suffering, a value of Jewish tradition from the time of the Babylonian exile forward. This notion held that the path leading to the Kingdom of God was marked by the most accursed and dreadful misery, even if such suffering directly contradicted—both today, as in days of yore—the hopeful message the Bible offered to the wayward, forsaken, and the blind. According to this interpretation, the only authentic signs of the path leading to the Kingdom were sickness, loathsomeness, degradation, want, misfortune, and pain, as long as such miseries were traveled as part of His path. Following the biblical example of God's suffering servant who was regarded as a living presence, whose successor, the suffering lamb "led to the slaughter" (Jeremiah 11:19, Isaiah 53:7) understood his affliction as a sign and portent of the salvation to come. Suffering was to be welcomed because it allowed one to bear witness, the sign of a new conception of martyrdom whose joyful fulfillment was first introduced into the world in this form. These were "religious heroes," to borrow and extend the phrase Leo Baeck used in 1901 to defend the Pharisees against Harnack's scornful derision. Baeck's description beautifully captures the spirit the Pharisees' medieval and modern successors, who have often taken up the cross as representative victims for humanity since this time this doctrine of the meaning of suffering first emerged. Defenseless and scattered throughout the world, and appearing in the varied shapes and hues of many different peoples, martyrs combine a willingness to sacrifice their own lives with a desire to testify to the presence of the divine will.

Though Jew-hatred remained wholly unjustifiable, a fact of life that could either be skirted or which Jews avoided whenever possible, some Jews were compelled to suffer so much of it that they began to view hatred of the Jews as a necessary and parallel phenomenon to their own existence. Some went so far as to regard it as part of God's historical plan. This mistaken view compounded an error that began in the days of the Jewish Sages. This interpretation argued that Ahashuerus, by allowing Haman to use his signet ring to authorize an anti-Jewish campaign, had in the end done more for the Jews through this act than the forty-eight prophets and seven prophetesses of biblical Israel combined (Megilla 14a). What could have possibly been more false? The hatred that constantly hounded the Jews did, to be sure, have the incidentally positive effect of strengthening Jewish solidarity. It also forced Jews who had left to the fold to return, allowing them to reacquaint themselves with a Jewish culture whose pleasures they grasped once more and expressed anew in a myriad of beautiful and authentic forms. This or that anti-Jewish campaign throughout the ages defeated in the nick of time—like Haman's assault on the Jews recounted for us in the Book of Esther—may likewise have done more good than harm. But wasn't the Jew-hater's self-devastation a kind of damage all its own? And didn't the Jews themselves fall prey to this sort of self-destructive behavior when, according to the Book of Esther, the Jewish community quickly cast aside the role of the victim of persecution and took up the cudgel of the persecutor? What sort of benefits could Jew-hatred offer if purchased at the price of such debasement? And whether any such benefits did in fact ensue remains an open question. How could these alleged benefits add anything whatsoever to the sovereign power with which Judaism had determined its own historical course throughout the ages, without any need of such self-degradations and its costly detours? Jew-hatred is always a fundamentally worthless phenomenon, and regardless of the various and competing explanations for it, or the extent of Jewish opposition it must confront at different times, its animosity lacks any deeper justification or worth, and is something to be avoided at best. Anti-Semitism is more worthless still, or to be more precise, fruitless in the strictest sense of the word: and Judaism bears no guilt for it whatsoever. Let it be said as clearly and directly as possible: anti-Semitism as a historical phenomenon is a byproduct of modernity, an unjust blaming of the Jews that falsely looks for its logic within Judaism itself. For in Judaism, anti-Semitism stumbled upon the perfect booty, a people seemingly made to order for anti-Semitic delusion, a nation that matched its delusive fantasies so precisely that it sometimes seemed as if Jewish persecution was in fact justified by actual qualities of the Jews themselves. But the problem of anti-Semitism lies entirely within itself. As a result, nothing the Jews have ever done to stem the anti-Semitic surge has ever had any effect: trying not to step on too many toes, keeping a low profile, submissiveness, public protest, and reasoned argument in refutation of anti-Semitic premises have all been tried in vain. Judaism's actual behavior plays no role whatsoever in anti-Semitic reactions (unlike Jew-hatred), for no matter what Judaism does, anti-Semites will construe Judaism as a threat, whether Jews actually represent a danger that must be combated or not.

What went wrong? Or to put it more precisely: what continues to go wrong? For with anti-Semitism, we are not dealing with some forgotten chapter of the past, or with some brief interlude in the history of German Jewry that has already come to a close. Anti-Semitism helped touch off a world war that finally revealed its infinite perfidy to the world in its truest colors, and that same anti-Semitism has not yet departed from the world's stage: now as then, it remains a contemporary presence and a threat to our

common future. What sort of phenomenon was it, and is it, that bestrode
its undeviating path toward murder?

While modern progress makes its advances, groups and classes who have
been left behind, and treated as remnants of the past, discover anti-Semitism as a kind of cure, a way of joining in dubious battle to thwart the
imminent downfall they sense is at hand. Groups such as these longed for—
and continue to long for—salvation from the ruination they sense by fusing
themselves with the fearful disaster. They seek their salvation from ruin by
flinging themselves against it, when all it asks of them is to make them part
of modernity, and thus to lead them forward, in order to flourish in a form
better suited to the modern world.

How did they—how do they seek such salvation? By persecuting a scape-
goat, heaping absolute blame on its back for everything that is new, or seeking relief by repressing every irritating form of existing or emergent life,
whether old or new, once and for all. In a word, they practice terror, sewing
fear far and wide by inducing panic, a mania that persecution excels at producing.[1] As the dark business goes forward, more and more power falls into
the hands of the persecutors, and eventually produces the system known as
totalitarianism. The totalitarian masters then subject the entire population
to their threats, including those not explicitly subject to persecution, terror-
izing those who are dismayed about what is going on, and before long turning them into collaborators who wear the allegedly dignified mantle of
power. Anti-Semitism's ascendancy permits the dispossession of these sectors of the populace to proceed without impediment, while at the same time
giving the dispossessed the sense that they are superior to the Jews. And all
this goes on as if these collaborators, all other social groups and classes,
and in the end, all peoples, would not eventually be subject to persecution
themselves. For anti-Semitism will never, under any circumstances, confine
itself to the Jews alone, and can more accurately be described as a kind of
weapons testing—using the Jews—for the murder that is ultimately being
planned, without exception, for all living irritants whatsoever.

This sort of "seizure of power" makes use of anti-Semitism regardless of
whether any significant number of Jews, or even any Jews at all, lay within
its grasp. Totalitarianism's persecution and terror are merely the guise assumed by a pervasive system of deception that needs to mask the plain and
simple truth that nothing of any worth whatsoever is being achieved or
created in such a regime, that nothing of lasting value is being developed or

produced. Anti-Semitism and nationalism became allies only when nationalism, mired in the early stages of its development, faced obsolescence when modernity offered the prospect of a universal, united humanity inhabiting an earth now fully explored. The national liberation of all peoples was a necessary development, and it remains a beneficial one: the community of all men and women can also be realized in the form of a confederacy joined between free peoples. But the goal of "world domination" first pursued in antiquity and later in the Middle Ages by the world's leading peoples became senseless in modernity, and remains a fruitless course to pursue. Nationalism, however, refuses to accept the fact that the process of nation building—a process that still awaits completion—no longer demands the defeat of other nations, the political pattern whose results are usually described as "nationalistic." Instead of expressing itself in a content and peaceful self-awareness and patiently taking up the work of securing its own freedom and prosperity, goals achievable only by coexisting peacefully with the rest of mankind, rabid nationalism lusts for conquest and shrinks from more difficult labors. Such nationalism is beset by a criminal arrogance, and afflicted with an impatience and egotistical self-importance that in the end become self-delusion. And it is here that the persecution of the Jews begins. These as well as other "reasons" drove nationalism into the arms of anti-Semitism, binding the two together until their idolatry and its forms of worship were complete. At least in the eyes of the murderers, killing other men on behalf of their nation came to be seen as a holy act.

Doesn't this explain why Judaism came to be seen as a "mischief maker" during the process of nation building—and continues to be seen as such? Wouldn't the recognition of the Jews as a minority entitled to equal rights under the law have made the seamless fusion of nation and nation-state impossible? It doubtless would have, and the nationalistic nation-state would suffer the same "mischief" and interference from every other human bond its citizens possess, and from each of their transnational affiliations, with Christianity serving as a perfect example. But in a period of virulent nationalism, such as the last third of the nineteenth and the beginning of the twentieth centuries, Christianity's autonomous status had come to be taken for granted in many states. Though placed on the defensive in others, Christianity for the most part posed no obstacle to nationalist fervor, and at times stood quietly by and allowed it to fester, when not itself forging

nationalism's weapons, until a militant church began to annoy the anti-
Semites themselves. At that point, anti-Semitism began to turn against
Christianity as well. And the anti-Semites were assisted by a nationalism
that was all too glad to lend a hand. Anti-Semitic and nationalist movements
were keenly aware that their programs were incompatible with the Bible's
message of love and peace, more aware of this unavoidable disparity than
Christian observers were, even though Christianity was itself the bearer of
that historical message.

Judaism and Judaism alone would be blamed for "disrupting" national
unity. And Jews today are still forced to deal with that charge, whether the
unity in question is that of a Christian society, or the wholeness of the
German state. At times, Judaism is simply said to represent a "distur-
bance"—according to certain socialist or Marxist perspectives—to "the secular state." This "disruptive presence"—sometimes a code word for
Judaism as a nation within the nation, or for the fact that it claimed a different nationality entirely, finally resulted in the Jews being called something
far worse: an enemy. This obviously false projection of guilt onto the Jews
was at the same time a charge that could always be revived, and still is, by
referring to what at first glance appears to be factual evidence. The tactic
allowed nationalism, already anti-Semitism's sworn ally, to prop up the fictional antagonist it so desperately required when modernity, having tamped
down past incitements to war, seemed as if it was going to be able to forestall future international conflicts through negotiation and compromise. By
taking up arms against the Jews, and portraying them as an armed enemy
—an opponent that had never lifted a finger against another state, and
therefore could not be brought before the bar of international justice—
nationalism found its raison d'être and more: a pretext to wage war for
"world domination." This objective was projected onto the Jews, and the
Jews alone, so that it could be "snatched away" from their grasp. The accu-
satory insinuation made everything else possible, allowing hatred to be incited in the midst of peace, the fires of war to be stoked, fear to be spread
far and wide and souls to be poisoned. Entire citizenries would be mobilized
and extorted until murderous violence was brought to bear against those
citizens themselves.

Every form of hatred incited against the Jewish "mischief maker" was
and is a delusion, for wherever trust has welcomed the Jews, the Jews have
responded with sacrifice and devotion that lasted until their last dying

breath. Persecuting the Jews as the "enemy" was and is nothing more than a distortion: as if the fact that the Jews possessed a national culture and identity of their own somehow made them the opponents, rather than supporters, of complete national rights for other peoples and nations. But this delusion, like all others, contained the grain of truth that proves it to be madness indeed. Judaism and modernity are bound up with one another, just as, on the other hand, anti-Semitism and nationalism share a common bond with an era that has passed. Just as the most redemptive future is said to promise not freedom but the sword (Matthew 10:34), Judaism actually did represent a disruptive presence and enemy to a past in inevitable decline as it confronted modernity's advance.

Judaism did not enter the modern world by following others, by taking well-worn, non-Jewish paths others had blazed in order to enter a world in renewal and upheaval. It is even less accurate to say that Judaism simply reaped the fruits bestowed upon it by friends who let the Jewish people retire from the fray, as if they were rewarding a worthy and veteran warrior of battles past for services rendered. Judaism achieved its entrance to modernity by making a revolution of its own, forging an independent movement for renewal that was part of the modern enterprise as a whole. The "Jewish Renaissance" that produced Judaism's outer development and inner renewal of the most recent past gives us more than ample grounds, based on Jewish efforts alone, to regard Judaism as a full participant and shaper of the modern era. Judaism was central to modernity, above all, because the very notion of the future as the goal and task world history must achieve originates in Judaism, and remains one of its most crucial discoveries as well as its primordial message. It is thus no accident that when the powers of yesterday defended themselves—and still do—against the future, they turned their ire against the Jews, just as it was never by chance that idolatry turned against Judaism as well. In fact, the Jewish people were guilty: of standing up for the unalloyed revelation of freedom, genuine joy, wholehearted piety, realistic progress, and absolute peace waiting to be realized in the historical future.

Yet this "guilt" was something completely different from the accusation that anti-Semitism had laid at Judaism's door! Such charges could not and still cannot be refuted, making it both superfluous and useless to investigate the "history" of anti-Semitic madness, as if the names, actions and dates connected with anti-Semitism amounted to anything more than a distorted mirror of its own delusive vision. The only thing resembling "history" in a "history of anti-Semitism" points us toward the historical path taken by its victims. The only "history" of anti-Semitism worth telling teaches us about the world history of its victims, the world history of the Jewish people, or about the unfolding course of the universal world history that happens to contain chapters of anti-Semitism only because anti-Semites cut a uniformly bloody swath through world history's path.

Even if one had assumed that anti-Semitism had good "reasons" for blaming the Jews during the twelve decades between the wars of liberation and 1933, or that anti-Semitism—assuming that the Jews were "innocent"—was a simple, hateful mistake that could be cured by education, the years between 1933 and 1945 laid any such suppositions to rest. National Socialism's pitiless annihilation of the Jews, which soon included millions from other groups and peoples who became subject to its delusion, greed, bloodlust, and craving for murder—that annihilation soon beggared all previous measures of comparison. Save one: the measure that holds a crime to be a criminal act and nothing more. Any possible recurrence must therefore be prevented, just as every new anti-Semitic flare-up must be controlled by legal means, for such outbursts will continue as long as the past strives to resist the future's sway.

Anti-Semitism is not some historical relic just because the powers of yesterday rally under its flag, a reminder to us of why those powers of the past have themselves already been superseded. Equally, the past has not been overcome just because modernity's future has been transformed from something simply awaited to a process that has already begun. The powers of regression remain powerful as always, representing a threat to mankind that must be taken quite seriously, and a threat to humanity that is never taken seriously enough! Judaism's power, however, consists in turning not against the past but toward the future.

NINE

The Final Step to Emancipation

Some ninety years after Lavater's suggestion that Mendelssohn convert to Christianity set off the first public debate on whether Judaism would become a full partner in the modern enterprise or be turned away at modernity's door, the final step toward full legal equality had been taken. In 1860, the Alliance Isráelite Universelle was founded in Paris. The event was comparable in its significance to the founding of the Verein für Kultur und Wissenschaft der Juden (The Society for the Culture and Science of the Jews). But the ambitious goal envisioned by the six founding members of the French organization was more far-reaching than anything Zunz might have imagined for himself and his six compatriots in 1818. "All members of the people of Israel are responsible for one another!" The motto of the Alliance transformed the Talmudic precept that "all Israel are sureties for one another" from a moral into a political claim (*Shevu'oth* 45–46), articulating a wholly new demand that would stand alongside the individual Jew's legitimate right to his "religious confession" and its concomitant obligation to "study." Israel's right to reestablish its community as an actor in history, an aspiration this people had sustained from its ancient past to the present day, now stepped forth as part of its modern identity, together with the right to its own religious expression and the Wissenschaft des Judentums.

Two years later, Moses Hess, with close ties to the Alliance and its founders, published a book that articulates this demand. Hess's book made him Zionism's founding father by laying out the Alliance's program and its fundamental elements in a form that would prove decisive. Hess's work linked the tenets of the Alliance with the religious and spiritual accomplishments of German Jewry, and did so, not coincidentally, by recalling Spinoza's importance and giving the modern significance of the Baal Shem Tov its due. For an Italy allied with France had, in 1859, just liberated the Italian region of Lombardy, freeing it from Austrian control. Hess's book of 1862 invited the French to compare an emergent Jewish national liberation movement with the Italian example, likening the Jewish quest with the Italian by calling his work *Rome and Jerusalem: The Last National Question*. Hess begins it with a ringing salvo: "After an estrangement of twenty years, I am back with my people. A thought which I believed to be forever buried in my heart, has been revived in me anew. It is the thought of my nationality."[1]

Not long thereafter, simultaneous with the founding of the Alliance Israélite Universelle in 1860, which also happened to be the year of Theodor Herzl's birth, Rabbi Zvi Hirsch Kalischer convened the memorable first conference on the settlement of Palestine in his residence in Thorn. The following year saw the publication of Kalischer's *The Restoration of Zion* and witnessed Kalischer's collaboration with Hayim Luvie in founding the Israelite Society for the Colonization of the Holy Land in Frankfurt on the Oder. Hess was already able to cite Kalischer in support in 1862, and while Luria was able to voice his enthusiastic support for Hess's position, he did so as a pioneer before his time, left in the lurch and soon forgotten. Oblivion would likewise shroud the fact that Moritz Steinschneider, destined to become one of the leading architects of the Wissenschaft des Judentums, had founded student chapters in Prague, Vienna, and Berlin under the name *For the Restoration of Jewish Independence in Palestine*. This earliest venture— shamelessly downplayed by those who later marched under its flag—had arrived, like the breakthroughs of the 1860s, ahead of time.

Many avowedly Jewish individuals, however, wanted nothing more in the period between 1860 and 1880 than to disappear into the nations that had granted them citizenship, together with the full civil enfranchisement they had fought long and hard to achieve. This generation, enjoying the peak period of individual emancipation, and having invented their own school of modern scholarship to go along with it, was content to go on savoring its fruits. The unity of the Alliance Isráelite Universelle was thus unable to withstand the extreme test posed by the Franco-Prussian war of 1870–71; by 1871 an Anglo-Jewish Association had already split off from the central organization, and in 1873 the Israelite Alliance of Austria followed suit. In the meantime, German Jews quietly abandoned any kind of cooperation on projects of mutual interest, and the founders themselves turned the Alliance Isráelite Universelle into a representational body for French Jewry that devoted itself almost exclusively to cultural work. Yet the idea of Jewish unity, extending beyond the domains of religion and modern scholarship, the notion that all Jews comprise one people, refused to vanish, because the Jewish masses represented an unavoidable fact—masses who had already been inspired to take action, in new political forms our discussion will soon describe.

The kind of pressure these events exerted to develop and express Jewish "nationality" became apparent in the memorable year of 1897, a year that witnessed no fewer than four responses that would embrace Jewry worldwide. The First Zionist Congress met in Basel at the end of August, where cultural Zionism gains momentum in its opposition to political Zionism when Ahad Ha-Am, attending as a guest, voiced his position in the most emphatic terms; Simon Dubnow catalyzed a different form of opposition, remaining in Zurich while the Congress took place and refusing to attend. In November of 1897, Dubnow published the first of his *Letters on Ancient and Modern Judaism* and began to codify the program that would come to be known as autonomism. In September, the General Jewish Workers' Union for Russia and Poland was founded, known as the Bund and the Bundist movement. More than a Jewish workers' party taking part in the worldwide struggle for the victory of socialism, the movement increasingly represented an assertion of the Jewish people's existence, the rights of a single people spread throughout the earth. While the differences between these four movements may have seemed great at the time, they were slight in comparison with the revolutionary significance, which, when seen together, their breakthrough to political maturity had in fact achieved. On the other hand, the differences between their programs should not be erased or minimized, since these same factions have consistently reemerged in sub-sequent Jewish history, and continue to divide Judaism to the present day.

The contention arose between two basic camps: political Zionists who wanted to establish a state there, in Palestine, and cultural Zionist who were first and foremost committed to a Jewish spiritual renewal here, in Europe. These terms were first established by Theodor Herzl and Ahad Ha-Am, then by Jakob Klatzkin and Martin Buber. The gap between these positions would be bridged neither by their common belief in the overriding signifi-cance of the land of Israel, nor by the state of Israel itself when it finally came into existence. Herzl and Klatzkin took up the work of establishing a Jewish state in Zion, while Ahad Ha-am and Buber sought to build up a spiritual center there. According to the political Zionists, an independent state would gather up the scattered forms of Jewish life in the diaspora and bring them to a fitting conclusion. The cultural Zionists, by contrast, ar-gued that the diaspora should never come to an end, though they believed it needed stronger ties to a national center. As an authentically Zionist point of view, this idea of a Palestinian national center was already out of the question for the Autonomists and the Bundists. Though culturalists, Ahad Ha-am and his supporters were Zionists through and through: for them, a Jewish state was preferable to slogans that called on Jews to stay put where they were. According to the cultural Zionist perspective, only when Jews came into actual contact with earth, the land of their fathers, and built up a settlement with the full range of normal occupations, with its own farmers, and working class toiling side by side with the intellectuals—only then would Judaism be able to renew itself from the ground up. Only then would the Jewish national center be able to blossom, and share its fruits with the rest of the Jewish world.

But the challenge Simon Dubnow posed to the Zionists was this: didn't the deep roots Jewish communities had struck in so many different states over the centuries offer Judaism its best chance, right there in their own surroundings? Hadn't Jewish life proved its resiliency precisely in the way it had always gone on developing, even in the midst of other peoples, prov-ing itself to be a full-fledged actor in the drama of world history? Wasn't it the diaspora itself, with its incessant to and fro of settlement and resettle-ment, that allowed the Jewish people to adjust to changing historical winds and bring one national center into existence after another? Didn't a people that had already traveled the road of statehood in antiquity remain a nation without reestablishing an independent, sovereign state? Hadn't the Jews constituted a single people and nation throughout the ages? Couldn't a people who had transformed and renewed itself so many times in the past be expected to do the same at any time, including the present? For Dubnow, the Jewish demand for autonomy was entirely fitting. He envisioned autonomism as the Jewish entitlement to complete self-determination, with the Jews granted all the rights and privileges of a national minority, accompanied by their loyal and willing acceptance of the sovereignty and obligations of the state in which they lived.

Unlike Dubnow's autonomism, the Bundists placed their bets on social revolution and demanded equal rights only as a way of setting that transformation in motion. The Bundists and Autonomists shared a perspective with both wings of the Zionist movement. They agreed that the settlement of Palestine should proceed, since extending Judaism's "geographical dispersion" to include yet another land bound to the Jews by age-old ties would reinvigorate and test the people and contribute to an inevitable process of renewal. But autonomism and the Bundists rejected political and spiritual Zionism to the extent that the Zionists privileged a single country, committing themselves instead to the world as a whole.

But the chief preoccupation of every camp from 1897 forward was securing Judaism's final step toward full equality: the recognition of the Jews as a people. This final step meant claiming Judaism's right to self-determination, of course, but also using Judaism's own resources to create those modern expressions of national life that are the touchstones of true political maturity. These took the form of two representative bodies founded in 1897 and 1936, respectively: the first Zionist congress in Basel, which gradually evolved and emerged as the parliament of the State of Israel, and the World Jewish Congress, that originated in Geneva, and could be considered Judaism's senate or upper house, final evidence that Judaism had achieved self-determination and political adulthood. More on this topic will be provided in chapter 13.

Other watershed movements of the 1890s, restricting their efforts to developing Judaism's spiritual strength, went so far as to announce their explicit opposition to any form of Jewish political assertion. But the very fact that these efforts had been mounted at all—and since they repeatedly pointed beyond all strict "cultural" and national boundaries—helped Judaism take its final step toward full emancipation. For a people's claim to full and legitimate recognition requires a self-affirmation that is never merely a matter of declaring statehood, regardless of the fact that the modern struggle for national self-determination had become a sine qua non for any people seeking their rightful place in the family of nations. The struggle to establish a Jewish state was never incompatible with the battle for the full civil equality of Jewish minorities in other nations. Zionism should have never been artificially pitted against that goal, much less used as an excuse to suspend Jewish civil rights or to hinder them in the future. The more central issue at stake then as now was the ability and the right of a people at any time to act in order to claim its place in history. Judaism's quest for nationhood was an expression of this common human responsibility, for becoming a nation was the only course that would guarantee the historical continuity of Judaism on the stage of world history, since only nations can act historically in the world. And since history's progress toward redemption of the world entire and Judaism's ultimate goal remain one and the same, history refuses to tolerate any premature departure of Judaism from the historical scene.

Sometimes in accord with their founders' intentions and sometimes against them, several other watershed movements helped strengthen Jewish national awareness, beyond the two Zionist camps and the Autonomists and Bundists. These included the Austrian-Israelite Union (Östereichisch-Israelitische Union), founded as early as 1886 in Vienna with the goal of furthering "Jewish scholarship" as well as "Jewish concerns," the Central Association of German Citizens of the Jewish Faith (Zentralverein deutscher Staatsbürger jüdischen Glaubens), founded in Berlin in 1893, and the Association for Jewish History and Literature (Verein für jüdische Geschichte und Literatur), formed in 1892 in Berlin by Gustav Karpeles, later to be honored for another deed, his *History of Jewish Literature*, a work that broke new ground in modern Jewish letters. It soon became clear that an umbrella organization for Germany would be necessary, and a year later the Union of Associations for Jewish History and Literature (Verband der Vereine für Jüdische Geschichte und Literatur) was founded, eventually to include more than two hundred branches. The Association for Defense against Anti-Semitism (Verein zur Abwehr des Antisemitismus) emerged in 1890 at roughly the same time, headed by Rudolf von Gneist and Reichstag member Heinrich Rickert, a group composed of both Christians and Jews. The year 1901 saw the founding of the Charitable Association of German

Jews (Hilfsverein der deutschen Juden), which gave assistance to Jews from the east and from Palestine. The first German chapter of the B'nai Brith was established in 1882, and the first Austrian branch in 1889, though the group had already been founded by émigré German Jews in New York as an independent organization in 1843.

While some of these groups disparaged the fact of their own nationality, calling it an "un-Jewish politicization," though their own actions had actually paved the way toward its realization, others became all too political. Alongside the claim to "collective emancipation," a position began to make itself heard that not only rejected any kind of connection to Jewish nationality, but expressed a lust for "collective assimilation": a desire to assimilate the nationhood of the Jewish people into that of all other nations. This assimilationist position abandoned any notion of Judaism's specific task. Their surrender consisted of locating the nationhood of the Jews and the building of a state as the singular essential ground, instead of recognizing the citizenship of the individual Jew as the only true foundation. The weakness and the temptation that motivated assimilationist Jews, however, could not be rejected out of hand, and still cannot be. Instead, their motives must be encompassed by a deeper and more plural vision of Jewish culture itself, an inward gaze that allows Judaism to take stock of its own errant paths and move forward. The "inner renewal" that German Jewry achieved in that process produced works that comprise its scroll of honor.

TEN

A Few Figures

The fact that many German Jews, including important figures, were shocked into self-awareness by the Eastern European Jewish refugees they met up with in Poland, Galicia, Romania, and Russia during the First World War is a story that has often been told. Many German Jews suddenly recognized that the Jewish people consisted of more than "citizens" of the nations of the West and that Judaism could not be forced into the narrow definition of a religious "confession," whose teachings remained a private, in-house affair. Instead, Judaism was revealed to them as an open, public way of life expressed in the manifold and energetic activities of a people on the move, a people who had demanded work and the rest of the satisfactions of modern life to which they were entitled long before the question of whether Judaism was actually "alive" was being debated in the West. "This People"[1] simply appeared before them, preempting any debate on the justification for a continuing Jewish existence and making any affirmative or negative answer to the question simply beside the point. A few figures, cited for the most part from the research of Arthur Ruppin and Jacob Letschinsky, can give us a partial indication of this inexhaustible reservoir of insight and talent that helped fuel the process of outer as well as inner Jewish development.

As recently as 1840, the world's entire Jewish population numbered 4.5 million, roughly the same as the number of Jews alive in the year 70 CE, when the destruction of the second Temple in Jerusalem and the end of the Jewish state marked the beginning of a Jewish decline. This amounted to one-twelfth of the population of the Roman Empire as a whole, making every twelfth "Roman" a Jew. By 1840 Jews made up less than one half of one percent of the world's population, in a world whose citizens were now fully and restlessly pursuing their own course in world history. Scarcely one of every two hundred citizens of the earth belonged to the Jewish people. Or to calculate the same fact differently: had the Jewish percentage of the world's population remained constant from the moment of the Temple's destruction forward, the Jewish people would have numbered not sixteen million, but seventy-five million by 1840. All too many slaughters and dire setbacks had nipped that possibility in the bud.

On the other hand, the nineteenth century witnessed the kind of population boom that humanity as a whole and Europe in particular had seldom witnessed before, an increase that took place after Europe's modern jump forward in population size had already occurred, thus only temporarily exceeded by the Jewish population boom. While the earth's population doubled between 1825 and 1930 and the population of countries where Jews had settled increased three and a half times, the Jewish population in those same lands increased either fivefold or ninefold, if one counts from 1650 forward. The Jewish percentage of Europe's population as a whole, however, went down, with the exception of several distinct areas of settlement, such as large cities and rapidly developing countries. Jewish population growth in these regions contributed to an exaggerated sense of the size of the Jewish population.

The rise of the modern Jewish people displayed a vigor and revolutionary intensity that dwarfed their numerical increase. Having been shut out for so long and left so far behind that their untenable isolation was hardly noticed any longer—though isolation had been the exception during their four-thousand-year history, and full participation the rule—Judaism's courageous ability to send out shoots from roots struck long ago began to make itself felt, and Jews acquired the wherewithal to delve into the possibilities offered by new ways of life. No less than a third of the entire people, around four million individuals, left Europe between 1880 and 1930, chiefly from Czarist Russia and the Austrian Empire. Broken down in standings that rank the number of émigrés from different countries, the period 1880–1930 saw the Jews move from twelfth place to fourth, behind the English, Germans, and Italians, with only five immigrants returning home for every hundred who took the trip, while for the period between 1908 and 1925, fifty-five Italians, nineteen Englishmen, fifteen Germans, seventy-six Romanians, and sixty-four Hungarians returned home for every hundred who left.

This powerful resurgence of Jewish vitality, perceptible in every important domain of Jewish life, made another salient characteristic clear: these émigrés kept the faith, and they remained Jews. Thrilled to become citizens of their new countries and ready to sacrifice for them, the immigrants at the same time built up new Jewish communities wherever they landed, and so testified to the relevance of Judaism's message and universal significance in all corners of the earth. Communities were successfully founded in almost every country on all five continents, and in three countries—located on three continents in three different linguistic regions—Jewish immigrants successfully established growing, capable, and active Jewish cultural centers: in North America, Palestine, and Argentina. Between 1840 and 1942, seventy-one of every one hundred Jews emigrated to the United States, ten to Palestine, six to Argentina, four to Canada, and two apiece to South Africa and Brazil. In addition, roughly a half-million Russian Jews migrated to Soviet Asia, a move long shrouded in secrecy but that nonetheless represented a significant modern Jewish population shift. In sum, six million European Jews moved their households during the last century, a number twice as large as the world's entire Jewish population around 1800—the same number of Jews who were killed between 1933 and 1945. In the end, too few Jews decided to emigrate, or were able to carry out their plans, but when all was said and done and despite the large number involved, too few, not too many, chose to leave.

The dark side of the immigrant experience should not be forgotten, despite the successful communities established throughout the world: the degradation, persecution, and misery that drove the emigrants from their homes, and the murder that overtook European Jewry in its homeland. All too many Jews continued to believe in the West, their homeland, even as it broke its trust. If there are any nations, somewhere in the world, who freely choose to emigrate for no reason, the Jews are not among them. The Jewish people gratefully struck loyal roots in good faith wherever Jews were allowed to settle, never willingly forsaking the land that became their home, because no piece of earth or land is essentially better than another, or to put it more precisely—all land is holy land. The Jewish people's self-understanding is not founded on land per se, and not on the "promised land," but in the covenant joined in the desert: in an oath sworn after Abraham had set forth from east Mesopotamia, his descendants had left the North of Canaan behind, and after Moses had left the south of Midian and the tribes had set forth from western Egypt to begin their exodus into the desert. These precursors lead up to and culminate in the Mosaic covenant, history's earliest affirmation and awakening to the promise of a universal redemption yet to come.

The Jewish exodus from Europe bore only a tangential resemblance to the modern Western nations' exploration and conquest of the earth, giving the Jews a fate distinct from that suffered by the West's other peoples. Jewish outmigration is evidence not of Jewish faithlessness, but of the hardheartedness the West displayed toward one of its oldest and most worthy constituents. The West's betrayal of the Jews—the West's self-betrayal, in fact—bears sole responsibility for the fact that by 1940, North America had given refuge to more than half the world's Jewish population, though it had been home to less than 1 percent of the world's Jewish population in 1840, while Europe, which had been home to roughly 90 percent of the world's Jews in 1840, a century later was home to a only a fourth. By 1939, barely one-third of all Jews lived in North America, with roughly twice as many in Europe, while six years later, the American third represented double the number of Jews left in Europe.

At the same time, Palestine, as a center for Jewish emigration, began to acquire an emotional significance that far outstripped the relative numbers involved, becoming the third-largest Jewish population center in the period after the United States and Russia. The modern resettlement of Palestine had begun in the same 1880s that witnessed the upsurge in Jews moving to North America, an outmigration triggered by the outbreak of pogroms in Russia in 1881. But of the Jews living in Palestine in 1945, some four-fifths had arrived after the First World War, while the majority of immigrants to

North America had taken refuge there before the war broke out. Emigration to Palestine increased decisively and took the lead only after 1926. At that point, the introduction of draconian immigration quotas severely restricted Jewish entry to North America: henceforward, a mere 10,000 Jews were allowed to immigrate each year, instead of the annual average of 100,000, who entered in the decade after 1904, and once more in 1921.

Roughly 80 percent of the Jewish emigrants leaving Europe in the first quarter of the twentieth century went to the United States, and a mere 4 percent to Palestine. But from 1926 to 1942, only 27 percent set foot in the United States, while by contrast 33 percent managed to reach a Palestine that had already taken the lead in another area, the proportion of the entire population made up of Jews.

Expressed in percentages, Jews comprised 11.1 percent of the population in the land of Israel in 1922, increasing to 18 percent in 1930, as opposed to 10.4 percent in Poland; 8.2 percent in Belarus; 7.6 percent in Lithuania; 5.9 percent in Hungary; 5.4 percent in the Ukraine; 5.2 percent in Latvia; 4.8 percent in Romania; 4.5 percent in European Turkey; 3.5 percent in both Austria and in the United States; roughly 3 percent in Mesopotamia, Spanish Morocco, Tunisia, and French Morocco; 2.6 percent in Czechoslovakia; 2.4 percent in Tripoli; 2.2 percent in Greece; 2.1 percent in Argentina; 1.7 percent in the Netherlands; .9 percent in Germany; .7 percent in England, Ireland, and Belgium; .5 percent in Switzerland; .4 percent in France; .2 percent in Denmark; and .1 percent in Italy and Sweden.

Palestine, in other words, was inhabited, in 1930, by six times as many Jews in percentage terms as lived in the United States, eight to nine times in Argentina, and twenty times in Germany, whose Jewish community will be described in statistical terms in subsequent sections.

And so the masses went forth. Facing their new trial and alert to its historic responsibility, the people found new territory, mastered its necessities, and brought that responsibility to fruition. These were men, women, and children who simply wanted to get on with their lives, exercising what in one sense was nothing more than the right of every creature to self-perpetuation. The apostates among them might have deluded themselves into thinking that Judaism's final demise was at hand; others were certain that its demise was nigh, and even Judaism's battle-hardened champions must at times have wondered whether they could go on believing that Judaism would be able to endure. Beneath them all, a powerful renaissance of

Jewish life burst forth and flourished. But this surging forth of life learned the expressible meaning of human suffering, and its torture, want, and tearful anguish, when delusory rapacity and bloodlust broke free of its reins and began—to use one of its own lunatic slogans—to "exterminate the Jews."

Before returning to the glorious and productive modern legacy produced to a significant degree by German Jewry, we must first grasp this reality in numbers. The numbers themselves describe death on a scale that shatters the limits of the previously imaginable, and have become a constituent part of every Jewish memory: and of human history for all time to come.

In 1939, nine and a half million Jews lived in Europe, including Russia. Six years later three and a half million survived. Six million were killed. These losses were not the "usual" casualties of war, but the destruction of two-thirds of what was a defenseless population, a fact that multiplies the catastrophe immeasurably, and left the surviving third of the population with a much deeper wound than can be expressed in what are already incomprehensible numbers. Women, future mothers, children, the generation about to emerge, and the entire intellectual and spiritual leadership, mostly consisting of the older and eldest generations—all these were killed. Were one to compile a list that would cite the dead by name, as in the memory books written after the persecutions of the Middle Ages, a hundred books would be required, each one thousand pages long and containing sixty thousand names each. Such books could never be produced, and even if they could be it would never be possible to grasp the full significance of six million individual names, each standing for the density and texture of a unique human life.

The arm of German domination extended its reach to the areas of Jewish settlement richest with children: the same number of children lived among the three million murdered Polish Jews as dwelled among the five million Jews of the United States of America. When the liberating armies arrived too late in these territories under German domination, scarcely a Jewish child under ten years of age remained alive. As the group of survivors lacked individuals who would soon have been of marital age, it was difficult for a new generation to emerge for some time to come. This colossal extension of loss forward into the future must be added to the bare numbers for the time being, for the loss of rising generations demands that we continue to ratchet down our expectations for the future. It is important to clarify again and again that, numerically speaking, these figures do not represent the "usual" losses of war, but instead that 90 percent of them were the most defenseless of the Jewish people. Women, the future mothers who were murdered—children, the new generation of youth—and their elders were wiped out, the precious and irreplaceable representatives and transmitters of a tradition handed down from the past and marking the course toward the future. Together, their loss not only beggars comparison, but represents a wound whose full effects will only make themselves felt as the event recedes into the distance in the coming decades.

Seeing these losses and their wounds as a single phenomenon gives us a more trenchant and serious appreciation of an already frightful prospect: namely, that approximately 90 percent of the Jews inhabiting Latvia and Lithuania in 1939 were to die, along with 80 percent of the Jews of Poland, Czechoslovakia, Germany, and Greece, and more than 70 percent of the Yugoslavian Jews and 60 percent of the Jews of Holland and Austria. The Jewish people lost a third of its entire population; Russian and Yugoslavian casualties during the war amounted to something more than a tenth of each country's population, while the Germans, combined with the Austrians and Sudeten Germans, lost somewhat less than a tenth, and the Poles a twelfth of their populations. The fact is that twenty-two times more Jews died than did United States soldiers in battle, and that seventeen times more Jews died than did English citizens during the war, with the latter including both civilian and combat losses. And if European territory alone is taken into account, Jewish losses were five times greater than those of Yugoslavia, which lost a ninth of its population, six times Russian losses, seven times those of the Germans, eight times those of the Poles, and nine times those of the United Kingdom—and five hundred and twenty times more than those of the United States, whose citizens gave their lives in Europe to create a better future.

ELEVEN

The Dual Legacy of Theodor Herzl

Theodor Herzl was born on May 2, 1860. His parents harbored the highest hopes for him early on, and the boy himself seemed to sense their aspirations, displaying his gifts precociously while setting his sights on a literary career. As a high-school student in Budapest, and later at the University of Vienna, his ambition was clear: to become a German writer. Terms such as journalist and feuilletonist did not as yet carry any negative connotations. By 1889, Herzl had already had the good fortune to see two of his comedies, *The Poachers* and *The Refugee*, produced at Vienna's Burgtheater, which represented a very great success indeed. Soon, *Neue Freie Presse*, Austria's leading newspaper, famed throughout the world, was carrying Herzl's columns. Before long, in fall 1891, the paper made Herzl its Paris correspondent, and four years later it entrusted editorship of the feuilleton page to his hands, a marquee position in the literary world of those years, providing Herzl with work, honor, glory, and actual power. But in that very same year Herzl was overtaken by a different vocation, a calling that launched him to heights of glory beyond his wildest dreams, but that also consumed his life before its time. Herzl died on July 3, 1904, having just turned forty-four, still the celebrated master of the Viennese feuilleton, a position he retained for the sake of his family, but he had by then become one of Judaism's greatest renovators and one of his people's greatest sons.

Seen from a distance, Herzl's short life falls neatly into two periods. His first thirty-four years comprised the first half, followed by the final decade, which began with the shock that sparked his new calling. On January 5, 1895, Herzl, working as a correspondent for the *Neue Freie Presse*, was an outraged eyewitness when Captain Dreyfus, stripped of his military rank, was humiliated by a mob whipped to a frenzied pitch by anti-Semitic insanity. But the task that was to shape Herzl's life and consume it during the final decade allotted him had cast its spell long before, as early as 1882, the year he himself recognized as his turning point. While reading Eugen Dühring's *The Jewish Question*, Herzl for the first time faced up to the deadly reality of modern anti-Semitism as a threat impossible to stave off with the specifically Jewish or universal remedies then at hand. With this in mind, Herzl's life is better divided into two equal halves, extending from 1860 to 1882 and from 1882 to 1904, periods that outline a transformation characteristic of most Jewish lives since Moses Mendelssohn—a transformative course destined to endure from the biblical Moses forward. This path leads first into the larger world of human affairs, and then, through that world, to Judaism, as soon as the world makes it apparent that Judaism's promised realm of freedom and happiness still awaits its fulfillment, the kingdom in which all strife and contention will someday be overcome.

Theodor Herzl's memorable life nonetheless marks a new point of departure that was his alone. The achievement that made itself manifest in his life's second half had been stirring within him from the start and had already made its demands known to him as a child. In his own retrospective account, Herzl would trace his self-awareness as a Jew confronting anti-Semitism to his early days in school. Herzl did not need to undergo any fundamental transformation to place himself at the forefront of his people as their leader: he needed only to stand up for who he was with increasing assertiveness and force and to take pleasure in his identity, becoming prouder and prouder along the way. He would always remain distant to Hebrew, to the synagogue, and to the other significant creations of the Jewish Middle Ages: the Talmud and the house of study, philosophy and Jewish mysticism. And while Herzl owed his Jewish identity to the continued existence of biblical Judaism that had been handed down for two and a half millennia, he did not return to these Jewish institutions. Instead, he added his own achievement to theirs, accomplishing a deed wholly foreign to the Middle Ages and quintessentially modern.

Herzl signals the political breakthrough to modernity. When crowds attending the ceremonial humiliation of Captain Dreyfus howled "down with the Jews," Herzl finally realized that the Jewish problem required a political solution. And that political solution was necessary even if the Jews, for whatever religious and spiritual reasons, remained what they had always been, an immutable if embattled community of believers, with the Wissenschaft des Judentums still subject to controversy. "Only an ignoramus," Herzl argued, "could see modern anti-Semitism as a repetition of Jewish persecutions of the past." In the modern world, Judaism meant the existence of the Jewish people as nation. And what became of that people would turn on statecraft and national power. This was, after all, "an international political issue to be solved at a council of cultured nations," a question with no solution other than the creation of the "Jewish State."

Soon thereafter, the decade began in which Herzl began to engineer the new "exodus from Egypt," a feat of superhuman exertion wrung from a heart that would soon be unable to bear the strain. After engaging in preliminary discussions with leading Jewish figures who remained hesitant, Herzl composed *The Jewish State* to spur the Jewish masses into action. At the same time, he began negotiations on equal footing with diplomats and heads of state as statesmen, with each step quickly following the next. And indeed, broad masses of the Jewish people were soon set in motion, displaying firm resolve and self-awareness, in numbers that dwarfed estimates that were far too modest and expectations that were far too small. The first Zionist Congress, convened on August 29, 1897, in Basel, Switzerland, displayed to the world an entity fully aware of its own powers. It was an event whose full significance the Jews of the world, their neighbors, and even Herzl himself had fully grasped, but that now stood before their eyes: the Jewish people were once again a nation with the power to act.

Herzl soon began to negotiate in his people's name, and he was taken more seriously than anyone would have expected or assumed. He met with the sultan, held discussions with the pope, and greeted the German kaiser at the gates of Jerusalem. Heedless of the pogroms whose screams shook the heavens above, Herzl, ever the politician, journeyed to Russia, visited England, and gained the support of leading Jewish figures and, more important, of leading statesmen: Gladstone, Chamberlain, Lansdowne, Balfour, and Lloyd George. England was unable to discuss what was then Turkish Palestine, but instead offered pieces of the Sinai Peninsula and, most important, Uganda. To Herzl, the latter seemed a clear step forward toward the "promised land." When writing *The Jewish State*, Herzl would have gladly accepted land anywhere in South America to establish a foothold for Jewish sovereignty, then switched the focus of his activities to Palestine. Herzl praised the glorious future of the Palestinian settlement in his *Altneuland*, Old-New Land—in Hebrew, Tel Aviv—a work he dashed off in the midst of his frenetic political work. But the idea of the "land of Israel" aroused feverish, messianic hopes in the Jewish masses Herzl had stirred to action, and the Uganda proposal, to Herzl a decisive step forward in the direction of the "holy land," led to cries of betrayal. By the time Herzl was able to vindicate himself in the acrimonious dispute that ensued, his heart had been broken.

Herzl's achievement, as we know today, was a stunning one: a living, breathing Jewish state was founded in his wake. But this magnificent and quite Jewish accomplishment represents but a fraction of what Herzl's vision might have realized had he lived until 1914, or for another five years until 1919, when he would not yet have reached the age of sixty. Herzl's diaries, begun after his awakening of 1895 and available since 1922, are a literary masterpiece and more: a text whose meaning for the future is yet to be exhausted, much less fulfilled. What stands out in Herzl's achievement is the dual legacy he left behind, laying claim to his own people's allegiance and the rest of the world's regard in a single deed which, like every great man's achievement, stands as an example for all mankind.

Herzl brought the Jews into world politics. That is, he showed the Jews how to become an effective historical presence, and thus how to stand the test of maturity that no people is spared in the modern world. It was only now that Jewish religious and spiritual life, rejuvenated during the struggle for civil equality in the nineteenth century, began to find its modern footing. Jews now claimed equal rights for themselves as a people, and demanded their place as rightful members of a national community that stretched throughout the world. The Jewish nation was comprised of citizens like those of all other nations, citizens responsible for their own country and for mankind as a whole. This was true whether Jews became citizens of the Jewish state or remained loyal members of any of the other lands they had faithfully served since Jeremiah announced his pledge to the Babylonian exiles. But there was a revolutionary core to Herzl's insight, and if anyone deserves the name of genius it was he, for Herzl had the genius to recognize the decisively new instrument that would shape every future strategic consideration in world politics: the power of modern technology. Why, Herzl asked, were political movements possible today that had remained nothing but fevered fantasy for centuries on end? The answer, he saw, was simple: "because we have machines." It was no accident that the year 1895, when Herzl's turning point took place, was also the year when X-rays were discovered and the work that would lead to harnessing the power of the atom began in earnest. The invention of the electric light, Herzl notes in another diary entry, was destined not just to provide us with light, but also to help us "solve the Jewish question under its illumination." The first side of Herzl's dual legacy is his grasp of the connection between politics and technology, or rather the fact that the politics of the future would require advanced technology to achieve its ends. Herzl understood the modern tie linking technology, on one hand, with the complete political emancipation of the Jews on the other, a connection that, to borrow the nineteenth century's most revolutionary catchword, was to turn the Jewish people upside down: from its head onto its feet. Herzl's second legacy was simply Herzl, the man himself.

"Who will dare forget this man?" Leo Baeck's pronouncement in his late work *This People: The Meaning of Jewish Existence* is fully justified in its estimation.[1] Yet anyone who tries to assess Herzl's Judaism using yardsticks applicable to antiquity or the Middle Ages is bound to be disappointed. Until, that is, one begins to sense the prophetic mission and message that runs throughout Herzl's endeavor, prophetic in keeping with continuing validity of the biblical task entrusted to this people in its simplest and most revolutionary form. Herzl made the Jewish people a modern historical force, and his achievement testified both to the modern force of their covenant and their loyalty to its bond.

Heeding the calling that overwhelmed him, Herzl sacrificed his well-being and his family's happiness during the last decade of his life, sacrificing his own fortune and his parents' as well. His reward was to be hated and despised, and to be spared no insult. Yet no one could relieve him of the unbearable responsibility he bore. Having brought the Jewish cause to the forefront of the world's attention, Herzl also carried the responsibility for exposing the Jews to the serious dangers such attention brought, a necessary trade-off, however, if the Jewish people were to be saved from a worse fate down the line. With his keen grasp of what was becoming possible in both politics and technology, Herzl was alone in seeing the true extent of dangers waiting just beyond the horizon. All the while Herzl remained completely selfless, as tolerant as he was patient, despite the trait he shared with all leaders of insisting that his troops stay in line, asking for nothing in return save a modicum of trust. Something quite Jewish was nonetheless at work here, as Jewish as the ancient prophets, the sages, and the martyrs of the Middle Ages. Not just Zionists and those who followed in the State of Israel, but all Jews dared not forget that this man was one of their own. Liberal Judaism was bolstered by the rebellious courage Herzl showed in replacing the old with the new, while Orthodox Judaism was heartened by the fact that Herzl's innovative program gave new life to the Jewish people's most fundamental beliefs. And the ranks of those who dare not forget Herzl extend even further to encompass a humanity that remembers him as one of those truly Jewish Jews, whose own people represented but a way station on the road to attaining peace, freedom, and joy for all mankind.

Herzl once had to make a decision that serves as something of a parable. When the name *Homeward* was the majority's choice for the newspaper to be issued in advance of the first Zionist Congress, Herzl rejected it. The title preferred instead preserved the sense of "homeward to humanity" that echoes throughout the Bible's longing for Zion, the longing that forms the substance of the deepest meaning expressed in Judaism's messianic hopes. The name Herzl chose, the one that finally prevailed, was *The World*.

TWELVE

The Lifework of Martin Buber

"So, we're just young people with no respect, are we, fighting you every inch of the way?" These were the words Martin Buber used to reiterate the charges Herzl levied against him and other defenders of cultural Zionism, including Chaim Weizmann, Berthold Feiwel, and David Trietsch. Buber had been editor of Herzl's Zionist organ *Die Welt* since 1901, and in this letter of May 26, 1903, he took up the battle head on. Buber and his supporters were answering Herzl's retort against cultural Zionism, arguing that Zionism was itself only part of a renewed Jewish culture that would accompany the political work Herzl had made the movement's centerpiece. "Our love for you was deeper and more beautiful, our admiration far deeper and far more beautiful than the affections tendered you by those *businessmen* you chose as your advisors," Buber declared. "You have been incapable of recognizing that the idealism burning within us, so ill-suited to courtly intrigue, and making us shun all thoughts of careerist advantage, was, along with your visionary idealism and example as a man of action, the only driving power our movement possessed. Your unflagging energy and our boundless enthusiasm carried an historic significance, and represented a living piece of our people's fate. They should have given us the chance to do great things."[1]

Buber was consistent in his oppositional stance from the start, as a cultural Zionist opposed to political Zionism, to the final position he took, which unconditionally rejected any restrictive factional commitment whatsoever, whether based on religious doctrine or school of thought. This stance is well represented in the articulation of his philosophic position Buber issued at the age of eighty-three: "I have no teaching. I merely show something. I show reality, a part of reality that is not seen, or has at least been too little noticed. I take he who listens by the hand and lead him to the window, open the window, and point outside. I have no teaching, rather, I lead a discussion."[2] Buber's lifework nonetheless remains firmly grounded in history. And for precisely those reasons he sets out in his statement, Buber waged a tireless battle, along with others, that strove to bear up responsibly to the forces of the present. He regarded the future with an absolute seriousness, considering it to be a joint venture undertaken by all mankind, and thus as a reality for which mankind as a whole would have to answer. His lifework falls into three discrete periods, which Buber's retrospective of 1929 divided into "three stages."[3] A fourth stage can be discerned in the period after the Second World War, the period he entered after passing through the abyss of the 1930s and 1940s and moved to the center of the twentieth century's concerns.

Before considering these stages, Buber's experience as a twenty-year-old in 1898 must be given its full due, since the direction it gave to his subsequent works would never face significant challenge. Where, he wondered, was life taking him? Buber's self-criticism leveled a no-holds-barred attack on the flashy intellectuality and flood of superficial productivity that characterized his early studies in art history, literature, and philosophy. Born in Vienna, Buber was two when his parents divorced. Afterward, he was raised by his grandfather in Lemberg (Lvov). There the fourteen-year-old Buber abandoned the daily ritual observance of the traditional Jewish life in which he had been reared, and immersed himself in the cultural temper of European modernism, moving east and arriving at its Viennese center. Nietzsche and Spinoza enthralled him. He attended lectures at the universities of Vienna, Berlin, Zurich, and Leipzig. Then, Zionism snapped him up; the First

Zionist Congress had just taken place. Now, Buber could be a Jew again, part of this people thanks to its historical reality, despite his disdain for its traditional religious forms.

But while becoming a Zionist and "rededicating himself" to Judaism gave Buber his footing, it did not provide an answer to his quest for meaning or point out the correct path to pursue. Buber constantly reminds us that although a "national conviction" does indeed stand as the precondition for every form of authentic creativity, it is not enough to provide the content and basis of one's life. As Herzl's close collaborator for a short period, working speedily on one project after another with his contemporary, Buber was active in a variety of pursuits that tried to give a new cultural depth to Zionism's political focus, but failed. The break with Herzl soon followed, producing Buber's first farewell to active participation in the world. Culture as a slogan was not enough. From 1905 onward, Buber became the champion of religious renewal, and while devoting himself to the study of Hasidism, he simultaneously published a series of social-psychological monographs in his series *Society*. The inaugural volume, Werner Sombart's *Proletariat*, bore an introduction by Buber that laid out his concept of the "interhuman" for the first time. Simmel's influence is also decidedly strong in this period, and Buber's friendship with the leading socialist activist of the period, Gustav Landauer, is quite close and plays a crucial role as well. Landauer's own edition of Meister Eckhardt's *Writings* (1903) exerted a powerful influence on Buber's *Writings on Hassidism*. Yet Buber had more than Judaism in mind in his campaign for religious renewal. His doctoral thesis, *From Cusanus to Boehme*, was a study of German mysticism. In 1909 Buber published his collection of mystical texts, *Ecstatic Confessions*. His *Speeches and Parables of Chuang-Tse* appeared in 1910, and in 1914 a book of Celtic sagas, *The Four Branches of Mabinogi*, along with the Finnish national epic *Kalevala*. In the meantime, a decisively Jewish hour began to toll, and Buber heeded its call.

Jewish youth called upon Buber the Zionist, who had been a champion of historical action, upon the Buber who had led the quest for religious renewal, and the prophet of Judaism's living message of redemption, asking him for help. Bar Kochba, the Jewish student association at the University of Prague, invited Buber to give a lecture in 1909, and yearly invitations followed. Buber's speeches given on those occasions, published as *Lectures on Judaism*, become a wake-up call for an entire generation. "Judaism and the Jews" was the topic of the first lecture, but the second followed immediately: "Judaism and Humanity." Buber's third lecture was a demand for "Renewal," and the fifth lecture's topic was "Religiosity"—not simply religion. The fourth lecture, delivered in 1912, spoke of "The Spirit of the Orient and Judaism." Here, Buber outlined a new perspective, linking the renewal demanded of every individual with the historic task of self-transformation enjoined upon all mankind. The Jewish people, Buber argued, who had themselves arisen in the orient, were to go forth once more from the Jerusalem that had been a cultural crossroads from time immemorial, between East and West. Now, they were to offer their faithful assistance to Asia's own long-justified awakening, and thus to live up to the obligation of a Judaism that had settled the length and breadth of the West: the reconciliation of East and West.

Disappointment, however, was once more in the offing. Though the magnificent journal Buber had once planned with Weizmann was published in 1916 as *Der Jude*, it went under because of the indifference of its Jewish readership. Buber's warning against nationalism, delivered at the first postwar Zionist Congress in 1921, met with just as little approval. Religious renewal had also failed to catch fire. "Religion," Buber wrote eight years later, "is not something that can be created by an act of will . . . boosting religion for the advantages it brings to human life, as something good for the nation, instead of as a way of sanctifying the divine within human life, is worse than no religion at all."

For the hour of Buber's "third stage" had arrived: "neither culture nor religion is crucial, but reality. This means the entirety of the real: God, the world and man," as part of "everyday life." No longer looking for slogans that might change the world, Buber now strived for renewal by seeking a way to stand up responsibly and confront the world's pressures, whatever form they may take. Such opportunities, of course, are hardly in short supply. Before Buber considered undertaking such a commitment, he must already have felt compelled by a sense of responsibility born of a face-to-face encounter. Though every face-to face encounter, whose deepest call is represented in the Bible, addresses its message to all peoples in a timeless fashion, both timeless and contemporary. Once answered, such a call demands and makes possible new forms of public action. Buber thus responded to Franz Rosenzweig's request and became part of the first modern

Jewish Lehrhaus just after its founding in Frankfurt. He also joined Rosen-zweig's grand effort to produce a new German translation of the Hebrew Bible. Another deed worth remembering: Buber's publication of the journal *Die Kreatur* from 1926 to 1930, in collaboration with the Protestant Viktor von Weizsäcker and the Catholic Joseph Wittig. And the first lectureship in Judaic studies that a German university dared to bestow was awarded to Buber in this same period in Frankfurt.

All the while, Buber never lost sight of Zion as the land and nation of Israel historically bound to Palestinian soil, the Zion from which the mes-sage of universal redemption, and redemption for Jews scattered throughout the world, would go forth. Buber thus differed with Hermann Cohen, who had argued in 1916, against Buber, that the Bible had already defined Zion in strictly universal terms. Cohen located the Zion that undergirds our hope for a messianic future not in Palestine, but in "the historical earth in its entirety." Here, Buber stood firmly behind the Zionist idea. His loyalty led him to accept an invitation to deliver a series of guest lectures at the Hebrew University of Jerusalem. That stint led to his appointment in 1938 to a professorship in social philosophy, while continuing his work in Germany, which, even after 1933, he carried forward with the greatest enthusiasm. For now, all of German Jewry had to bear up responsibly to the force of reality, and to do so as Jews. The consequences of Buber's life's work now began to make themselves felt in the broadest possible context. Any expla-nation for the fact that his work failed to flourish in German must be sought on German soil alone, and did not and still does not represent an argument against this work's fecundity.

As Buber continued his work in Palestine, the Jewish state was declared in 1948, a harvest reaped from the seeds Buber had helped to sow. Yet despite this affirmation of his own labors, and the fact that Judaism's com-plete return to historical reality dwarfed any kind of self-confirmation, Bub-er's "third stage" once again ended in bitter disappointment. His later work at the middle of the century shows numerous signs of this turn. This period is not a standstill in Buber's development, but another period of taking stock that allowed him to move forward with new vigor. Buber's short work of 1952, *At the Turning Point: New Lectures on Judaism*, contrasts the prophetic word's earlier predicament of nonfulfillment with the modern world's new state of affairs. Today, Buber argued, forms of fulfillment can be found aplenty, though they lack prophetic inspiration, a situation Buber's significant treatise of the following year would call the "Eclipse of God." Of course, "the dimming of God's light" does not mean it has been "extinguished . . . for tomorrow, for that which has interposed itself between that light and ourselves may recede," though today, its shadows may prevail. But the same Buber who issued this pessimistic pronouncement remained an indefatigable worker committed to his labors, demonstrating an attitude that was itself a guarantor of a light that was not to be quenched.

One of Buber's later achievements most worthy of our admiration was his new edition of his *Tales of the Hassidim* (1949), which edited out all the extravagant excesses of the complete edition of 1928. Everything in the volume now worked together to illuminate the fact that the religiosity of the Middle Ages had vanished, and that the religiosity of modernity was a project still underway. The Bible translation begun with Rosenzweig, set aside during the German horror, was taken up once more and carried to its completion in a new and simplified linguistic form. These projects were accompanied by a rich array of works on the Bible, along with his philosophic, pedagogical, and psychological writings; Buber's commitment to religious socialism never flagged, but was instead renewed in cultural and religious-Zionist form in his *Israel and Palestine*. The founding of the state of Israel—as Buber notes in the foreword to the German edition of 1950—was not a bypass around the demands that religious socialism posed.

Buber gave the talks that would comprise his new *Lectures on Judaism* in Jerusalem, London, and New York, steadfastly meeting the obligation imposed by Judaism's universalism and its relevance to listeners worldwide. Buber spoke wherever he found an audience open to his message, even returning to Germany. Topping the long list of his other achievements, Buber's greatest deed of honor was to have become a tireless advocate for Israel's Arab neighbors and for his Arab fellow citizens in the State of Israel, standing up to much more powerful currents pushing in the other direction. Martin Buber testified to the enduring power within Jewish modernity, to the possibility of a common human future: the substance of Buber's lifework was evident as he truly labored a lifetime to resist and withstand reality's sway, endowing his work with a living vitality that endures.

THIRTEEN

The Jewish State and the World Jewish Congress

Two different political bodies founded by the Jewish people announced that Judaism's outer development was complete, putting an official seal on the fact that the Jewish people had mastered its own path into modernity. The emergence of two different representative entities—with the state of Israel and the World Jewish Congress comprising a national, and transnational parliament, respectively—offered mutual protection against whatever exaggerated forms of accommodation either side might take. The achievement of Jewish emancipation was not regarded as an end in itself, as the resonant and seductive slogan of "Equality!" might suggest. Equality was instead the motive force pushing Judaism to create institutions that would embody its difference and help it secure its identity as something more than an existence that differed from others. Jewish identity insisted on a greater goal, and in the end on the only truly productive one: that the Jews remain true to themselves, just as other peoples were, that is, by retaining their Jewish character. The state of Israel defends against the danger that the World

Jewish Congress might come to resemble other exclusively transnational entities, such as world religions. The World Jewish Congress meanwhile guards against the Jewish state's becoming too much like other nations, lest it become content with squandering its energies on statehood and its autonomous power, that is, with "sovereignty" alone.

The intellectual path on which this dual set of national and transnational rights and responsibilities was achieved will be discussed shortly, as part of the "inner renewal" we are about to sketch. This dual set of obligations, of course, confronts every citizen who belongs to a state as well as the world; the two must be fulfilled together. The significance of the creation of these two political bodies, however, has not yet been fully appreciated. The founding of the state of Israel and the World Jewish Congress occurred quickly, almost hastily, rushed into existence by external events before the people who struggled to achieve them had acquired the maturity and outlook that would allow them to adjust. The constant political horse-trading and shifting membership between the two groups, allowing Nahum Goldmann to become president of first one and then the other organization over time, displayed a kind of intellectual immaturity preventing the Jews and kept them from taking full advantage of the deeper opportunities offered by these events. Eventually, the existence of two different representative bodies justified itself in "theory," in precisely the Greek sense of the word meaning "to look at": not as the sign of a development brought to fruition, but as a preliminary prospect on the kind of meaning future labors might create.

The Jewish state and the World Jewish Congress came into being after arduous labor, the results of both intensive planning and frantic groping after the proper course. Emerging as only a partial fulfillment of their original aims, these two political bodies have become the practical attempt to realize much larger ideas, for seen together, they represent the authentic message of Judaism's mission, tried in the unavoidable test of practical circumstances. Today's modern world demands a maturity that is apparent in both Israel's achievement of self-determination in a land of its own, and in the commitment of the World Jewish Congress to the freedom and solidarity of all the earth's peoples. That commitment evokes the collective hope, unity, and feeling of affinity shared in all lands of the earth. Neither hate nor disbelief nor mere reserve can erase, dim, or simply pass over the fact that Judaism's outer development, reaching its summit in the Jewish battle for emancipation, testifies to the same message this people had proclaimed in every age. Emancipation harkened to a promise transformed and renewed from the biblical exodus forward: a message of exodus, national awakening, and covenant that will continue to sound until that day when peace is fully achieved.

And so, as the fitting self-designation puts it, the "Jewish state in progress" began to gather in the form of the Zionist congresses convened in Basel, London, the Hague, Hamburg, Vienna, Karlsbad, Zurich, Prague, Lucerne, Geneva, and Jerusalem, well before any territory for an independent state had been acquired. This precondition for statehood could be dispensed with in Judaism's case. The Jewish people's ancient experience as a sovereign state had continued to mold their character from antiquity forward. That heritage produced a kind of political self-awareness apparent in the decision of the Zionist Congress, a forerunner of the Israeli parliament, to allow its representatives to divide into parties, even though its delegates hailed from communities spread throughout the world. When some of these same representatives gathered as the World Jewish Congress in Geneva, in Montreux, and in Stockholm, that different rationale of that organization responded to different imperatives. The Congress rejected party membership and regarded its delegates as representatives of the districts, countries, or national entities that had elected them. The World Jewish Congress is made up of delegations from states whose Jewish representatives remain loyal and devoted citizens of their respective lands, while the Congress itself expresses the fact that these Jews belong to a nation of their own. That national identity was so crucial, in fact, that the Jewish response to the world's demand that they justify their continued existence in modernity was to found a state with a territory of its own.

The constitutions of both organizations—whose profound appropriateness makes them almost artificial—imposed themselves through an irresistible logic of their own, against the dominant tendency of a people who from time immemorial had shied away from its own prophetic mission. Within four decades, the World Jewish Congress would stand together with the Zionist Congress in 1936, an organization that met for the first time in 1897, thirty-seven long years after the Alliance Israélite Universelle had first attempted to convene a worldwide Jewish assembly. And again, two decades have passed, and many more might go by until the Zionist Congress resolves its overlap with the parliament of the state of Israel it hoped to initiate, by merging itself into that body.

The party system of the Zionist congress was produced by a different kind of representative overlap: the chaotic admixture of Jewish political parties and communal groups in Europe that would eventually require the bicameral form of Jewish political organization that emerged. Before that, the Zionist Congress was plagued by a dual burden, with its program committed both to the establishment of a Jewish state and to the unity of the Jewish people as a whole. When the Zionist Congress began to act as if statehood was Judaism's crucial and singular form of expression, their actions spurred the Jewish people's ability to think and act in historic terms, and thus helped to enable the mutual and supportive efforts that the World Jewish Congress undertook. The first Zionist congresses were thus correct when they regarded their delegates not as simply representatives of their parties, but of the Jewish people as a whole, in all their complexity, delegates who, by paying their membership fee—the shekel—became Zionists, voters, and representatives as well.

But Zionism's ultimate goal—fighting for "the creation of a publicly and legally recognized homeland for the Jewish people in Palestine"— increasingly pushed all other questions to the side. Herzl had indeed expressed the second Zionist congress's sentiment when he called Zionism "a homecoming to Judaism" that would occur "before our return to a Jewish land." But the more the congress's daily attention came to be absorbed exclusively with questions of Jewish settlement and acquiring land, the less delegates found the time was available for other concerns. "Coming home to Judaism," with its broader focus on Jewish self-assertion, modern self-awareness and the need for fundamental self-renewal, receded to the background, especially after Herzl's untimely death, when the "practical" Zionism he so resolutely opposed won the day against his strictly "political" Zionism. So-called practical work became Zionism's central concern, despite the fact that the homeland was far from being publicly and legally secured.

As early as 1903—while Herzl was still alive—the first splinter group of the Mizrahi Party had broken away, followed by the Poalei Zion in 1907, the former representing religiously observant Jews, and the latter the party of the workers. Both parties were forerunners of like-minded parties that would emerge, not unjustifiably, in what would be mandatory Palestine and later the state of Israel. The Sixth Zionist Congress of 1907 decided to promote settlement, economic development, and better organization for the settlement in Palestine, all of which began to take effect in 1908. This emphasis on practical work led both present and future citizens of the nation to a deeper involvement with the land of Israel itself, and soon, domestic policy began to take the upper hand. The inevitable split between the political left and right began to make itself felt, and the rapidly developing spirit of party and faction asserted its primacy over all other ties, tearing at the fabric of the Jewish communal organizations that made up the Zionist Congress. Those communal groups were themselves splintered by even deeper factional division when an additional body emerged from their midst. Representatives of the Jewish community in Palestine began to claim the Congress as their own, wanting the body to be constituted of their parties with their adherents throughout the world, but not representatives from other groups.

For all of these reasons, the interim World Jewish Congress convened in Geneva on August 8–15, 1936, after three preparatory conferences held there in 1931–33, did not compete with the Zionist Congress, which met in 1935 and 1937 for the nineteenth and twentieth times, in any way. Here, delegations from every Jewish community once again had their own say. The process established by the World Jewish Congress, which had limited delegations to a single representative from every recognized state, was broadened to allow the formation of new Jewish delegations to represent Jews who, though able to vote, lacked effective representation or were prevented from making their voices heard. Delegates from the Jewish community of Palestine sat side by side with representatives of the rest of Jewish people, just as the World Jewish Congress convened shortly after the declaration of the state of Israel saw Israeli delegates take their seats amidst the almost seventy other delegates attending to the people's common affairs. The World Jewish Congress aims to assure "the continuity of the Jewish people and to strengthen its unity." This makes it a welcome extension of both the Zionist Congress and the parliament of the state of Israel, and of all other independent Jewish communities and organizations, as well as the umbrella organizations of every Jewish community throughout the world. For the World Jewish Congress expresses that which can be embodied by no single voice or group: that vision they affirm in common. The World Jewish Congress alone—unshackled by a particular citizenship—can extend the national voice of the state of Israel and all Jewish communities, for only a worldwide federation of the Jewish people can stand up for those unable to be present among them.

This is exactly what happened in August 1936 when representatives of the world's Jewish communities finally met in Geneva. Both Russian and German Jewry were absent from the solemn festivities of that event meant to symbolize the full equality the Jewish people now claimed as their own. Russian and German Jews together made up one-fourth of the world's Jewish population, though they contributed a much larger portion of Judaism's intellectual and spiritual energy. New rulers in each country had pitilessly revoked the rights Jews had struggled to achieve in exemplary and upright devotion to their lands. Jewish citizens in both had proven themselves loyally devoted to both the Jewish communities and their states by irreproachably fulfilling their civic duties, fully vindicating the civil rights they had won. Now they were forbidden to be Jews. That is, they were denied the chance to obey Judaism's commandment that enjoined them to sustain their identity as a people, a nation of biblical origin that had preserved itself in diaspora throughout the Middle Ages, and were now scattered to the four corners of the modern world.

But the more the new Russia became intoxicated by its own salvific message, the more jealous it became of others, and vented that jealousy in an antireligious frenzy that sought to disavow the religious origins of its own redemptive scheme. The Soviet Union demanded complete assimilation from its Jews in exchange for its offer of full equality, requiring that they shed all ties to Judaism's own historical commitment to redemption. Germany meanwhile kept its ultimate and sinister aims hidden, demanding at first only that the Jews give up full legal enfranchisement as such, in exchange for the illusory right to remain in their own country, a Germany that purported to bear salvific tidings of its own. Germany nevertheless kept the opposite alternative open even in the year of 1936, offering a "permission" to emigrate that Russia had long restricted. Yet Germany prevented Jews from attending the World Jewish Congress that year unless they wished to sacrifice their German citizenship, and Russian Jews were simply denied the chance to attend the convocation.

As a result, the World Jewish Congress became part of the legacy of German Judaism while German Jewry was still alive: one of the cornerstones of Jewish modernity German Judaism had helped establish, but a body from which it found itself barred, cut off from the whole. This sort of historical contribution cannot be measured in the abstract, nor by counting the proportionally large number of German names who attended that World Jewish Congress, or helped in founding the Jewish state, whether by planning, smoothing the way, or carrying its numerous tasks to completion. The World Jewish Congress of 1936 marked the completion of modern Judaism's outer development. And that achievement resulted not from the efforts of a few well-known figures, but from the collective efforts that Moses Mendelssohn's move to Berlin in the fall of 1743 helped set in motion. That movement came to an end two hundred years later, in the summer of 1943, when the Berlin police closed the last State Office for the Jews of Germany. At the beginning of this period, Judaism seemed to be a relic or a culture about to die out: at its end, Judaism stands up powerfully against those who would have taken its life, in the midst of its path toward the future.

Boastful pride over such accomplishments would be quite unseemly. Too many innocent victims litter the path to the future, numbers that increase the closer we come to the end. What an incomprehensibly gruesome mystery it remains, with horrible wounds all its own, that it was German citizens who indelibly inscribed their place in Jewish history by the spilling of so much innocent blood. The only unshakable certainty left is that world history remains a redemptive history in which Judaism lives on for the sake of the future—and dies—so that its prophetic message, heralding the kingdom of freedom, joy and peace, can be heard by all of mankind, all of creation, and the universe as a whole. The reawakening of that message will always remain one of German Jewry's achievements, the fruit of its inner renewal, and the most precious legacy it left behind.

PART THREE

FOURTEEN

The Essence of Judaism

German Jewry's quest to define its essence—its attempt to name the "essence of Judaism"—was perhaps its most characteristic endeavor. The word "essence" invokes both the distinctive uniqueness and weakness of German Jewish society, and of German intellectual life as a whole. German and Jewish intellectuals shared a predilection for abstraction and a tendency toward inner withdrawal, a desire to retreat to an inward reality cut off from the concerns of everyday life, and without influence over it. Yet the phrase we are about to consider, "the essence of Judaism," also signifies one of the most important debates in world Jewish history, though in quite German fashion, the phrase itself became the title of but a single book. The controversy over "the essence of Judaism" ultimately produced one of the most crucial intellectual breakthroughs and victories of Jewish modernity.

The whole affair began innocently enough. Adolf Harnack, theologian at the University of Berlin and scholar of the Prussian Academy, the Kaiser's trusted advisor and a towering scholarly authority in his own right, held a series of interdisciplinary lectures in the winter of 1899–1900. The lectures—published immediately as *The Essence of Christianity*, and gaining a wide readership—in their own way tried to take a wholly progressive, open-minded, and modern tack, and compared with other points of view, they might even be said to have succeeded. Harnack contrasted Christianity with Judaism to the benefit of the former as not just the newer but the higher religious form of religious life, the new dispensation that had long ago rendered Judaism's message obsolete. Harnack reserved his scorn for the "belated" productions of those "rabbis and theologians," who, according to Harnack, pirated the sources of an emergent Christianity in the first centuries of its existence and exploited its teachings in order to breathe fresh life into a supposedly exhausted Jewish sources. It is as if those Jewish sources alive two thousand years before had, by dint of their own authority, continued to flow and passed through the Christian world history that would carry them forward to their destined future.

Harnack thus took the same position Lavater had 130 years before when he challenged Mendelssohn in 1769 to convert to Christianity, contending that Judaism had been superseded, and that modern political life and citizenship would be possible for the Jews only if they accepted Christianity's embrace. This time, the gauntlet was dropped at the threshold of the twentieth century, as if the modernization and renewal of Judaism Mendelssohn had set in motion had not taken place at all. Harnack, in other words, acted as if Jews had not acquired full individual equality decades before, as if the Jews had not made equal rights for the Jewish people their watchword throughout the 1890s. He ignored the fact that Jewish religious feeling had recently burst forth into a new self-awareness, and that the Wissenschaft des Judentums was already powerfully at work. Harnack acted as if Jewish historians were not busily pursuing their trailblazing work.

In the face of these achievements, Judaism's core principle was about to bear even richer fruit. Its inner resources had not yet been able to claim the shining recognition they deserved, and the dispute Harnack had sparked was about to allow Judaism to do just that. The Jewish response his lectures provoked would articulate a self-conscious vision of Judaism's own capacities and historic achievement, a vision insufficiently appreciated by its cultural contemporaries and by Jewish activists alike. This step could be taken only when the intellectual and spiritual response to Harnack had been given its decisive form, anchoring the achievement that became the legacy of German Jewry. The Jewish entry to modernity was outwardly complete, its program fulfilled insofar as the formal acquisition of equal rights spoke to Jews as men, citizens, and a nation of their own. The inner Jewish revolution that accompanied this process was about to receive its unequivocal statement, echoing beyond the confines of the nineteenth century into the millennia to come. The debate over the essence of Judaism would allow Judaism to acknowledge and affirm the depth of its own spiritual power, and to define the validity of its truth as fully equal to the modern challenge. Both Judaism's ancient and original and the vibrant forms of its contemporary religious expression would declare themselves to be equal in every respect to Christianity, Islam, the rest of the world's religions and to socialism as well. Judaism would define itself as the equal of every vision of redemption the world has known or is yet to know, and as capable in science, philosophy, art, and technology as every other people of the past, present, and future.

One of the first and most impressive expressions of this conviction was expressed in a review of Harnack's lectures that was published in the spring 1901 volume of the *Monatsschrift für die Geschichte und die Wissenschaft des Judentums*. Four years later, Leo Baeck's contributions to that journal became the basis of his book of 1905. *The Essence of Judaism* marked Baeck's intellectual emergence: though a mere twenty-eight years old, he had the temerity to take on a scholar of Harnack's stature. And as a figure on the German intellectual landscape, Harnack was as influential and famous as Baeck was isolated and intellectually unknown. Baeck, in fact, might well have stood for one of those "rabbis and theologians" Harnack had derided for "retrospectively imbuing Judaism with a living vitality that entered the world with the advent of Christianity alone." Baeck rose up, accepted the challenge, and vanquished his opponent. His argumentative style eschewed any defensive posture, and he refused to waste time or squander his energies by trying to refute Harnack's central charges, not to mention the tawdry counterattacks and vain "refutations" advanced by his opponent. Instead, Baeck laid out a vision of the future that made intellectual and religious space, next to his own Jewish "essence," where the authentic "essence of Christianity" had a right to reside and persevere as well. Making his case in contemporary terms, Baeck argued a wholly modern perspective that was at the same time fundamentally consonant with the inner vision of Jewish tradition.

Baeck's first point of opposition to Harnack concerned the importance of Jesus' Jewish provenance, a subject well understood by Jewish scholars since 1838 at least, when the issue emerged with the publication of Joseph Salvador's *Jésus-christ et sa doctrine*, and was finally taken up and confirmed by Christian biblical scholarship. "Jesus was a Jew among Jews," Baeck argued contra Harnack: "one must understand the Jews if one wishes to understand the Gospel." Baeck's point crystallized a specifically modern, a "dialogic" outlook, if you will. His unshakable conviction originates from the insight that both participants in the modern dialogue possess legitimately divergent viewpoints that are nonetheless contingent upon one another, making it impossible for either interlocutor to dictate the dialogue's course. This divergence, of course, is what called for dialogue in the first place. Modernity demands that we come to terms with the greatness of different traditions without subordinating one to the other, or compelling a minority tradition to submit, because the validity of different traditions is constituted relationally. The fact that Jesus was a Jew does not rob Christianity of its redeemer, any more than proving that Christianity begins with Jesus refutes the covenant to which the Jewish people swore allegiance in the Sinai Desert.

Baeck's second major contention would eventually be borne out by biblical scholarship as a whole. *The Essence of Judaism* argued that the ancient Jewish sects active during the origin of Christianity were hardly the ossified and benumbed remnants of a tradition that had "pharisaically" gone astray. Instead, Baeck showed that "the sieve, in which Israel's chaff was sifted away," was not in place until the Babylonian exile and the revisions of Ezra and Nehemia; not until the Maccabean revolt and its spiritual demands gave the Jews the strength to resist both Greece's dominating intellectual influence and the oppressive force of Roman political power. The Pharisees themselves had waged a passionate campaign, dedicating their lives to the insight that the demands of piety must be obeyed, setting themselves against the Sadducees, Essenes, Zealots, Sicarii, Hellenists, Jewish Christians, pagan Christians, and other Jewish offshoots and foreign temptations. The Pharisees replaced the sacrificial rituals of the second Temple with the House of Study and the Synagogue. They thus also created the religious service comprised of the word alone of the church and the mosque, which would become a part of both the Christian and Islamic service, a change that ended the domination of the Temple priesthood and its clerical establishment. Confident and courageous, the Pharisees ventured beyond the commandments enumerated in the Torah in their "liberal" affirmation of the validity of the oral tradition and the Talmud, arguing that the Torah and the Talmud together represented a single and common injunction: "Study!" According to Baeck, "They stood as a group apart, a society of religious heroes . . . the world's great non-conformists."

Baeck's third great contention against Harnack showed that the Pharisees, religious heroes who masterfully constructed the bridge that linked Jewish antiquity with the Middle Ages, had given the humanity of its era a great gift that was wholly new, a new religious ethos exemplified in their own lives. The Pharisees had introduced the notion of religious martyrdom, the idea of a complete dedication to God's service and an acceptance of suffering equal to that symbolized by the cross, that would later become Christianity's symbol. The ardor with which Baeck underscored the meaning of martyrdom—and this in 1901—is all the more disconcerting for being so at odds with the calm and peaceful security that characterized the first decade of the twentieth century. Enthusiastically celebrating and praising martyrdom's appearance in history as a Jewish discovery, Baeck hailed its concept of religious sacrifice as a symbol of Judaism's deepest meaning, preserved in acts that history would witness time and time again:

> If it is an unconditional duty to decide for God, then the limit of life is no limit to duty. Against the vastness of man's task life itself seems insignificant and even the fullest existence means little when contrasted with the infinite ethical demand. . . . The martyr exalts his love for God above his life; he manifests the eternal value of his soul. . . . This is the victory which man wins through his freedom, for in the very face of death he still exercises his choice. He chooses the will of God, through death he chooses life. In martyrdom death is no longer a mere end of life, a mere fate. It becomes a deed of freedom. . . . It is the pride of Judaism that it created the idea of and the call to martyrdom. From Judaism men first learned that they belonged to God, and to hold fast to him. In this way sorrow becomes a path toward freedom, hallowing the name of God. Nor was this a deed accomplished by the select few while remaining an indefinite mood among the Jewish masses. Jewish history shows us the contrary: martyrdom was never a mere passive fate but always an active deed, a singular and unique testament to heroic conscience, to the idealism of decision, a testament showing us

how religion for the Jewish people was always its life, a people whose confession of faith was action.[1]

Baeck contributed to the growing rediscovery of the importance of Jewish antiquity to Western culture. This scholarly effort would flourish in the following decades, reaching farther and farther back, beyond the Pharisees and the prophets to Moses and Abraham of the distant past. This reexamination of a four-thousand-year period stretching from the Middle Ages back to antiquity itself brought scholars to rethink the significance of Judaism's primary sources, and to begin to understand them as the cultural wellspring of Jewish modernity. Abraham's setting forth from Ur, his abandonment of the world of Mesopotamia, and that other crucial turning point, the Jewish people's exodus into the desert that left behind Egypt's temptations, once again took center stage. But the Jewish covenant towered above them all. This oath to an unbreakable faith, along with the ten commandments aimed at men's hearts, was accompanied by the other doubtlessly Mosaic achievement: the twin adjurations to "love your fellow as yourself," and to care for the stranger: "you shall love him as yourself: for you were strangers in the land of Egypt" (Leviticus 19:18, 19:34).

Baeck's formulation of this tradition gave new and clear expression to a central tenet of the Jewish people's self-understanding, restating a conception of Judaism that Buber would summarize in 1913 in his fifth "Lecture on Judaism." There, Buber argued that the religious life of other peoples should be defined as the "sum total of the customs and the teachings articulated and formulated by the religiosity of a certain epoch in a people's life; its prescriptions and dogmas are rigidly determined and handed down as unalterably binding to all future generations, without regard for their newly developed religiosity, which seeks new forms." Religiosity, on the other hand, was an expression of the human desire to "create a living community with the absolute," the desire to "act in such a way as to give living reality to it by making it part of the human world. Authentic religiosity seeks to transform what is unconditional into the material of this world," and this makes it "Jewish religiosity" as well.[2]

Another question, however, provoked Baeck's fourth contention against Harnack, and became apparent only at this juncture of the debate. The issue of Christianity's alleged priority had in fact been raised anew. Once Judaism and its culture, already flourishing for four thousand years, was taken into account, and once it was recognized that the modern Jewish world, so alive and changing, had been just as vibrant at the time of the Pharisees, how was contemporary Christianity, or even the Christian past, to be viewed? How could Christianity define its own distinctive mission and creative contribution once Judaism was taken into full account? Should Judaism, for its part, recognize Christianity's vital and living path, which had emerged, after all, from Jewish sources? Or should the negation Harnack had hurled at Judaism simply be thrown back in Christianity's face? Baeck avoids this sort of premodern tit-for tat not by simple goodwill and civility, but by an affirmation deeply rooted in his own tradition that allowed him to recognize both his own Jewish essence and the essence of Christianity. "The day had come when Paganism could finally begin to assimilate Israel's teaching," he asserts, describing the complex of Jewish-Christian relations in familial terms: "A mother never hates her child, but the child often forgets and betrays its mother."

Baeck grants Christianity its own specific task and provides the basis for a joint affirmation of the Jewish and Christian traditions. He grants that it was Christianity that, "in the fullness of time," had carried the message of revelation to the pagan world. Judaism, to be sure, is acquainted—or better still, was well acquainted with this mission already laid out in detail in the forty-ninth and fifty-sixth chapters of the Book of Isaiah. The call itself had been received during the era of Babylonian exile and taken up, until five hundred years later, every twelfth "Roman" was a Jew. But as far as completion goes, the decisive act that made this task a part of a broader redemptive history belongs to Christianity alone. And while Christianity's mission may have resulted for the most part in persecution, slander, and repression where Judaism was concerned, Christianity's redemptive historical task and achievement must at the same time be seen as part of a redemptive framework whose point of departure originates with Judaism itself.

That task and message had begun, Baeck reminded Harnack, with Judaism. For Baeck, coaffirmation means that a deeply believing and confirmed Jew—a witness to the covenant who is both filled and fulfilled by its meaning—can hold fast to his own tradition while recognizing that Christianity and its covenant possess their own validity, and in fact ought to do so. Because the absence of such mutual recognition soon leads to its opposite and contradicts the religious self-certainty of one's own vision of redemption and humanity. "A mother never hates her own child," even when the child continually forgets his mother, disavows and even persecutes her! Here, Baeck takes his cue from the solution to religious coexistence pioneered by Yehuda Halevi and Moses Maimonides, the two most influential Jewish thinkers of the Middle Ages, who argued that different traditions of expounding revelation that had sprung from Judaism's sources could coexist with it. Baeck's image of the mother and her children continues their thought, envisioning an unqualified affirmation of all Judaism's "daughter religions": Christianity, Islam, and Socialism, for the last, too, belongs to the "essence of Judaism" as well.

Another German Jew thirteen years Baeck's junior, Franz Rosenzweig—whose essay "Education Without End" provides the title of a chapter to follow—reduced the thriving variety of the world's religions to Judaism and Christianity alone in his *The Star of Redemption* (1921). That is, Rosenzweig viewed the Jewish and Christian traditions as central, and he refused to grant other religious traditions the same authenticity and validity. The reciprocal difference and completion that constituted the Jewish-Christian encounter, he argued, was unique, a difference and reciprocity I have elsewhere described as a "division of labor in redemptive history." Yet however one judges his contribution, Rosenzweig surpassed Baeck by conceiving the relation between the Jewish "mother" and her Christian children as equal in every respect, a relation better described by calling them "sister religions," since both are the modern children of a past held in common trust. Baeck, however, had already made the breakthrough to this revolutionary reconceptualization in *The Essence of Judaism*, not just by refuting *The Essence of Christianity* but also by offering a completely new vision of Jewish-Christian relations better grounded in modernity's terms. Baeck argued that neither Christianity nor Judaism was meant to replace the other, as if this were some type of either–or question, but that both were capable of continued development, and indeed, were meant to go on and flourish.

Exactly fifty years after *The Essence of Judaism*, Baeck followed with another visionary account. Baeck died on November 2, 1956, just two days after finishing its second part. The first had appeared in 1955 as *This People Israel: The Meaning of Jewish Existence*, with the concluding chapters seeing publication in 1957. It is with admiration and respect that we read Baeck's final work, which combines all the gifts of Baeck's advanced age with his unique talent for portraying Judaism's self-understanding, and both are apparent throughout his magisterial and culminating exposition. Baeck's book was quite literally wrested from the very martyrdom his youthful writings had anticipated with such clarity, and welcomed so enthusiastically in advance. And though the full extent of that martyrdom still remains scarcely conceivable to us today—horrors beyond any measure, yet which many people nonetheless survived—Baeck's final work grasps this not as evidence against the continuity of "Jewish existence," but as a new and pronounced authentication of "this people."

Baeck composed much of the book during his imprisonment in Berlin, then Theresienstadt, ready to surrender his own life at any time, but because of that the more resolute in testifying to his own message, standing steadfastly by those fundamental, universal concepts that shape Jewish existence: covenant, exodus, revelation, wandering, and the land of Israel. The exposition itself follows an inward gaze, with part 1 examining only biblical figures and several key Jewish thinkers up to Spinoza. Baeck writes at a remove from the tumult and variety of world history, intent as he is testifying to the particularity of his own message. By fixing his gaze in this way, Baeck finds himself curiously free of the need to delimit the bounds separating his particular tradition from others, and from the universal. In Israel's daily and representative sacrifice as a people, Baeck sees a nation—God's champion and suffering servant—who lives, suffers, and dies alongside all other peoples and nations. "As for this nation, so for all": these seven immortal words bring the first part of *This People Israel* to a close, spanning a course that leads from his contemporary world-historical moment, fraught with terrible dangers as well as spiritual intensification, to a new instauration of the deepest and most basic truth that guided Judaism through millennia past and to come: For all!

As Baeck puts it in his preface to the second half: "When the book *This People Israel: The Meaning of Jewish Existence* began to make its way to its readers, it also confronted the author again. This encounter awakened reflections."[3] One can sense the pressing magnitude of the twentieth century's dark realities as they impinge on his presentation throughout, and Baeck engages those realities directly in his retrospective reflection at the start of the new edition. A biblical injunction expressed the new task, joining the one that directed both parts of the work, and proving it: "The people I formed for Myself / That they might declare my praise" (Isaiah 43:21). The second part of Baeck's work bears a motto taken from the hymn of praise sung by the people of Israel after crossing the Red Sea, a hymn of more than victory alone, which celebrates a standing summons: "Till thy people pass over, O Lord / till the people pass over, whom thou hast acquired" (Exodus 15:16). For Baeck, a different kind of temporal affirmation exists alongside the timeless immediacy of covenant, exodus, revelation, desert, and the promised land, a temporal affirmation that takes them as its origin and telos: the continuing history of "this people," concretized in the historicity and world-historical meaning of "Jewish existence." Concluding his work by calling our attention to the message embodied in the full scope of that meaning, the final page of Baeck's work reminds us that it stretches "throughout the life of man, and throughout mankind."[4]

The five chapters of *This People Israel* span the three epochs and four thousand years that make up Jewish history. Three are devoted to the Middle Ages, while the fifth, treating the modern period, is almost as long as the rest of the book put together. The chapter "Growth and Rebirth" begins the chapter that stretches from Jewish antiquity to the first of the "Jewish Renaissances," which occurred during the Babylonian exile; "The Way and the Comfort," "Prayer and Learning," and "The Kingdom of God" discuss the Jewish Middle Ages. The title of the chapter on Jewish modernity comprises a single word that manages to encompass the watchwords that stand over all the preceding sections: "The Hope." This was Baeck's powerful and consoling act. A Jew who came to represent Judaism itself arises from death's abyss not just as a survivor, who goes on with life, but as a living and enduring witness of what transcends our current moment, and looks toward tomorrow, bringing joyful tidings of a future yet to come.

FIFTEEN

Philosophy Out of the Sources of Judaism

The philosophic and at the same time Jewish legacies of Philo, Maimonides, and Spinoza preceded the legacy of German Jewry, but our account of German Jewry's legacy to philosophy does not need to take separate account of their pioneering philosophical work. We thus mention only in passing Philo's philosophic synthesis of Moses and Plato, written in Greek, which became a foundational work of medieval philosophy and the chief model for the church fathers and the exegetical method they would deploy. Philo's synthesis was thus a crucial source for the high scholasticism of the Middle Ages, and for Moses Maimonides. Writing in Arabic and building on Saadia Gaon, Maimonides constructed a bridge between the philosophically more rigorous Aristotle and a Judaism that had in the meantime flourished as never before. We must also recall that as the Middle Ages waned, Spinoza—writing in Latin and building on Leone Ebreo's writings in Spanish and Italian—paved the way toward a modern philosophy by taking a philosophic approach to biblical exegesis, blazing the trail that modern Judaism would follow as well. However, the philosophic legacy of German Jewry consists of its comprehensive reacquisition and reworking of this philosophic tradition. With their perspective rooted in a different linguistic medium, German Jews were completely at home with the most advanced intellectual methods, testing and reaffirming Judaism's message and casting its philosophic tradition anew.

The year was 1915—ten years after the appearance of Leo Baeck's *Essence of Judaism*—when Hermann Cohen, a leading neo-Kantian and the head of the Marburg School, gave his followers a peculiar surprise. After publishing a series of historic and significant works on Kant and a theory of knowledge grounded on reason alone, Cohen began the process of laying out his own philosophic system after the turn of the century. *The Logic of Pure Cognition* appeared in 1902, followed by *The Ethics of Pure Will* in 1904, and *The Aesthetics of Pure Feeling* in 1912. All that was needed was a "psychology" to reunite these separate faculties as "pure consciousness." But in 1915, the concluding volume of this system failed to appear—it would never be written—and a different work took its place: *The Concept of Religion in the System of Philosophy*.

Religion, however, had been Cohen's concern for decades: sublated, to be sure, in his "philosophical system" as one of philosophy's "preliminary stages." Cohen had regarded religion as a "natural condition," nothing more than a "surrogate" and stand-in for a philosophy whose reason was not yet wholly mature. Religion's message, the core of its revelation, was said to represent an "idea," and an ultimately knowable one. Belief, as distinguished from knowledge, was seen as nothing more than a stage to be passed through on the road to a knowledge that would eventually be grasped in its own terms. Suddenly, Cohen had published a work that contradicted all that, making room for "the concept of religion," and granting it a place in his "philosophical system." While skeptical of religion's autonomy, Cohen still sees it as possessing a specific character all its own. And while posing no threat to the ultimate synthesis of reason on which Cohen's philosophic system rests, religion is still allowed to confront reason in its own terms and to follow its own particular path.

The argument that played itself out here was not unlike Leo Baeck's dispute with Harnack, except that this time the dispute was carried on within the soul of a single individual. The outcome of this debate between Cohen's philosophy and his religious sense would be decided four years later, when *Religion of Reason Out of the Sources of Judaism*, finished just before he drew his last breath, was published in early 1919. Now Cohen argued that the future belonged to both religion and philosophy alike. But Cohen remained so much the philosopher in his final work's style that many "Marburgians" regarded his *Religion of Reason* as nothing but a detailed reaffirmation and completion of their master's life's work, evidence of his continued loyalty and commitment to "pure cognition" alone. Others, led by Franz Rosenzweig, read Cohen's testament to the "sources of Judaism" as proof of a fundamental shift in his thought, though the simple fact that he had remained loyal to his religion did not mean that he had therefore broken faith with philosophy.

As we have seen, the fact that Christianity had branched off from a living Judaism, alive then as now, does not defame Christianity's independence but reaffirms it. The Jew who demands equality for Judaism likewise becomes a better, not a worse citizen. And the same holds true for the relation between philosophy and Judaism. A superior philosopher will never deny what is best within him or her in their quest for what is universally best in philosophy. This notion is progressive in the strictest sense of the word, demanding that the work of philosophy continue until every kind of human particularity becomes part of a philosophic project that can encompass the common inheritance of all peoples with negating their particularity, a goal that remains to be reached. Human particularity is indispensable in this quest, and Judaism certainly need not shy away from its own. Hermann Cohen's late work testifies to this fact by bringing Judaism's "messianic humanity" into full philosophic view for the first time, under the new philosophic premise that "peace is the crown of life."

Cohen's integration of Jewish cultural particularity into philosophy succeeds, by showing that the summit of "pure cognition" is not defamed but instead, fully developed for the first time in the process. The result is a new way of philosophizing out of the sources of Judaism. Cohen's achievement remains quite distinct, however, from an earlier effort in the philosophy of religion that sought to do justice to philosophy and Judaism in turn. This previous effort to bring Judaism and philosophy into relation was represented by figures such as Salomon Ludwig Steinheim, Salomon Formstecher, and Samuel Hirsch, whose innovative and praiseworthy efforts appeared in 1840 as *Revelation According to Synagogue Practice*, *The Religion of the Spirit*, and *The System of Jewish Religious Observance and Its Relation* to *Paganism, Christianity and Absolute Philosophy*. Moritz Lazarus was still following their lead in 1900, and was succeeded by the remarkable Oskar Goldberg and later Joachim Schoeps, and finally by Julius Guttmann's *The Philosophy of Judaism* in 1933. Yet the narrow definition of Jewish religious identity characteristic of these works hobbles their grasp of the subject time and time again. The limitations of this "philosophy of religion" approach characteristically become apparent in a dependence on other disciplines for its fundamental principles. What is needed, instead, is an attention to the religious material itself that would allow it to produce the guiding principles the investigation itself demands. Religious principles per se, of course, cannot be put aside in such investigations, but philosophy must not be conducted according to religious dictates either. Philosophy for the sake of philosophy can be undertaken only when full self-acknowledgment becomes philosophy's point of departure, and its ultimate measure as well.

My own short outline of Cohen's *Philosophy Out of the Sources of Judaism* was published as *For a Jewish House of Study in Zurich*, given at the opening of courses there, and became part of *The Message of Judaism* (1960).[1] That book was shaped by Cohen's *Religion of Reason*, which it reformulates to approach the book's original meaning, in order to do justice to the unique combination of the religious intensity of Cohen's sudden reawakening to Judaism with the philosophical self-awareness he displays throughout. Cohen's project of tracing those ancient Jewish tributaries that flow forward and feed modernity could be accomplished only by deploying an unfettered critical reason, using the most advanced concepts available and following developments wherever they might lead. Neither a religion of reason nor a reason based in religion would suffice: such a venture could be mounted successfully with the resources of reason alone.

Guttman's philosophers of Judaism represent only marginal figures when compared with this powerful stream issuing from the sources of religious Judaism. This larger vision becomes even more apparent if we enlarge the list of religious philosophers mentioned above to include thinkers whose Judaism is obvious, or chose to identify themselves as such, and whose work embraces already universal concerns, from Moses Mendelssohn and Salomon Maimon and Moses Hess to Heymann Steinthal, Manuel Joel, Martin Buber, Jakob Klatzkin, Hugo Bergmann, Max Brod, Felix Weltsch, and Franz Rosenzweig. Other writers who count as Jews, whether they prefer that designation or not—that is, whose creativity owes a great deal to their

Judaism, and who often were its witnesses and messengers—doubtlessly include Friedrich Julius Stahl, Karl Marx, and Ferdinand Lasalle, as well as Sigmund Freud, Georg Simmel, Edmund Husserl, Constantin Brunner, Franz Oppenheimer, Walther Rathenau, Gustav Landauer, Alfred Adler, Max Scheler, Theodor Lessing, Ernst Cassirer, Rudolf Maria Holzapfel, Otto Weininger, Leonard Nelson, Georg Lukács, Ernst Bloch, Eugen Rosenstock-Huessy, Ludwig Wittgenstein, and Herbert Marcuse.

We will soon examine the issues raised by these figures, and soon thereafter the question of "Jewish self-hatred" that arises just as often. But their number would be incomplete without listing those great mathematicians who could just as easily be considered philosophers, such as Carl Gustav Jacobi, Leopold Kronecker, Georg Cantor, Hermann Minkowski, and Albert Einstein. Let us also recall the following individuals, including Edith Stein and Walter Benjamin, listed here by year of birth until 1900: Lazarus Geiger, Adolf Lasson, Joseph Popper-Lynkeus, Otto Liebmann, Kurd Lasswitz, Fritz Mauthner, Paul Rée, Wilhelm Fliess, Ludwig Stein, Emanuel Lasker, Raoul Michael Richter, Emil Lask, Aron David Gurewitsch, Arthur Liebert, Max Picard, Max Horkheimer, and many more.

Such a list provides little more than a hint of what a full investigation of this topic demands, and an adequate treatment would require a book of its own. Treatments of this subject exist, and while delivering what they promise, still fall far short of the definitive, with Siegmund Kaznelson's collection of 1959, *The Jews in the German Cultural Sphere*, a case in point. The "questionable" assumption behind such books, however, calls for a certain clarification. This sort of cultural history is bound to raise the question of precisely who should be counted as Jewish, since a not inconsiderable number of those involved no longer considered themselves to be Jews, and others never even knew they were Jewish. And how are we to categorize those who mistake holding citizenship of one kind or another with belonging to a people, despite the fact that national identity and citizenship can be two different things? Where do we put those secular types who believe that holding Israeli citizenship or that of another state absolves them of their Jewishness? Do those children of their people who consider themselves to be without religion cease being Jews? What about self-styled freethinkers, or those who consent to be baptized, or who become Marxists? And finally, do those who succumb to anti-Semitic delusion cease being Jews?

Since Judaism means belonging to a people, though a people established by covenant, one becomes Jewish at birth in accord with the custom followed by all peoples or "nations." These constitute, as the German term has it, "communities of origin" (*Geburtsgemeinschaften*). But this by no means rules out the possibility of moving from one community of origin to another, and no one may be refused acceptance who makes such a move in good faith. The full significance of what it means to enter or leave such a community, however, dawns on us only with our children, and our children's children, just as it does for other peoples. But from a historical perspective, Judaism can be said to be at work in all the offspring that Jewish progenitors produce. What emerges from the vantage point on German Jewry we obtain by listing its most outstanding figures is not just their significance, but the astounding import conveyed by the sheer number involved, and the remarkable breadth of their influence. In drawing nourishment from the sources of Judaism, these individuals sustained their own Jewish existence, and at the same time they contributed to those forceful and powerful tributaries whose convergence produced the modern era of world history.

Let us return—or better still, let us move forward and consider Cohen's philosophy out of the sources of Judaism in its own terms, a work that dared to take a self-consciously Jewish position, and makes the same claim upon us today. Instead of emphasizing a unity and oneness that would rule out plurality in advance, Cohen takes a position athwart every conventional philosophic approach: the point of departure of *Religion of Reason Out of the Sources of Judaism* is the uniqueness of revelation. This opening move forestalls any mistaken attempt to confuse the "religion of reason" with the kind of sophistic, hair-splitting rationalism that has nothing but metaphors to offer where religious truth is concerned, given the fact that "we are acquainted with the human intellect alone." In Cohen's conception, the fact that humanity has finally reached "adulthood" defines modernity as a new kind of human maturity: the uniqueness of revelation, for Cohen, while setting ethical boundaries that keep us from going astray, at the same time represents the principle of beginning itself, the potential for opening up new fields of human action. Modernity has given humanity a power previously thought to be superhuman and taboo, a responsibility for the universe as a whole. Our task, according to Cohen, is to meet this modern challenge wisely, as a being "not meant to become as a God, but rather, to become more human. His task is to become fully human."

Here, mankind's ethical relation with others assumes a central role. The biblical "neighbor" becomes the crucial figure of "the fellowman." Once what Cohen calls "the discovery of man as fellowman" has taken place, as the title of his eighth chapter tells us, the meaning that flows from that discovery is nothing less than revolutionary! Cohen's concept of the "fellowman" signifies his break with the classical philosophical tradition that insists on a truth that is available to every individual intellect. For Cohen, by contrast, perception and the quest for truth necessarily turn every individual into a "fellow" or neighbor, a person who lives with others. Cohen develops this discovery of the fellowman at different points in his presentation as both a "new problem" and a "new paradigm" for philosophy. This new conception of philosophy parallels those revolutionary breakthroughs of his contemporaries that created the new physics, a new biology, and a new psychology, and challenged the commonplaces of the natural sciences as well. Every acting individual is implicated in his actions, every truth implicated in the respective perceptions that produce it, and both are thereby absolved of any claim a governing consciousness might make to absolute self-determination. Philosophy, in other words, had been conceived anew as dialogics.[2]

But while the old truths still retained their validity for Cohen, the "new thinking"—as Franz Rosenzweig called this new philosophic turn—asserted its validity just as strongly, defining the limits of the tradition and bringing its pockets of intellectual isolation into clear view. The new philosophy, in other words, was able to absorb the terms of traditional philosophy which themselves denied the validity of the new. It should therefore come as no surprise that Cohen himself did not regard his philosophic breakthrough as a new way of doing philosophy, or as overturning the traditional philosophic concerns that shaped his point of departure and textured his work throughout. Albert Einstein, in a different context, never recognized the groundbreaking upheaval he had set in motion, even at the point of his death in 1955. Nevertheless, both cases represent breakthroughs on a revolutionary scale. According to Cohen's conceptual breakthrough, a person who achieves self-awareness discovers not only the liberty to encounter his fellowman on equal terms, but the freedom to confront the enduring core of a revelation that is no less subsumable, and which cannot be reduced to humanity alone. With philosophy's ban on considering revelation lifted, its attendant neglect of humanity is lifted as well.

Hermann Cohen's *Religion of Reason Out of the Sources of Judaism* as a whole is an unmediated testament, gripping the reader with the force of a revelation. For despite many weak passages and its author's own inhibitions and prejudices, the work represents a breakthrough to a new philosophy and concept of religiosity. Not since the Baal Shem Tov and the Hasidic movement had such an event of such significance come to pass, this time overpowering the "enlightened" reason of one the most rigorous of contemporary philosophers. Cohen's turn to revelation could not be written off as some remnant of enlightened philosophy's "outmoded" past, but had to be recognized as a harbinger of the future. All this was very much in the spirit of Hermann Cohen's Purim greeting of March 19, 1905, sent to the rabbi of Marburg, Leo Munk, the year Leo Baeck's *Essence of Judaism* was published: "Boldly onward, then, into the future millennia!"

SIXTEEN

World History of the Jewish People

It was no accident that when Simon Dubnow left Germany in 1933—thanks to a life spent studying world history and its vicissitudes, he was all too aware of what the National Socialist seizure of power of would mean—he moved not to Palestine, despite invitations that came with the highest honors, but to Riga. From Dubnow's "autonomist" perspective, the preservation of Judaism could be accomplished by acquiring a form of self-government within Europe, for this was a people who had already experienced statehood once before. Self-government would permit the Jews to exercise collective rights guaranteed them as a national minority, while they in turn would unconditionally accept their responsibilities as citizens of the respective states in which they lived. By returning to the Eastern European Jewish world, Dubnow meant to keep faith with the vast majority of his people, just as he had affirmed his people's diaspora as Judaism's essential, productive, and historic ground. The same reasoning had already moved Dubnow to reject an invitation in 1897 to the first Zionist Congress he had received while in Switzerland, remaining in Zurich instead of traveling to Basel.

Nor was it an accident twenty-five years later when Dubnow, now seventy-two, eleven years before being driven out, moved to Germany when forced to leave his Russian homeland after the Bolsheviks had gained control. For what English and American Jewry have still not succeeded in bringing about in the four decades since—translating and publishing Dubnow's ten-volume *World History of the Jewish People*, written in Russian—had already been accomplished in Germany. Dubnow's warm reception had had its origins in the fact that his history took its intellectual lead from the earlier work of German Jewish scholars. And like all truly great men, Dubnow was eager to express his gratitude, acknowledging the extent of his dependence on German Jewish scholarship in the introduction that appeared in the first volume toward the end of 1925: "As I now offer my work to the public of a land where a century ago, the bases for a scholarly Jewish historiography were laid, I cannot keep myself from observing that I see this connection as a symbol of continuity as well. If I depart from my predecessors both in my general conception as well as in many particulars, I at the same time remain steadfastly aware that without a full century of research by the school of Zunz, Geiger, Frankel, and Graetz the current level of Jewish historiography could never have been attained."[1]

But Dubnow had done more than sustain the continuity of Jewish historiography, done far more than simply carry on work others had begun. Dubnow had given Jewish self-awareness a new degree of historical anchorage, providing it with a breadth and depth it had never known before. Dubnow's history reaped the harvest of a century of great Jewish scholarship that began with Jost's *History of the Israelites from the Times of the Maccabees to Our Days*, published between 1820 and 1828, exactly one hundred years before *World History of the Jewish People* appeared from 1925 to 1929. It also absorbed the fruits of the greatest works of nineteenth-century German philosophy and historiography. Dubnow was therefore able to understand Jewish history as world history. The confluence of forces was a remarkable one indeed. It was as if a stream fed by the best representatives of the German spirit, extending its tributaries throughout the earth, had converged with Dubnow's mastery of Jewish sources, flowing toward the same humanity, and merged to create the broad context in which Judaism's inner development could be seen. Dubnow's "world-historic" style of historical exposition brings the particularity of Jewish existence—whose separateness is established for the sake of the universal—to a new level of modern expression.

To borrow Aaron Steinberg's fitting phrase, whose translation of Dubnow demonstrates a deep spiritual affinity for his work, Dubnow's *historia rerum gestarum* itself belongs to the *res gestae* of the Jews: *World History of the Jewish People* was a work that itself made history. This fact cannot be observed without recalling Leo Baeck, if we are to grasp the full significance of Dubnow's achievement. The argument suggested by the title, revising the superficial notion that the Jewish people had led a restricted and severely limited historical existence, corresponds with Leo Baeck's claim for Judaism as a "world religion" advanced in this same period. According to Baeck, the "particularity" of Judaism—distinguished from other religions by virtue of the fact that belonging to its covenant at the same time constitutes being part of a people—exists only for the sake of the "universal" message that Judaism in particular bears, in order to bear witness to the prophetic message:

> And the Lord shall be king
> Over all the earth.
> On that day the Lord shall be one,
> And his name one. (Zechariah 14:9)

Jewish national and religious difference does not signify any kind of exclusion of the universal, or seclusion from "the world," but just the opposite. Jewish particularity stands as a symbol of the breakthrough needed to leave the antinomy of coexistence and opposition behind, an understanding that would pave the way toward a universal solidarity, "that day" when particularity will come to an end. Judaism therefore stands, and stands up for the redemption of all the earth in its entirety, for the One and Only whose kingdom will unite all men and all things.

The watchword guiding Dubnow's *World History* can thus already be found in the first edition of *The Essence of Judaism* of 1905. There, Leo Baeck deploys "World Religion" as his term for Judaism's redemptive truth. Of course, this particular "world religion" is at the same time the "people's religion"—just as Dubnow's *World History of the Jewish People* always remains the world history of the *Jewish* people, that is, a history of the Jews as a specific historical nation. In both cases the term "world history" signifies not an all-determining universal trajectory, but a Judaism that transmits a message of universal significance to the world while acting out a history of its own. The meaning Judaism carries transcends the Jewish people who carry its message, continuing a Jewish history that is of universal relevance. But only a specific people, whose "particularity" tries to look beyond autocratic motives and attend to the "universality" of the universe and its scope, can transmit that message. Until the kingdom first glimpsed at the covenant in the desert, whose true meaning awaits its realization, will finally come to pass.

Leo Baeck's essay "National Religion and World Religion" of 1931 made this point in summary fashion: the notion of world religion does not exclude the national roots a religion strikes in its people's heart, but it does rule out the idea of its becoming a state institution or a state religion. The distinction was crucial to Dubnow as well. "The universal does not oppose nationhood per se, but does set itself against statehood, against purely political aspirations whose execution is so often dictated by a state's particular and self-interested motives." Such a "statehood," and every "state religion," whose "self-interest" aims at empire, must be resisted, and seek its ultimate foundation, along with Judaism, in "the kingdom of God."[2] The Jewish people carries this message as one that cannot be claimed by any single people, no matter how legitimate or powerful its state, and no matter how extensive its empire might be. Judaism instead announces the promise of redemption for all the peoples, states, and realms of this earth. "World religion," Baeck writes—and his point holds true for Dubnow's "world history" as well—"signifies an independence from the political . . . a move beyond the means and ends of state politics, beyond reasons of state and their goals. World religion shows human ends to partake of the realm of the universal, beyond the state."[3]

Dubnow's *World History of the Jewish People* thus became one of the most significant milestones in German Jewry's consolidation of its inner renewal, though Dubnow's history does not fully capture its ultimate peak after the turn of the century, ending its account in 1914, "the last decade" before the war. Dubnow's life's work bears witness to the fully modern culture that German Jewry helped to introduce. His work is also noteworthy as an achievement of Eastern European Jewry as well, a "synthesis"—to borrow a favorite expression of Dubnow's—unique in the twisted and constantly sundered path the Jewish people have followed throughout the course of world history. And the last but not the least noteworthy aspect of Dubnow's achievement was the insightful confidence his account of German Jewish history displays. Dubnow's work makes determinations and discriminations that slip by the notice of the most rigorous "sociologist," insights all the more striking for their accurate grasp not only of the German Jewish community's two-thousand-year history, but also the future it was about to confront.

Let us recall, for example, Dubnow's unforgettable celebration of the shift from Franco-Spanish hegemony to Spanish and German dominance that occurred over the course of the fourteenth century, the point when German Jewry became the unquestioned leader of Europe's Jewish communities. At this point late in the Middle Ages, German Jews did not need to take bold action in order to distinguish themselves from a French Jewish world in decline, or from the Jews of Spain: patience and suffering was required for them to hold onto to their creative mandate. The Inquisition's expulsion of the Jews from Spain only partially explains the demise of the Jewish community in Spain, as Dubnow reminds us when describing the choice between conversion and apostasy or death that thousands of Spanish Jews faced:

> While the Jews of Germany groan under their martyr's fate and disenfranchisement, they confront these storms boldly and defiantly, standing up to the most formidable pressure without yielding. And as the German Jews assert their national preeminence over the French, sharing it with the Jews of Spain . . . Their powers of passive resistance at the same time increased immeasurably. Even the most horrible massacres fail to bring about a mass exodus of German Jews from their faith: victims of persecution characteristically refuse to relent and renounce their faith, and the martyrs go bravely to their deaths, never giving sham baptism a moment's consideration as a way of saving their skins. In more peaceful times, German Jewry carries its yoke of disenfranchisement in utter humility, bending, but never breaking. Spanish Jewry presents us with an entirely different case.[4]

This description is to be compared with Dubnow's "Epilogue" to his *World History* finished in 1928 and published in 1929. Dubnow's concluding vista looks forward to consider the world's three largest Jewish settlements in Eastern Europe, American, and Palestine. Here both the historical significance of Dubnow's own "synthesis" and the threat of Hitler, which would eventually prove decisive, emerge in all their significance, and not for the last time:

the dominant center of Western Jewry clearly belongs to Germany. Its stratum of assimilated Jews appears to possess a surplus of unexpended national energy, and the phenomenon of Jewish "marrano-hood"—that is, of closet Jews—is by all measures in marked decline. Prominent Jewish figures in the fields of science, literature and politics openly proclaim their sympathies with Zionism. And in the earlier aversion that German Zionists had displayed toward "diaspora," or *galut* autonomism has begun to disappear. The rapprochement between Western and Eastern Jews provides a strong impetus in this direction, and represents a significant event of unforeseeable historical consequences.[5]

One year later, when expressing his gratitude for the good wishes he had received on the occasion of his seventieth birthday on September 18, 1930, Dubnow addressed himself to those who had raised their voices as well as those who—like the Russian Jews—who had fallen silent: "the resonance my historical perspective has found in Germany gives me particular pleasure, as it was there that I was destined to complete my lifework. I have always viewed German Jewry as a steady fortress of our culture perched on the boundary between east and west. My hope is that she will continue to be an active participant in our national renaissance."

SEVENTEEN

Science from a Jewish Perspective

The inner renewal German Jewry had begun, marked by a new self-understanding that creatively reimagined Jewish existence in wholly modern terms, was also subject to frequent interruptions and reversals, with its ends even perverted at times. Yet the productive consequences of that process could never be held in check. German Jewry continued to make important contributions to Jewish, German, and human development as a whole, even faltered onto many painful, erroneous, and wayward paths. Leo Baeck's caution in his tenth anniversary address to the American Federation of Jews from Central Europe of 1951 is well taken in this regard: "Whoever dares to discuss this matter should do it in only the most respectful terms." Our discussions of "Science from a Jewish Perspective" and "Jewish Self-Hatred" that follow are obliged to take the measure of these failures and reverses. For without their contrasting shadow, the light of other achievements would shine less brightly, and these reversals themselves often provided the material from which a stronger vision of the Jewish present would eventually emerge.

By the time of the Enlightenment, unique facets of the Jewish situation in Europe had almost erased the memory of Judaism's close ties to the German tradition, a long-standing and productive connection with deep roots. An intimate bond existed between the Jewish people and the covenant, and Jews identified strongly with the powerful force of a "world history" stretching back four thousand years. Jewish confinement to a ghetto existence extended a pervasive influence on the Jewish attitude from the late Middle Ages to the early modern period. All these factors had combined to deemphasize the identification of German Jews with Germany. But with the advent of emancipation, assimilation seemed to offer a more attractive face to the Jews than it did to other nations with whom the Jews waged the battle for universal liberation. Judaism had already suffered countless and of course unjustifiable rebuffs in its quest for modernity, and the beginning of a new era of freedom and profound peace for all mankind now seemed at hand. To Judaism's Jewish champions, preserving the Jewish culture that had always stood behind them now seemed to be almost a secondary concern. It was at precisely this historical juncture that the Prussian Decree of 1822 discussed earlier banned Jews who insisted on retaining their faith from teaching at the universities and secondary schools, notwithstanding the fact that the Jews had been granted full citizenship only ten years before. Then, of course, Prussian Jews had been useful to the state as fellow soldiers in the wars of liberation—and how much more useful they could have been!

Franz Rosenzweig's fate, for instance, was to be denied unrestricted opportunities to pursue an academic career. And this occurred only two years before the outbreak of World War I—exactly one hundred years after Prussia granted the Jews "full civil rights" on March 11, 1812—and after earning his doctorate with distinction. Rosenzweig seriously considered the option of baptism, overcoming the temptation at the very brink of apostasy, when his authentic energies roused his inner resistance. Others were not as strong. Before we rush to judge them, we should first reflect carefully on the kind of pressure Jews had to confront as they rose in society, along with the rest of Germany, as the decades passed. Keeping the faith in the face of such insistent pressure often meant abandoning any hope of intellectual advancement whatsoever. Such self-denial was not only contrary to the driving, entrepreneurial spirit that characterized the European nineteenth century as a whole, but ran counter to their own best gifts, when their extraordinary talents, and the creative forces of Judaism, were breaking new ground in German culture.

In the end, many of the most creative Jewish individuals were willing to accept baptism, paying the price of disavowing their identity in order to go on with their cultural work. This is what motivated Julius Stahl, founder of the conservative theory of the state, and what drove Karl Marx, author of the communist vision of redemption, just as it impelled Eduard Gans, Hegel's leading collaborator, who had just left office as president of the Society for the Culture and Science of the Jews, just as it drove a pious Johann August Neander, who, when all the dust had settled, received an important professorship in Berlin. This same urge to realize Jewish creativity drove the conversions of the incomparable Rahel Varnhagen and Ludwig Börne, Heinrich Heine, Felix Mendelssohn-Bartholdy, and even Ferdinand Lasalle, who while utterly detesting the idea of baptism, was in equal denial about the sources of his best energies. This list goes on to include Eduard Simson, president of the German National Assembly in 1848–49, who led the deputation that offered the kaiser's crown to the king of Prussia, and would make the same offer once more as deputy of the German Reichstag at Versailles in December 1870. When he died, Simson was serving as the first president of the German Supreme Court.

Jewish creativity drove these men, as it did a large group of effective and proven Jewish women too seldom given their due, pushing them until they could accept the disavowal of their Jewishness, though others kept the faith. Among the latter was Gabriel Riesser, four years younger than Stahl and four years older than Simson, whose "great deed" we have already discussed. Leopold Zunz remained steadfast as well, despite numerous sacrifices, temptations, and disappointments, until the proud edifice of the Wissenschaft des Judentums had been placed on a firm footing, and collaborators had been found to continue his work. Frankel, Geiger, Graetz, and Steinschneider have already been mentioned. Younger scholars joined the effort, and were welcomed by the old master. Their number included figures born in 1851 and 1852 such as Wilhelm Bacher and David Kaufmann, as well as scholars outside of Germany proper: Nachman Krochmal in Tarnopol, Salomo Yehuda Loeb Rappoport in Prague, Samuel David Luzzatto in Padua, and Salomon Munk in Paris. Born in Glogau, Silesia, Munk was to become one of the greatest Orientalists of all time, and he would eventually succeed Ernest Renan at the Collège de France. In 1828, however, bitter poverty forced him to leave his homeland after a difficult period of soul-searching, and to seek his living elsewhere. Munk left with the following notification in his pocket, from Karl von Altenstein, Prussia's minister of education, received just a short time before:

> This ministry hereby informs you that, so long as you continue to profess the mosaic religion, it will not be in a position to guarantee you any support for your future scholarly activities.

But as Jewish creativity pursued extra-Jewish ends, the Wissenschaft des Judentums continued its work alongside them, promoting an awareness of Jewish existence and its active, four-thousand-year destiny through research, public presentations, collection of new source material, and what were often decisive contributions to intellectual history as whole. The significance of this research transcended the world of scholarship—though this wider significance would only meet with misfortune and disappointment, for which Germany never made full amends—inspiring Jews to return to their Judaism, and offering its own scholarship as a testimony to that process.

Because of that influence, the new scholarly discipline was denied all support and deprived of the essential basis that would allow its practical fulfillment: a tenured professorship. This denial occurred despite the fact that scholarship as a whole recognized the crucial importance of the discipline's subject matter and the crying need for its institutionalization. How Zunz struggled for such a position, and waged his fight precisely because he understood the crying need to connect his subject matter with the rest of public life. An isolated Jewish existence would not suffice, but neither would a "Jewish" scholarly discipline split off and excluded from the universities. Zunz proposed the "establishment of a tenured Chair for Jewish History and Literature" at least twice, in April 1843 and once more in July 1848, as the revolution he so passionately supported reached its peak, but both times his efforts were in vain.

The opinion leading to the rejection to Zunz's petition by the Berlin faculty, for which Dean Trendelenburg and Professors Boeck, Petermann, and Ranke were centrally responsible, insists that Judaism is a dead subject matter. That opinion expressed their concern that a branch of scholarship of importance to Jewish cultural life might well swell Jewish numbers at the university, and increase Jewish self-awareness to boot. Ranke, to be sure, opposed the increasing fragmentation of the disciplines as a matter of principle. But even when this argument was thwarted by the steady stream of cutting-edge research the new discipline of Judaic studies brought forth, no reconsideration was forthcoming, despite the clear recognition that Judaic studies was a required discipline for any "university" that could truly be considered "universal." Though Zunz, his spirit finally broken, continued to carry the banner of the Wissenschaft des Judentums, it would eventually be taken up by the rabbinical colleges, and finally by its own "Academy." His campaign would even lead to the establishment of a normal professorship in Jewish studies at the University of Frankfurt am Main from 1924 through 1933. But this was nothing more than a rearguard skirmish in a battle that German Jewry, and indeed Germany as a whole, had already lost.

It is idle to speculate about the positive results this sort of recognition in 1848 might have achieved. Judaism's cultural significance would have carried a far higher cultural profile in Germany, and the Jewish sector of the population might have cut a more worthy and impressive figure in the eyes of the German intellectual elite. This might have led—perhaps—to an altogether different kind of reaction when that intellectual leadership was forced to make their choice in 1933, a moral examination they miserably failed. The bitter and painful truth is that the Wissenschaft des Judentums, conceived and founded by German Jewry, had already become their "legacy" before Jewish life in Germany came to an end. Blighted on its native ground, their movement led to the establishment of chairs of Judaic studies in the United States as well as other lands, and was responsible for creating the Department of Judaic Studies at the Hebrew University of Jerusalem.

Yet as significant as the establishment of Judaism as a field of academic study was and remains, this was only the penultimate step in the process of Jewish self-awareness returning to its sources. Judaism would grasp the full measure of its own independent achievement only when Jews became full participants in all the disciplines: when they were able, as scholars and professionals, to sustain a Jewish point of view.

How was such a perspective possible without a compromise of intellectual integrity? Precisely because science must be undertaken for the sake of its subject matter, without interference of any kind, it must remain as self-conscious as humanly possible of any external factors that might affect research. In some cases, factors such as one's background must be excluded from the field of investigation; in others, when exclusion is impossible, a full accounting of their effects will suffice. But in either case, the only way a scholar can give scholarship what it truly deserves is by refusing to deny his or her origin in any way, shape, or form. With such clear acceptance as a solid starting point, the scholar's background can either be bracketed off from the study, or self-consciously made part of the field of investigation, whichever method proves more productive. Only a Jew who acknowledges his or her Jewishness to the fullest extent can give his or her best toward creating a Jewish scholarship worthy of its people, or to the other fields that Jews may join. Such self-awareness never leads them astray, but always allows what is best within them to spur them on to great efforts.

This quest for accomplishment, to achieve one's best, has influenced every aspect of Jewish endeavors. Sigmund Freud referred to it when he spoke of the Jewish penchant for nonconformity and Judaism's resistance to preconceived ideas when he addressed his B'nai Brith lodge brothers in May 1926. Albert Einstein attributed the same trait to the "democratic ideal of social justice" that originates with Judaism, and which it had always held dear, connecting those values to the traditional Jewish respect for intellectual achievement in all its forms in his essay of November 1938. This desire to realize the best that is within one—part of Judaism's messianic impulse—ultimately represents the core conception behind the idea of the kingdom of God, whose message this people were the first to transmit. The Jews remain living proof of that message's entry into history, the guarantors of its historicity that still awaits its fulfillment, bearers of the message of the kingdom from its origin in the past to the future beyond. Judaism continues to transmit the biblical conviction that the universe as a whole still requires the work of redemption, if freedom, joy, and peace are to characterize the world to come.

Let one contemporary example suffice to illustrate the close connection between science and the Jewish point of view, closely connected as it is to the end of German Jewry. The powerful Jewish belief in a redemptive future, for instance, helps explain the disproportionate number of Jews who furthered the development of the modern natural sciences. That science has now given us "the power to produce matter by gaining mastery over its nuclear building-blocks," and taught us that our consciousness itself is "co-determined by the unconscious," enabling us to "trace the very structure of our awareness back to its earliest origins." Many factors played a role in this overall development: the political situation between 1933 and 1939 provided the strongest push in the race to split the atom. And the sociological fact that minorities wanting to remain historical players often forge ahead in the boldest fields of investigation may explain in part why so many nuclear scientists were Jews. But another, more basic Jewish attitude was also at play. A large part of the motivation impelling Jewish researchers forward was the traditional Jewish notion that "faith as well as knowledge must be given full and unfettered rein along with the increasing freedom required for their realization, despite the dangers that attend such a course. . . . Faith must be allowed to become an enthusiastic conviction, without placing any limitations on knowledge's capacity to acquire unlimited mastery of a world faith seeks not to possess, but to redeem. This cooperative relation between faith and knowledge cannot help but produce contention, of course, but it is also the source that will produce the ultimate achievement of peace, and the kingdom to come."[1]

Today's physicists look beyond the confines of their field and seek guidance from some higher source, despite the fact that their revolutionary discoveries have played no small part in making modernity an irrefutable fact. The same is true in the natural sciences and the humanities, and for the same reason: the logical structure governing both has long proved itself incapable of fully illuminating the questions each field must necessarily raise. All this should serve to remind us of the powerful force that provided the springboard for Jewish scientists, and of the forces that impelled others in different fashion, even if they themselves never explicitly accounted for their motives in precisely these terms. The fact that we can hail their scientific achievements as work spurred on by a Jewish perspective takes nothing away from science. Such recognition instead serves to outline a source of cultural energy, giving us a measure for the ultimate fulfillment of peace.

EIGHTEEN

Education Without End

We have now reached the proper moment to examine what was in a literal sense the most "advanced" period of German Jewry's inner renewal. The German Jewish legacy touched a future realized in Germany for a brief moment, and attained a horizon that other Jewish communities have yet to match. Wherever these achievements were continued—achievements that set the standard for subsequent decades, and still do—later "advances" were only partially realized, or all too ephemeral.

"Of the making of books there is no end" was once the sigh of Ecclesiastes (12:12). "Education Without End" became Franz Rosenzweig's lament, playing off the well-known biblical passage. But Rosenzweig's slogan would eventually issue in the educational vision he called "the new learning," despite the legitimate critique of his phrase and its apt summary of the pedantry it took to task. When Rosenzweig coined the title of his essay "Education Without End," the wondrous decade of the 1920s, destined to realize its own, quite different promise, was still in the offing. The 1920s was to be a period as unique as it was precarious, characterized by a welter of experimental bustle and ferment, saturated with new educational publications and fully stocked with scholars of every stripe. "Education Without End" was not a call to go on piling up new books, but to move beyond them. Rosenzweig's guiding notion was that the time had finally come for Judaism's own truth, expressed time and again in written form, to find its "realization": that is, for Jewish principles to be transformed into action. Jewish education, understood as the writing of books on Jewish subjects, was instead to become a living embodiment of Judaism, an act of joyous devotion to all things Jewish, a living affirmation that would be of consequence in the here and now.

This was the same Rosenzweig who was the great-grandson of Samuel Meyer Ehrenberg, head of the Samson School in Wolfenbüttel since 1807. According to the account of Leopold Zunz, the school's most illustrious pupil, the school originally restricted its curriculum almost entirely to the teaching of the Talmud, but its program contained less and less Talmud as time went on, until eventually the Jewish Realschule, or public school, was created. Roughly one hundred years later, Ehrenberg's great-grandson Franz Rosenzweig—after serving four years at the front during World War I, writing *Hegel and the State* and completing *The Star of Redemption* (1919)—decided at age thirty-four that he would henceforth devote himself to Jewish education alone. Rosenzweig had just been engaged to be married, the capstone of the masculine maturity he sought: like his contemporary Franz Kafka, Rosenzweig, at this late stage in his life, gave his engagement a distinctly parabolic and exaggerated significance. In January 1920, the essay "Education Without End" suddenly "delivered itself . . . not written, but danced" in the space of a few days. The plan for the modern Jewish Lehrhaus, or house of study, had emerged in all but name.

"Who has a better name for it?" The essay itself seeks a better title for its program than the notion of "a college for continuing education" (Volkshochschule). For the revolution Rosenzweig announced was already pressing in from all sides: new educational trends racing through the Jewish community were affected by educational movements that had been in ferment for decades; institutes for adult education were springing up everywhere. The urgent contemporary need for "continuing education" brought with it a fundamental rethinking of what teaching and learning actually meant, since adults wanted neither a grade-school education nor a university course, especially since their "teachers" possessed the same level of maturity as their "students." Like its contemporaries, Judaism met this common challenge head on and responded, like those others, with a different, and fitting model of its own. Had Jewish adult education adopted the system of the German Volkshochschule wholesale, the result would have been an imitation that disregarded the specific and authentically Jewish tradition of learning. Copying the German model would have betrayed what the true meaning of equality demands: for although individuality is meant to be enjoyed in common with others, authentic equality permits the unique difference and particularity of every individual to shine forth.

In the case of Jewish education, Judaism represents the subject matter to be "learned": for nothing less than Jewish existence itself depends on the success of the enterprise. Whether in the territories to its West or in the land or state of Israel, Judaism, rooted in its covenant sworn in the desert, consists before all else of its "teaching." Above and beyond the various, natural conditions of Jewish existence, connected to humanity throughout the earth, Judaism can be "propagated" effectively only by study and action. Affirming the meaning and validity of Judaism by studying the truth of its message, of course, cannot replace those worldly knowledge and lessons that can only be learned through concrete praxis. Just so, lessons that can only be learned at a particularly historical moment—however indispensable, replete with insight and vitally significant they may be—can never replace "teaching," the font of Jewish life. The Jewish adult education movement itself may have been a creature of its era, a reaction to the Volkshochschule movement, to give the larger push for continuing public education its due. But Judaism demanded an entirely different form of the educational endeavor: and though Rosenzweig sought a new and "better name" for his new institution, the designation was ready at hand, waiting for him in the system of Jewish teaching and study that had been in existence for thousands of years.

That name was Lehrhaus, or House of Study, a Jewish institution of such ancient and enduring significance that the Talmud allows a synagogue to be transformed into a Lehrhaus if the community lacks one, but prohibits changing the Lehrhaus back into a synagogue. Learning takes precedence over all (Megillah 26b). Similarly, the five books of Moses conclude their greatest confession of faith—"Hear, O Israel: the LORD our GOD; the

LORD alone. You shall love the LORD your GOD with all your heart, and with all your soul, and with all your might"—with the following injunction:

Take to heart these instructions with which I charge you this day.

Impress them upon your children. Recite them when you stay at home and you are away, when you lie down and you get up.

Bind them as a sign on your hand and let them serve as a symbol on your forehead.

Inscribe them on the doorposts of your house and on your gates. (Deuteronomy 6:4–9)

The original Jewish Lehrhaus, first mentioned by Jesus ben Sirach (51, 23, 29), had already been built next to the synagogue during the first Babylonian exile, or shortly thereafter during this first of the Jewish Middle Ages. The epoch of the first Lehrhaus waned after the return to Palestine and the rebuilding of the temple in Jerusalem. The Talmud offers a moving description of the phenomenon as it unfolded, portraying the new institution of the Lehrhaus as an innovative way of fulfilling an eternally binding obligation. The Sages trace the origins of the Lehrhaus back to discussions held in the House of Study back to Shem's son Eber, who is said to have attended a heavenly Lehrhaus all of his days.

"But today," Franz Rosenzweig declared at the opening of the Freies Jüdisches Lehrhaus (the Free Jewish House of Study) in Frankfurt am Main on October 17, 1920, a "new learning" transformed from the ground up was required. This new form of education was to be conducted without regard to age, and without harming the immutable obligation to study as such. Speaking in his capacity as the official head of an institution previously built to conduct "Jewish adult education courses," Rosenzweig's call was a signal that the seclusion of the Middle Ages had been shattered once and for all. The bookish enclave of Jewish existence had opened itself up to the world, and the Jews—that is, every Jew—had now struck roots outside of Judaism proper and set up a more expansive residence. "There is no one today who is not alienated, or who does not feel partially alienated; even a 'Goethe' would be," Rosenzweig confessed. But in passionately affirming this Jewish inclusion of the "foreign," which medieval Judaism condemned as an abandonment of Judaism itself, Rosenzweig was in fact referring to a Jewish modernity whose outward ties had left it transformed and enriched. A return to Jewish sources, to be sure, is immediately referred to as well, but Rosenzweig envisioned that process as an inclusive one, requiring a broad and decisive move forward to keep up with the contemporary significance of his audience's own Jewish tradition.

The educational method of the Lehrhaus, the "New Learning," was to proceed in reverse, "no longer moving from the Torah into life, but rather from life back into the Torah!" And if everything was now "to be referred back to Judaism," then by the same token "nothing" in their wholly modern lives was "to be sacrificed, nothing disavowed." As Rosenzweig put it to Buber in a letter in 1922, "from some people [we hear that] everything belongs to the curriculum of the Lehrhaus, from the theory of relativity to instructing patients and their families on how to relate better to their physicians, while from others, no topic is quite fitting, even if it were the essence of Judaism or to the study of Palestine."[1] But the "most capable teacher," as Rosenzweig explained at the opening of the Lehrhaus, would nonetheless be the person who "carried the maximum of what is alien with him, and thus precisely not the expert in things Jewish. In any case not the Jewish expert as expert, but only in so far as he is alienated, searching for his home, returning."[2]

The fissure torn open at the entrance to modernity, establishing a chasm between modernity and the Middle Ages, was impossible to bridge by returning to Judaism's medieval isolation, no matter how modern the conduct of new Jewish "experts" might be. On the contrary: for Rosenzweig, the gap between modernity and tradition closes of its own accord as soon as the modern individual begins to realize he is called upon and likewise fully capable of remaining a Jew through and through. "It is not a question of establishing relations between Jews and non-Jews—that's been going on for long enough. The point is not to engage in apologetics, but to gain access to the heart of our lives. And to remain confident that this heart is a Jewish one."[3]

The Jewish path to modernity had thus far consisted of individual steps in religious life, scholarship, nationality, or of efforts to pinpoint Jewish religiosity's transhistorical or historical basis. Jews had been encouraged to define Judaism in strictly statist, or in non-national terms. But it was also true that this push to become modern had given short shrift to other levels of the Jewish tradition, or rejected them wholesale. These steps toward modernity had at the same time established firm ties with realms of knowledge and experience that had heretofore been considered "un-Jewish," or at least marginal to an authentically Jewish existence. Beyond such partial steps and

half-measures, Rosenzweig was now in a position to embrace his whole existence as Jewish. Modern Jewish education, he argued, should neither reject
"non-Jewish" experience, nor retreat one single inch into a privatized Jewish sense of self: nothing in the modern self was to be sacrificed, nothing
disavowed. As in all confident epochs of Jewish world history, the heart feels
confidently Jewish long before any closer definition of its Jewish identity
takes place; afterwards, "literature" provides the key to what has occurred.
But "Jewishness as I conceive of it," as Rosenzweig put it in "Education
Without End," "is not literature. Producing books does not get at what it
is. Nor does reading books. It is not something that one—and all modern
minds will have to pardon me for saying so—'experiences.' It is at best
something lived. Perhaps not even this. It is something that one is."[4]

One *is* Jewish, but, as everyone knows, this is not true for every individual, or everywhere at all times. For Rosenzweig, Judaism was the very heart-
beat of existence that confirmed the Jewishness of the Jew, without any
explicit Jewish action or declaration, and was not to be defined by some
arbitrary point in time that would determine the "Jewishness" of one or
another of his contemporaries. Nor was one's Jewishness to be determined
by scholarly "study." The notion that "one *is* Jewish" refers to the "Plat-
form for a Jewish Life" Rosenzweig advanced in "Education Without End,"
a proposal that "would do justice to the bookless present" and to those who
entered the Lehrhaus: "the mere fact that they enter the lecture hall of
the Jewish College for Continuing Education—who has a better name for
it?—already shows that a Jewish soul is alive within them."[5]

Only for those, in other words, who came to the Lehrhaus—the better
term Rosenzweig found—and found meaning in the "new learning" practiced there. The Lehrhaus was founded on the notion that the Jewish spirit,
which exists prior to any literature, and makes itself felt to us as a bookless
and forceful contemporary presence, can realize itself only through the interplay of study and action. The breakthrough achieved by the New Learning decisively transcended the kind of either/or choice that had been so
characteristic of Jewish modernity to that point; the Lehrhaus, as Rosenzweig described it in a letter of May 1, 1917, transformed those divergent
paths into a "unity of purpose." And it achieved this even though in this
new "learning," each single step is henceforward to be taken in utter seriousness, but no individual path arrives at the ultimate destination. The goal
of the Lehrhaus is not defined by any sort of "literature," but takes its point

of departure from life as it is lived and learned, a life whose "bookless" heart sets out from the contemporary world, and builds something new within it: a confident trust.

This kind of confidence was to be heard in Rosenzweig's inaugural lecture at Frankfurt's Free Jewish House of Study. That speech recalled his earlier plea in "Education Without End," which declared, "The more rigidly all formulas are adhered to—be they orthodox, Zionist or liberal—the more laughable are the human caricatures they produce. . . . There is only one formula that can assure a person's Jewishness, and because he is a Jew, lead him to a Jewish life: that formula is the fact that there is no formula. . . . Our sages had a beautiful word that expresses this perfectly: the word is confidence."[6]

How long it had been since anything like this had occurred! How long since a Jew confidently raised his voice without feeling as if he had to defend himself at the same time, or that he would be attacked, confident in the certainty that he himself, his people, as well and their teachings just as they stood, were indeed alive—and that this was enough!

Considering the actual heights the Lehrhaus and its moment achieved, it makes little difference that its conquest of this peak scarcely lasted two years. Rosenzweig, beset by a difficult and eventually fatal illness, was unable to carry forward that spirit of inner freedom, prophesied in "Education Without End," that he himself had made so manifest: he failed to find a successor who was his equal. German Jewry's fate as a whole could be seen as a similar one when it was denied any possibility of realizing the future the Lehrhaus had glimpsed in their own homeland, a land to which Rosenzweig belonged as no one else. Hadn't something utterly new been disclosed on its ground? In this sense, the Lehrhaus represented only the first step in the authentic and encompassing process that all Jewish communities of the future would follow, pointing out the path toward self-realization in modernity.

The "New Learning" and the modern Jewish Lehrhaus have already been seized on as a model and continued in many forms. They will go on reappearing wherever an enduring Judaism, without longing for days of yore, catches up with the Jewish past as an integral part of its present, and discovers its message for the future.

NINETEEN

Jewish Literature

"This study has been undertaken without fear or favor, and its presentation has not been shaped by any sectarian standpoint or dogma."[1] So begins Gustav Karpeles's *History of Jewish Literature*. Appearing in 1886, his work was the first full-dress treatment of the history of Jewish literature. We can better characterize Karpeles's contribution by placing it in context, recalling the fact that it preceded Baeck's characterization of Judaism as a "world religion" by two years, and likewise anticipated Dubnow's conception of Jewish "world history" by four decades. "The efforts that comprise this work," Karpeles wrote, "are to be understood strictly as an attempt to add Jewish literature to those many building blocks already gathered together in the grand edifice of world literature constructed by all nations and languages. The subject of this book is a literature that is both one of the world's oldest and one of its newest, surely not the least significant in world literature, though it has certainly taken up the rear, if not been accorded the least significant place among national cultures."[2]

Karpeles lists the precursor studies without which his own effort would have been impossible at the start of his work: Zunz, Steinschneider, Rappoport, Luzzatto, Jelinek, Frankel, Graetz, Geiger, Munk, Delitzsch, Cassel, Berliner, and Joel. His own work is divided into six periods with a section dedicated to each: Biblical, Judaic-Hellenistic, Talmudic, Judaic-Arabic-Spanish, Rabbinic commentary, and Modern Jewish Literature. Along the way, shortly before the end of his more than 1,100-page work, Karpeles finds the time to offer a few illuminating words on the place of modern "Poetry and Belles-Lettres." Those reflections and their tone anticipate the evocation of the contemporary scene that makes up this memorable conclusion. There, Karpeles reminds us of "the sons of the Jewish tribe involved in all intellectual endeavors, in religious research, advancing knowledge and yearning to act, pursuing advanced education in all its forms and teaching, mediating the acquisition of knowledge and studying every populated region of the earth and every historical period, undertaking every shape and form of creative activity: and doing so by waging an unrelenting struggle against hostile powers and the gods of ignorance, fervently seeking the highest ends, and before all else, acting from an unshakable faith and with an unparalleled devotion to their god."[3]

The Wissenschaft des Judentums carries on the "basic teachings" of Judaism, like the *Halacha*, which comprises half of the biblical and Talmudic texts. These teachings, along with the postbiblical commentary and additions to "the law," make up the Talmud. Modern Jewish literature likewise sums up and carries forward the tradition of biblical and largely Talmudic *Haggadah*, the "narrative" transmission of doctrine characteristic of antiquity and the Middle Ages. Modern Jewish literature is thus hardly an anomaly within the Jewish tradition, or a contemporary upstart or foreign impulse at the fringes of the Jewish mainstream, as Karpeles reminds us: "These two strains of Jewish writing can be traced from their biblical origin forward, until Halacha and Haggadah separate off into the spheres of science and poetry."[4] Karpeles goes on to rejoice at the prospect of contemporary Jewish writing, and justifiably so, given the splendid examples of modern Jewish literature available for his perusal: "Before our very eyes, we can see our lovely *Haggadah* receiving the honor it was due of old, ancient rights that have been withheld from her long enough."[5] Literature, like other realms of culture, springs directly from Judaism's living core, making up a crucial chapter in the story of its people's burgeoning reawakening.

Jewish writing presents us some of the most public evidence possible that the energies of Jewish writers were fully up to the challenge that modernity posed.

Heinrich Heine, Karl Wolfskehl, Alfred Mombert, Else Lasker-Schüler, and Franz Kafka—these are but five of the unquestionably great writers among the boundless multitude of different kinds of artists, both women and men, that German Jewry produced. They helped bring German Jewry's inner development to fruition, taking their place alongside others who joined in the process of Jewish renewal during the previous two centuries. As literary figures, they occupy a worthy place next to the greatest contributors to Jewish culture going back thousands of years, and Franz Rosenzweig's remark about Franz Kafka provides a case in point. As his spiritual twin, Rosenzweig felt a deep intellectual and spiritual affinity for Kafka, who was almost the same age. Rosenzweig's estimation of Kafka's achievement, ventured in his letter of May 25, 1927, is no throwaway remark, but an appraisal of the utmost seriousness, asking us to take it as seriously as its biblical term of comparison suggests: "The authors of the Bible apparently thought of God in the same terms as Kafka. His novel *The Castle* reminds me of the Bible more strongly than any book I've ever read."[6]

Adding to the rarity and significance of this poetic achievement—one of the greatest mankind can claim—was that its victorious peak included many significant women writers, an occurrence all the more unusual given how rare the appearance of an authentic writer truly is. Else Lasker-Schüler is joined by Margarete Susman, Nelly Sachs, and Gertrud Kolmar. A literary circle in which both men and women writers mature and flourish to this extent is bound to find a worldwide audience and influence. Not even the abyss that lay in German Jewry's path could prevent its creative energies from overcoming the most extreme tests that intellectual life can confront. This literary circle would not be kept from realizing a freedom and maturity that far exceeded Rosenzweig's hope that "confidence" would allow German Jews to leave all Jewish "formulas" behind. For unlike the scientist, the artist detaches himself completely from his or her material. That is, since one cannot be an artist without such material, getting to the heart of it requires that no subject matter be ruled out in advance, and of course this includes the artist himself or herself. In this respect, both Mombert and Kafka were typical. As the authors of works that are supposedly the freest of explicitly "Jewish" material, writers whose Jewishness is by no means "obvious," both Mombert and Kafka were constantly aware of and reflected on their Jewish identity, as we are learning from the papers they left behind. The more each of them became a pure writer, the more honest and authentic the relation to Judaism each writer was able to sustain.

It is therefore also important to remember the seemingly endless numbers of Jewish men and women of the German-speaking world who garnered their share of honors as writers or gained laurels in other cultural endeavors. We must recall composers like the great Gustav Mahler, for instance, or Arnold Schoenberg, one of the greatest musical innovators of all time, along with earlier figures such as Felix Mendelssohn-Bartholdy, Giacomo Meyerbeer, and Jacques Offenbach, not to mention other figures on the artistic margins. Heine, Wolfskehl, Mombert, Lasker-Schüler, and Kafka in the field of literature, and Schoenberg in music: these represent but a few of the literally hundreds or even thousands who set out on this same arduous artistic path. The enthusiasm, readiness to sacrifice and selflessness of this endless multitude was not the least reason that for the greatest among them, there would be no turning back in what they achieved.

In 1922 Gustav Krojanker published a collection of essays on contemporary writers, *Jews in German Literature*, noteworthy both for those portrayed in its articles and those who penned the portrayals. The collection presented and discussed a fragmentary selection of significant figures. Krojanker offering his readers essays on Franz Werfel by Rudolph Kayser, Georg Hermann by Hans Kohn, Alfred Kerr and Alfred Döblin by Ernst Blass, Franz Kafka by Max Brod, Albert Ehrenstein by Ernst Weiss, Alfred Mombert by Martin Buber, Otto Weininger and Richard Beer-Hoffmann by Oskar Baum, Hugo von Hofmannsthal and Rudoph Borchardt by Willy Haas, Else Lasker-Schüler and Paul Adler by Meir Wiener, Peter Altenberg by Albert Ehrenstein, Paul Kornfeld by Leo Sborowitz, Arnold Zweig by Moritz Goldstein, Moritz Heimann by Julius Bab, Carl Sternheim by Arnold Zweig, and Max Brod by Manfred Georg, along with Jakob Wassermann, Maximilian Harden, Martin Buber, and Arthur Schnitzler. Alfred Wolfenstein's "conclusion" surveyed the significance of "the new Jewish world of writing":

> The knees of our era, after a first mistaken fall, may be flexed for a great leap forward. And the Jew will acquire a new form as well: he will emerge as a distinct figure amidst the uproar of the present—life, death, and literature, have already

proclaimed as much, making his spiritual mission that much more decisive and clear. Literature will play a decisive role not because the essence of Judaism will become spiritually stronger, but because the new forms it assumes will increase its expressive capacities. Many now seek a new land. But the independence of new forms of Jewish literary expression is more splendid still. A land can be lost, and fate can furiously be repeated because it has not been understood, producing an eternal diaspora—Jerusalem can be destroyed once more: but Judaism's transcendent mission, never. This mission transcends every state, envisioning an open world that belongs to God, and that citizens of its various states receive from him.[7]

The *Philo-Lexikon* (columns 663–671) of 1937 lists no fewer than three hundred Jewish writers and poets writing in German who were born between 1800 and 1900. Another wave precedes this crest, from Moses Ephraim Kuh to Heine; similarly, the turn of the twentieth century does not mark an end, but a beginning, enlarging on the nineteenth century's achievement with both male and female representatives of the other arts. What devotion these unsung, largely unknown figures displayed, and what passion they showed in the long, difficult, and selfless struggle they waged!

In measuring this achievement, we must recall the constant struggle of all artists to perfect their aesthetic vision while earning their daily bread, until the public finally accepts an artistic movement, or until one of its exponents finds recognition, if not favor. In addition, Jewish artists were forced to wage an unimaginably difficult campaign, barred from career paths that artists would normally follow, and constantly forced to justify their entitlement to basic civil and human rights. The Jewish artist was repeatedly forced to demonstrate that he or she was in fact a genuinely authentic and pure flower of their native land. As if they had not been intimately acquainted with their land and its language for centuries and countless generations on end!

Added to the mix was a fateful set of circumstances that affected German Jews and Germany as well. Lessing had established a standard of interfaith cooperation and tolerance that presupposed a magnanimous spirit wholly lacking in the great and greatest German masters who followed. His friendship with Mendelssohn turned out to be a one-time affair. The memorably close and productive relationship between Karl Marx and Friedrich Engels is of course worth recalling, but it was not an incidental factor in their friendship that both were German émigrés and that Marx had fallen under the spell of Jewish self-hatred. We could also adduce the friendship between Stefan George and Karl Wolfskehl, a bond tremendously important for Germany and highly productive for intellectual history, a connection rewarding in human terms over a long period of time. George, however, would painfully abandon Wolfskehl: as the abyss approached that threatened to destroy their common efforts, George was unable or unwilling to make a final break with the past. In the end, Wolfskehl's achievement allowed him to set sail alone and chart his own course.

For though figures such as Alfred Mombert and Else Lasker-Schüler were befriended, and for all the actual collaboration and mutual support that did indeed occur, Jews never gained warm or grateful acceptance as fellow artists. This was due in part to a specific aspect of their public predicament: the Jews had become full participants in German life just as Germany was experiencing its boom, its greatest period of intellectual progress. But when German intellectual energy had stalled or had been directed to other fields of endeavor, Jewish creative powers were reaching their peak. Jewish success came to be seen as an aspect of the Jewish character, despite its entwinement with the deepest impulses of the German language and its soul, expressed in German thought and art. It became possible to lament rather than celebrate the tireless group of Jews who, toward the end of the nineteenth and the beginning of the twentieth centuries, began to devote themselves to artistic pursuits in German-speaking countries. Jews replaced other sectors of the population who had once led the way, but now lagged behind.

The completely senseless debate over loyalty to Germany and to Judaism—whose senselessness made it no less poisonous to the soul—could never be settled in a way that would satisfy every nagging question or malicious demand. The anguish involved exposed Jewish citizens to scornful derision in a climate that was at worst hatefully set against them, and at best exerted a subtle pressure to accept Christian baptism. This "conversion," of course, would then be thrown back in the face of the Jews as yet more proof of a Jewish mendacity and faithlessness that ought to exclude them altogether, whether baptized or not, from the artistic sphere. On the other side of the ledger, an all too self-righteous Jewish community was neither able nor willing to support its artists, yet never hesitated to damn the artist—born a Jew, but also an artist—who could no longer bear his marginalization on account of his Jewish faith.

We will consider how this situation fanned "Jewish self-hatred" into an angry, self-inflicted despair, but also how this heart-rending detour unleashed active and original energies that spurred Jewish productivity forward. The next chapter will leave this dark episode behind to consider the beacon that Judaism's enduring message represented for German Jewry. The Jewish commitment to transmitting that biblical message never flagged, always striving to realize its message of liberation until German Jewry reached its "end." That demise will call for its own exposition and analysis—a task that can longer be deferred. Looking at it more closely, we will see how that end transformed German Jewry's creative presence into a past, whose future could exist only in the form of a legacy, a legacy that would truly belong to the future as a task to be fulfilled.

With this in mind, let us recall our measure for defining "Jewishness," so important for discussing the representatives of "Philosophy from the Sources of Judaism" and well illustrated in our earlier portrayals. This measure includes Jews who had been baptized as well as those descended from one or from several Jewish progenitors, and it includes Jews who doubted their Jewishness as well as those who cursed it, encompassing Berthold Auerbach, Karl Emil Franzos, Stefan Zweig, Ernst Lissauer, Lion Feuchtwanger, Arthur Silbergleit, and Joseph Roth, not to mention these unambiguously Jewish figures not yet mentioned in any context, but also Karl Johann Philipp Spitta, Paul Heyse, Georg Ebers, Karl Kraus, Friedrich Gundolf, Hermann Broch, Kurt Tucholsky, Ferdinand Bruckner, Walter Hasenclever, Johannes R. Becher, Ernst Toller, Carl Zuckmayer, Elisabeth Langgässer, and Anna Seghers. This criterion for Jewishness is grounded in the fact that Judaism, though a community with roots going back to the desert covenant that owes its continuing existence to that covenant alone, must at the same time—as part of the world-historical process that same covenant set in motion—constitute a people, whose membership is decided by birth.

We often worry about Judaism's potential dissolution into other nations—a process whose full effect is felt only with the children and grandchildren—via conversion. And we also reflect often enough on the opposite case of those who wish to convert to Judaism, a conversion that Jews never deny anyone whose intentions are serious at heart. We must therefore also consider the equally important prophetic concept of "the remnant of Israel" and include it in our reflections. The remnant is what is left over, a fraction of the people as a whole, since many unquestionably "Jewish" members of the community are in fact only pro-forma Jews and will not remain such over time. What truly matters in the end and counts, as it were, is whoever remains Jewish when all is said and done. But to sit in judgment over who counts as a Jew and who does not is not the task of their contemporary. He would do well to deploy broader rather than narrower criteria when considering Judaism's shaping influence in creative works. Testimony to Judaism's message can be found in many people who have fallen away, and consciously try to reject their Jewishness, in people born into another faith and raised as members of a different people, as well as in those unschooled in their original covenant and distant from it. Unbeknownst to themselves and without conscious intent, such individuals offer evidence of a lasting message that remains, transcending all sworn and unsworn testimony, a message that is older and at the same time more vital and full of future promise than any of its individual messengers.

While our consideration initially focused on Heine, Wolfskehl, Mombert, Lasker-Schüler, and Kafka alone, we must also remember the work of many others, since "there would be no turning back for the greatest among them in what they achieved." And while each member of this almost unlimited multitude deserves a thoughtful biography and careful assessment of his or her contribution, central consideration must be accorded those figures at the forefront who carried Judaism's message and achieved one of Jewish modernity's greatest victories. Their work made everyone aware of Judaism's vital, contemporary significance, and that this people was capable of the highest, purest form of literary achievement. Loyalty to one did not weaken or compromise the writer's commitment to the other: instead, these dual commitments furthered and completed one another. It was, is, and still remains possible to ascend every artistic, patriotic, and linguistic peak without ever straying from Judaism's paths.

For Germany, however, this recognition arrived far too late and hesitantly to counter an increasingly hostile environment. But this insight, part of the German legacy after all, remains an encouragement to Jewish life as it exists there today, and in many other lands and languages as well. The example of German Jewish artists encourages Jewish artists everywhere to achieve that complete outward and inner liberation that remains the substance of Judaism's call.

TWENTY

The Empty House and *Shofar*

Karl Otten concluded his prose anthology of 1959 with an admonition. "What use would it be for the German people," he wrote, "to reach the heights of worldly power and influence, if they were nothing more than strangers, passing by the empty house?"[1] That house, once bustling with life, which will be haunted by the souls of German Jewish writers "until the end of time?" Otten's anthology, *The Empty House*, included selections by Paul Adler, Ernst Blass, Albert Ehrenstein, Efraim Frisch, Gertrud Kolmar, Paul Kornfeld, Simon Kronberg, and Ernst Weiss. Otten, not a Jew himself, acted on behalf of the Jews and out of a sense of the horrible injustice done to them. But Otten also wrote from a profound awareness of the terrible loss the German people inflicted on themselves by destroying the Jews. He explained his effort as "the return of a few Jewish representatives of German intellectual and creative life, from the shadowy mists of complete oblivion, to the homeland that is rightfully theirs, a land that was all too little concerned with espousing their cause while they lived."[2]

The Empty House thereby avoids the common tendency to place the spotlight on "belles-lettres" alone, or to choose the best-known, most accessible, or best-loved works wherever possible, the common course most editors eagerly follow when anthologizing literary documents or producing a memorial work. Otten therefore forgoes short prose fiction, though such pieces would be more easily grasped, and does not hesitate to include entire novellas such as *Nämlich* (Namely) and *Die Zauberflöte* (The Magic Flute) by Paul Adler, or Efraim Frisch's masterwork *Zenobi*, a genre twin of Thomas Mann's *Felix Krull.* Two literary works are presented here for the first time: Ernst Blass's *Der Blinde* (The Blind Man) and Gertrude Kolmar's *Susanna*, while Paul Kornfeld's gripping *Legende* of 1917 appears in a new light, both for its similarities to and differences from Kafka, who had in the meantime emerged as a major figure. Also included were Ernst Weiss's *Daniel*, Simon Kronberg's *Chamlam*, and Albert Ehrenstein's *Selbstmord eines Katers* (The Tomcat's Suicide) and *Wudandermeer*.

Seven male writers and one female are included. Together their works are able to encompass the world's heavenly heights and hellish depths. Today's reader can, with the blessing of hindsight, grasp the tension between these two poles as a brilliant, shocking, and ingenious expression of the abyss that would, in a few short years, transform these literary works into a martyr's testament in the most authentic sense. It was permitted to Ernst Blass alone to die in 1939, before the volume's remaining contributors would be swallowed up by murder, suicide, and exile. The unique power of the literature in this collection is almost strong enough to part the curtains of mourning that darken the house of Jewish writing in German. That dwelling, now bereft of its creators, is almost roused to life, if but briefly, by the sense of satisfaction and joy that still emanate from these recovered works, as is always the case with creative works of real achievement.

Three years later—and one year before his death on March 20, 1963—Karl Otten published a second and yet more splendid anthology brought together as *Lieder und Legenden jüdischer Dichter* (Songs and legends of Jewish writers), under the title *Shofar*. "The *shofar*," Otten writes in his introduction, is that " instrument made from the twisting cone of the ram's horn, which was first responsible for bringing down the walls of Jericho before it became the instrument blown on the Jewish High Holidays, New Year and the Day of Atonement. The instrument's tone resounds with a gripping and soul-searching lament. Here, the *shofar* stands as a symbol for the waking of the dead."[3] Which dead are to be awakened? To what end this raising of the dead? Twenty-six Jewish writers who wrote in German, men and women—each significant in his or her own right, and some, truly great writers—are to be snatched from the jaws of oblivion. But the vacuum created by the elimination of the Jews from German intellectual life, Otten asserts, cannot be filled: "Never again will such a creed, such a summons to humanity sound forth for the German people in its language. This voice has been silenced forevermore."[4] Literary works produced in that voice, which have either never fully fallen out of our awareness, or which, thanks to Karl Otten, have been brought to our attention once more, ought never to suffer the fates of their creators.

For *Shofar* succeeded in demonstrating the lofty heights German Jewry had achieved as they had seldom been shown before, peaks this Jewish community had mastered in the name of others as well as itself. In the process, the "message of Judaism" had been given a new and modern form, and a legacy had been left behind—the legacy of German Jewry—transmitting the basis and essential truths in whose name surviving Jews and humanity as a whole would seize the future. Let us return once more to Otten's Introduction, an achievement in its own right: "In reading the works assembled in this collection we must overcome our habitual desire for the same old literary thematics, the adventurous, the exotic, the erotic, but in any case psychological. None of the writers gathered here tries to produce such fare.... The significance of these Jewish poems and legends is based on the historic position they occupy within the course of German history and its events. In as much as they tower over the dynamic of those not destined to occupy such a fateful poetic position, each word they utter is surrounded by something unspoken that can only be sensed. Their works are Jewish in the way they give things meaning, in the way they lay claim to an eternal significance that transcends what is merely human, a meaning that we, whether consciously or unconsciously, whether believers or faithless, all recognize as the law on high. For it was to this law, in the end, to which these Jewish poets harkened, the law that from the time of Moses to our own has affected and influenced mankind's creative drive most deeply."[5]

The common Jewish thread running throughout Otten's collection of German Jewish writing is finally this: Jewishness is understood as an expression of humanity's drive for freedom and profound peace. This literature

expresses Judaism's religious message, in other words, in thoroughly modern terms, as a commitment to a future already set in motion by modernity's
revolutionary upheavals. The great Jewish authors of the *Shofar* anthology
in this way move beyond those traditional forms of expression still characteristic of the Jewish way of life and its many forms of self-understanding,
such as late biblical and Talmudic legalism, ritual observance, and the liturgy of the synagogue. But the religious ardor, grounded in an awareness
of "belonging to the oldest of religious people is omnipresent . . . and
proves," as Otten correctly observes, the continuing "identification of the
Jewish people with its God, the prophets and the fate which—directed by a
German hand—brought it to the brink of the abyss."[6] Four of the twenty-
three poets were murdered; four others saw no other way out and chose
suicide; and two fell during the First World War as German soldiers. Richard Beer-Hoffmann, born in 1866 is the oldest, and Gertrud Kolmar, born
in 1894, the youngest in the *Shofar* collection, and in between we find Else
Lasker-Schüler, Karl Wolfskehl, Efraim Frisch, Paul Adler, Arno Nadel,
Ludwig Rubiner, Martin Beradt, Leo Perutz, Ernst Weiss, Carl Einstein,
Albert Ehrenstein, Jakob van Hoddis, Alfred Lichtenstein, Paul Kornfeld,
Franz Werfel, Ernst Blass, Yvan Goll, Simon Kronberg, Franz Janowitz,
and Ludwig Strauss.

An Alfred Mombert, an Arnold Schoenberg, or a Franz Kafka could well
have found a place in such a volume. But Otten may have regarded them,
along with others left out for similar reasons, as introspective writers atypi-
cal of their era of narrowly classical or naturalistic styles. Their contribution
to the aesthetic realm was seen as dubious by the writers represented in this
volume, regarded as falling short of mimetic clarity and its demands. The
editor's marked and idiosyncratic taste in this regard must be accepted by
the reader, and not least by the Jewish reader, for this same decidedly personal perspective generated the drive that made this extraordinary volume
possible in the first place. Otten passes severe judgment on Christianity in
his introduction, making statements that are not grounded in the Jewish
texts, but that he reads back into them because of his deep sense of personal
commitment. We nonetheless come to appreciate him as something more
than a historian, seeking to salvage the bounty of the past. Instead, Otten
comes into focus as a deeply motivated and committed soul with a poet's
temperament, someone unafraid—precisely because he comes to Judaism

from without—to call his own German and Christian world to account for its manifold guilt toward Judaism. The volume is a labor of love, and the anger so strong only because without it, love would never have found the strength to create this *Shofar* from the "songs and legends of Jewish writers."

TWENTY-ONE

Jewish Self-Hatred

The shadows darkening the brilliant picture of German Jewish creativity with which we must now come to terms resulted in no small measure from missteps and detours German Jews took together as a group. The light cast by their achievements cannot be praised without considering the shadows it also produced. "The world we are about to enter is a heartbreaking one," as Theodor Lessing explained in his *Jewish Self-Hatred* of 1930.[1] His book was a slender masterpiece. While not fully plumbing the depths of self-hatred as a phenomenon, Lessing's work achieved a significant grasp of the subject, while presenting its findings with boldness, courage, and honesty. Here, a Judaism that has fully come to terms with its modernity demonstrates the maturity needed to look its own shadow squarely in the face. The last step on the road to complete autonomy was thereby taken. By facing up to its shadow image, German Jewry would both acquire and affirm the true extent of its authority and dignity as a community, by accepting that shadow's burden as their own. The world we are about to describe is a painful, indeed a shameful one: but without integrating it into our account, a crucial aspect of the modernity that German Jewry achieved would be missing from our story.

What a consolation it is that the Bible itself had already reckoned with that very same shadow! In the scriptures, all previous forms of worship could be branded idol-worship only after the biblical advent of divine revelation. The oath sworn to the covenant was therefore also the origin of the apostasy that pulled the other way. History becomes a site of value and judgment only from that moment when history's course is revealed as the difficult path leading toward redemption. In the same way, self-hatred exists only after the conflict between the individual's "natural" or "logical" desires and the demands of a higher calling have been felt in full. Self-hatred, in other words, can come into being only once the individual has set out on the path that demands that the individual conquer the inescapable and irrevocable force of individual will:

> It is a terrible conflict, with one force set against the other: the sea of blood and tears trailing history's path, constantly welling up and almost succeeding in effacing history's course, though the lying falsity of that course has been exposed. Delusion may replace faith, just as obsession may displace authentic emotional possession, since both faith and emotion truly exist.[2]

To borrow Theodor Lessing's all too accurate figure, a heartbreakingly large number of those left wretched by self-hatred have already joined this dark and dismal procession of temptations, tests, and disappointments as it makes its way through the desert. This new struggle to justify one's own existence, and its failure, begins as early as Moses, a boy who grew up with an Egyptian name far from his family. The leader destined to return to his people found them only after triumphing over the twists and turns that mark the road of return. From the time Abraham set forth from the city of Ur to follow the divine call, one's choice would never again be an inconsequential matter. After Abraham, the choice was between following the one and only path of the commandments, or to break faith and desert it for others. No third path was allowed.

Self-hatred comes into existence along with the command to heed the message of revelation. The psychological malady originates with the covenant itself, and accompanies every subsequent form the covenant's bond would take. He who feels himself closed off from a happy, active, and productive life under the covenant begins to hate the covenantal people, who then become decisive, in a negative way, as a determinant of his own existence. Hating his own brothers and sisters, and finally the cultural forms in which the covenant finds continued expression and vitality, he finally hates the one who expresses the existence of this covenant along with them: himself. This loathing for his Jewish brethren becomes all the more furious the less the individual is able to rid himself of a Jewishness that demands expression as an ineradicable, constituent element of his being. Many self-hating individuals in the end choose death over such a life, burying one's origin and existence in a single stroke.

But does Jewish self-hatred have to come to this, and did it? What inescapable barrier prevented modern Jews from taking pleasure in their Judaism and its bounty? What forced them to revive this ancient trauma and to reproduce it to be suffered in this modern form? And can Jewish self-hatred as a discrete phenomenon even be said to exist, since self-hatred accompanies every form of covenantal agreement and every corresponding form of apostasy? At the same time, the form of the covenant under discussion here has been impossible to abandon, as its founding constitutes an uplifting force that remains irreversible. Given this, can a special form of "Jewish" self-hatred be singled out for discussion? The questions we have posed already provide the basis for an affirmative answer: the uniquely "Jewish" form of self-hatred has a threefold foundation, resting on Judaism's status as minority culture, the guilt feelings that are specific to the Jews, and their particular calling.

Hatred can be fanned into self-hatred, a deadly and aggressive aversion to one's own existence, whenever individuals suffer from inner feelings of inadequacy. Such self-contempt is more easily aroused when an individual or group can be singled out as an identifiable minority. That minority may exist within a state, as a state within the community of nations, or as in the predicament faced by contemporary Israel, as a state faced by the surrounding Arab majority in its region. The feeling of being a minority has not even been spared today's Jews in the Jewish state. Like Jews throughout the world who for centuries, and into modernity proper, had to defend their religion against a majority that either practiced idol worship, or continued the biblical tradition in faiths of their own, today's Jews have not been spared feelings of inadequacy. The revolutionary Jewish breakthrough that invented the idea of history at the same time created powerful ties no Jew can break or dissolve, giving the Jewish people a minority position in a world in which social justice has not yet been achieved. A minority, of course, scrutinizes itself more carefully, and as a result, its self-confidence is weaker, and its self-criticism harsher. Feelings of dissatisfaction take a greater toll on someone who already experiences his exceptional status as a burden. The constant temptation in such a situation is to switch sides and join a self-assured majority whose status seems beyond question, a majority drunk with its own success, and to turn against the minority, even if the price is self-inflicted harm. The Jew possesses fewer defenses against such damage than do members of other minorities, because as a Jew, his tendency is to find the chief source of his malaise within himself.

How is this characteristic Jewish tendency toward self-accusation to be explained? Theodor Lessing provides one answer, overlooking the fact that continuous self-scrutiny is accompanied by an uplifting moment of greatness that makes the abyss of self-condemnation that much deeper in cases of apostasy from one's original faith. The argument for a specifically Jewish form of self-hatred rests on the attitude toward everyday life that the Jewish people have displayed ever since it was forged with the covenant at Sinai. The very meaning of guilt for Jews is to abandon the demands of the covenant. When he sins, a Jew sins against adherents to the covenant who have made the radical turn to goodness and love. He sins against the faithful, though they may in fact be as or far more guilty. History—the path toward a united humanity that is also Judaism's own—is twice judged: that is, a kind of temporal trial decided by choosing a certain direction, or missing it. The price paid for this exodus, the new dispensation it represents, and its commands—the price, in short of this new "bond" of covenant—is guilt. To quote the prophet Amos, the covenant, in groundbreaking fashion, includes Africans, Philistines, and Syrians—all peoples of the earth (9:7). "To Me, O Israelites, you are / Just like the Ethiopians. / True, I brought Israel up / From the land of Egypt, / But also the Philistines from Caphtor / And the Arameans from Kir." But the covenantal burden of the Jews is a special one: "You alone have I singled out / Of all the families of the earth— / That is why I will call you to account / For all your iniquities" (3:2).

The path Judaism was commanded to take by revelation may have carried the Jewish message throughout the entire world since the time of the covenant, but it was also a summons to judgment. The Jewish path raises the question of guilt from the very start, but at the same time blesses Jews with the capacity for insight into their own iniquity. That is, the choice is always open for every individual and people to turn away from evil deeds. When such searching self-examination brings about a change of heart, humanity's most exalted dignity and noblest calling has been realized. The exercise of moral autonomy represents the summit of human achievement, allowing the self to come into its own as a self-possessed individual. Though judged, the individual also authors a judgment of his own, that is, enacts a transformation that changes part of the universe along with it. Such power remains a burden to the self-hating Jew who is not up to its demands, until he finally gives in to what he perceives to be his "guilt." But it also carries the loyal "remnant" out of every such abyss, giving it the courage to look every individual and communal failing squarely in the eye. The individual can see guilt as something provisional, so that he can join in the struggle once more, until victory has been achieved.

But the quest for this ultimate "victory"—the "kingdom" of God—creates another opportunity for a characteristically Jewish form of self-hatred to reassert itself, because the task of carrying this message is a never-ending one. While other forms of self-affirmation may be easier, striving in this case means taking the harder path, more difficult than the seductive possibility of self-negation. To claim an individual identity as part of a biblical tradition means having to assert one's difference from one's surroundings and "beloved" course of habit. The covenantal identity goes against the grain of every supposedly "natural" human impulse, counter to all "logic." Claiming it means rejecting all tolerance for those omnipresent forms of idol worship that so often commands human worship, love, and support. In Baeck's quintessential formulation, this covenantal impulse motivates the world's great nonconformists, its religious heroes and martyrs. But that same drive can also invert itself and become a peculiar form of self-hatred in those unable or unwilling to follow its flag. But why did modernity in particular produce such a large-scale outbreak of Jewish self-hatred? How could such self-hatred represent such a barrier to the many forms of Jewish self-fulfillment available, reviving its ancient sorrow and reinventing new forms of suffering its throes?

One part of the answer lies in Germany's rapid seizure of the heights in both its outer and inner development. As Germany's cultural and economic successes began to peak, so did the challenges those revolutionary developments posed from the eighteenth century to the twentieth, as all peoples had to come to terms with the fact of revolutionary change. At the same time, progress constantly encountered roadblocks that brought great dangers, defeats, and their corresponding temptations. While German Jewry's flourishing success may at first seem shockingly, and even repulsively compromised by its mistakes and moral missteps, such long shadows could only be cast by the heights of achievement German Jewish development had already scaled. That success carried every individual Jew and every Jewish group along with it without exception, making it much more likely for Jews to be forced onto false paths, or to lose their way, than to simply be left standing still.

Theodor Lessing laid out the basic elements of this process in an unforgettable memoir entitled *Einmal und nie wieder* (Once and never again), published as part of his literary remains in 1935, following his insidious murder on the night of September 30, 1933. Here it must suffice if we detail two of the most extreme paths leading to the confusion that is Jewish self-hatred. One scenario presents us with parents who were model, loyal German citizens through and through. Yet, despite their formal legal equality, they were persistently and mercilessly refused the chance to realize their ambitions and to advance as high as their intellectual gifts, rights, and dreams would take them. In order to give their children a better life, such parents would often baptize their children to better their chances at success. A second scenario involved children who had received a Jewish education, but who were unable to go on living as Jews, regardless of whether that Judaism had been "renewed" in liberal, orthodox, or Zionist form. By baptizing themselves or as Marxists, "pure" scientists, or espousers of one or another utopian program for redemption, such individuals felt themselves better equipped to confront the challenges of the modern world. And while accomplishing great, and indeed the greatest things, much of their accomplishment was rooted in a Jewish outlook and character they sometimes minimized, but most often despised and hated.

This self-effacement and self-deception was part of the calamity that beset the Jewish people as a whole and exposed every element of Jewish society to its temptations without exception. We know, for instance, that of Moses Mendelssohn's children who survived him, with the exception of his oldest son Joseph (1770–1848) and his daughter Rechel (1767–1831), four converted to Christianity. Aside from Alexander Mendelssohn (1798–1871), Joseph's son, all of his grandchildren became Christian, just as Theodor Herzl's only son Hans accepted baptism. The great-grandson of Samson

Raphael Hirsch, Karl Jakob Hirsch, publicly renounced orthodox Judaism in 1946, authoring a work called *Heimkehr zu Gott* (Coming Home to God), a pointedly blasphemous title given his family background.

Chapter 17 has already sketched the variety of different factors that helped German Jews achieve scientific breakthroughs, but which also thwarted and dispersed their cultural force. Our analysis in no way intends to diminish the significance of these achievements that were completed, so to speak, under a foreign flag. Nor do we mean to cast any doubt whatsoever on the validity and richness of other religious traditions, for they too, in their own way, pursued an end akin to Judaism's own, and enlarged upon Jewish efforts or were enlarged by them. It is another question altogether, however, whether a Jew who denies his Jewishness can produce his best work. And it is another question entirely—regardless of any Jewish content in his work—whether such a person does not literally become *extravagant*, even if the import of his own achievement remains the same. Is it truly possible for someone who denies his own origins—which of course can never truly be fled—to escape the grip of self-hatred? Doesn't the very wellspring and source of his energy undergo a change, and not for the better: burdened by hate instead of furthered by love?

Theodor Lessing documented his book on Jewish self-hatred with six short biographies. He offered accounts of Paul Rée, whose work was an important influence on Nietzsche, Arthur Trebitsch, a leading figure in political anti-Semitism, Otto Weininger, a major influence on "intellectual anti-Semitism," Maximilian Harden, who helped Germany's hypernationalism get underway, Max Steiner and Walter Calé, who brought their own lives to an untimely end. These exceptionally insightful analyses eventually made Lessing one of the leading figures in the development of psychology, an endeavor advanced by a group comprised largely of pioneering Jews. Their transformation of the field of psychology made a major contribution to modern thought as a whole. Some of the first suggestions of its "Jewish" origins can be found in the concept of self-hatred that Lessing pioneered.

A terrifying Jewish trauma accompanied the Jewish entry to modernity in the difficult conditions we have described. But all the psychological subterfuge and divided consciousness that process created were at the same time responsible for many of the creative insights that created the field of modern depth psychology and allowed it to flourish. A few names will suffice to spark associations and provide a feel for the astounding number of

German Jewish men and women of intellectual stature who devoted their life's work in creative efforts to this field and to the humanity it served. Along with Sigmund Freud and the countless number of his Jewish students, supporters, and successors, such a list would also include Joseph Breuer, Wilhelm Fliess, Hugo Münsterberg, Max Dessoir, Alfred Adler, William Stern, Max Scheler, Richard Hönigswald, Max Wertheimer, David Katz, Kurt Koffka, Siegfried Bernfeld, Charlotte Bühler, Emil Utlitz, Leopold Szondi, Erich Fromm, and, last but not least, Theodor Lessing.

But the eye prefers light to the world of shadows, taking the grandeur of that light even more seriously and appreciating it more deeply when its effects have become apparent by penetrating all. Such insights are not won easily: they require hard, arduous, and honest effort. Nevertheless, this teaching and its message do not address life from without, connecting to it at will—not since Judaism's ancestral founders joined the covenant at Sinai, and made every one of their descendants a part of their exodus and national awakening. Instead, such teaching and its message can only exist as the living point of orientation for an individual's life. For without such critical self-reflection, not just truth, but life itself begins to falter. Even Jewish self-hatred, that irreconcilably hostile foe, exiled from its own place of origin, in the end testifies only to the fact that this origin—its Judaism—wherever it comes to life, remains indestructibly alive.

TWENTY-TWO

The Jewish Quest for a German Bible

In an earlier chapter, we described the dual breakthrough to modernity Moses Mendelssohn achieved in 1783. Mendelssohn had by then published his own "declaration of independence," as it were, his book *Jerusalem, or On Religious Power and Judaism*. He had also issued his new German translation of the Hebrew Bible, including the five books of Moses in Hebrew characters, and his version of the Psalms already published in German. The formulation we used then is worth repeating here: "Since the Babylonian exile, no full Jewish life has existed without translating the Bible into the language of the land in which that life was bound to develop. Only when a foreign language could be fused with Judaism's own religious message, when that message itself was able to merge with the intellectual and spiritual depths of another linguistic world, could a Jewish community be said to have struck roots, enabling its message to blossom and ripen to fruition."

German Jewry's translations of the Hebrew Bible represented such a linguistic reawakening of the Jewish people's authentic and essential spirit, following in the footsteps of Jewish communities that had achieved the feat of translating the Bible first into Greek, then Aramaic, and finally Arabic. Their success was achieved in the face of stiff opposition that awaits any modern revision of the biblical text that might give it new life, giving their project an exemplary significance. And their accomplishment was no less significant for the fact that their final translation arrived too late in the day for German Jewry itself. The German Jewish translation of the Hebrew Bible reached other Jewish communities, and humanity as a whole, but in the form of an inherited legacy, a gift from a foreign, German linguistic realm.

The Voice Speaks was the title Karl Wolfskehl gave the splendid and memorable book of poems he published in 1934. This was the same Wolfskehl who felt connected to Martin Buber and Franz Rosenzweig in his own quiet way, influencing their translation of the scripture. His title, whether consciously or not, took its cue from Buber's notion that giving new life to the Bible was not the work of a book, but of a living voice. Buber's series of lectures held in November 1926, "The People of Today and the Jewish Bible," carried out this idea in detail: "It is not a matter of a 'return to the Bible.' It is a matter of the renewed reception of a genuinely biblical, unified life by our whole time-enmeshed being, with the whole weight of our contemporary many-sidedness lying on our souls, and the incomprehensible material of this historical hour taken into account in full. It is a matter of bearing up responsibly and dialogically against the pressure of our own present situations, with an openness to belief in accord with the biblical vision. Do we mean a book? We mean the voice. Do we mean that people should learn to read it? We mean that people should learn to hear it."[1] As Buber and Rosenzweig formulated the idea in "The Bible in German," written that same year: "We believe that every moment, our own as much as any in the past, is distant and hostile in relation to the word that in the Bible has become Scripture. We also believe that this word preserves in every moment the power to take hold of those that hear it. The moment is passive, the word active. If we only preserve the word, only conserve it, only let it be borne along by the moment, we blaspheme it. The word wants to speak—to every moment, into every moment, against every moment."[2]

Three different, innovative changes, and one in particular, caused Buber, Rosenzweig, and Wolfskehl to move from Jeremiah's repeated warning to "Listen to the voice of the LORD" (22:29, 11:4,7, and 38:20)—a warning still heeded by Franz Werfel in 1937, when he titled his important Jeremiah novel of that year *Listen to the Voice*—to the gripping and immediate "The Voice Speaks." No peak can be scaled in a single leap. Buber and Rosenzweig's resolution of 1924 to translate the Hebrew scripture into German, carried to its completion by the surviving Buber in 1961, marks a turning point they reached in stages, in common effort with others. The first volume appeared in 1925, and the last in 1961. But their work was able to benefit from the collective efforts represented in an extraordinary number of earlier biblical translations completed after Mendelssohn who started it all, but not without predecessors of his own going all the way back to the thirteenth century. A brief survey of these is now in order.

The spiritual crisis brought on by the Crusades was in part responsible for the translation of portions of the Bible chanted in Hebrew in the synagogue service, first into middle high German and then into Yiddish. Previously, the liturgy had become more and more closed to female participation, and its Hebrew was beginning to exclude an increasing number of men as well. The letter by Wolfskehl to be cited in a moment points out another factor at play, namely a pervasive and powerful love of life, part and parcel of a burgeoning spiritual energy in the period that was pushing to find an expression of its own. Women, the common folk, and eventually German Jewry as a whole began to insist that their everyday language be allowed to convey the biblical teachings, and demanded Yiddish versions of its texts, which eventually resulted in the translation of the Bible as a whole. In any case, the manuscript evidence that might support what Karl Wolfskehl called in a 1943 letter from New Zealand "the most urgent desire of my declining life, to see that the great medieval biblical Epic receives scholarly editing, and to see it in print," is not our present concern. Until recently, the field of Yiddish has been punished by an enforced scholarly ignorance. Wolfskehl nonetheless wrote the following to Isaiah Sonne, professor at the Hebrew Union College in Cincinnati:

> As you know, Joshua, Judges, Samuel and Kings are done, all in Nibelungen verse, often full of poetic felicities. Everything else remains to be done— producing the text itself, clarifying the issue of authorship, and ascertaining the date of composition with precision. It is my firm conviction that the earliest sources of these epics go back as far as the fourteenth century. . . . They are truly Jewish epics, perhaps the only extant epic poetry of such scope and breadth in

the post-biblical era. . . . [This is] evidence for a complete and intimate connection with the surrounding medieval world, that exile was nonetheless not a period lacking illumination at all.[3]

Yiddish translations of the five Books of Moses, the Psalms, and the *Megillot* (The Song of Songs, The Book of Ruth, Lamentations, Ecclesiastes, and the Book of Esther) by contrast, are extant only as early as the sixteenth century. Two translations of the Jewish Bible in its entirety—the Old Testament of the Christians—were published between 1676 and 1679, and both were printed in Amsterdam, one by Yekutiel ben Isaak Blitz of Wittmund, the other by Josel Witzenhausen. As Mendelssohn declared in his Hebrew introduction to his modern German translation of the Bible, which appeared a full century later: "It has since occurred to no one to improve on what has gone bad, and to translate the holy Torah properly into the language of our day. Jewish youths who can grasp the meaning of the sayings of the fathers must hunt about, and in the end learn the word of God from translations done by the Christian sages."[4]

Does the fact that Mendelssohn's German translation was printed in Hebrew characters explain the immediate acceptance and acclaim that transformed it into the sign that a new historical hour was at hand? Or on the other hand, did those same Hebrew letters impede the reception of his translation? Or was it the stubborn and persistent medieval Jewish outlook already blocking his path that condemned in advance any innovation threatening its hegemony? Traditional Judaism cloistered itself away from any such changes that aimed at, and eventually succeeded in, recasting Judaism's fundamental core principles in a different form. Or was the French Revolution and its aftermath the underlying cause? By bringing the centuries-long ghettoization of the Jewish population to an end in all too rapid a fashion, the revolution forced a full reassessment of the Jewish world's intellectual and spiritual premises to take a back seat, while the political battle for full Jewish civic equality was being waged. More than thirty years would elapse before Mendelssohn's German text would be published in German letters, and another twenty years would elapse before the first translation of the entire Bible would be complete.

This noteworthy achievement was the work of Leopold Zunz and his collaborators Heymann Arnheim, Julius Fürst, and Michael Sachs. Their effort followed on the heels of the *Deutsche Volks- und Schulbibel für Israeliten*

(The German People's and School Bible for Israelites) put out by Gotthold Salomon. "As sixty years ago, so today, one biblical translation for German Jews vies for preeminence with another," Zunz wrote in a letter of August 28, 1836, alluding to Josel Witzenhausen's attempt to outdo the biblical translation of Jekutiel ben Isaak Blitz. This remark by the founder of the Wissenschaft des Judentums evokes the living and enduring connection from century to century, and across the expanse of the millennia as well, always present to Zunz. His translation was and remains a landmark: *Die vierundzwanzig Bücher der Heiligen Schrift, nach dem masoretischen Text, unter der Redaktion von Dr. Zunz* (The Twenty-Four Books of the Holy Scriptures, according to the Masoretic Text, edited by Dr. Zunz) was published in 1837 and has since been reprinted many times. Zunz's achievement, however, was unable to spur a deepening of interest in the Bible of any consequence, and failed to become a subsequent reference point for Judaism's religious sector. This phenomenon, of course, is hardly unique to the Jews. Movements hostile to any form of religion had already taken hold, and created divisions within Judaism that became ingrained, preventing his work from gaining any impact. Zunz's translation did, however, suffer what could be called an inevitably Jewish fate, given the fierce debate and internecine strife it unleashed. A not inconsiderable number of rival Bible translations soon appeared. Some settled for translating only parts of the scripture, though all made significant contributions to the successful conclusion of the Jewish quest for a German Bible. Here, four examples must suffice.

Ludwig Philippson, founder of the Israelitische Bibelanstalt, or Israelite Biblical Institute, as a bulwark against the rise of baptism-oriented Protestant biblical institutes, unintentionally spurred the Jewish conservatives into action. His translation became the impetus for the Orthodox Bible institute and its Bible, the work of Seligmann Bär Bamberger, Abraham Adler, and Marcus Lehmann, who opposed the supposed modern liberties Philippson's translation took. These conservatives—like Philippson himself—shared the common goal of preventing Christian translations from gaining the upper hand. Between 1839 and 1853, Philippson published the *Israelitische Bibel* (Israelite Bible), which aimed at fidelity to the original, popularity, and stylistic grace, and was accompanied by introductions, explanatory notes, and commentary. Philippson had his translation appear as the *Heilige Schrift der Israeliten* (The Holy Scripture of the Israelites), otherwise known as the Doré Bible, after the translation was checked for accuracy by Wolf Landau and Paul Isaac Kämpf, and after his own revisions had brought it into "accord with the latest scholarly standards." Adorned with 150 of Gustave Doré's images and numerous ornamental decorations, the edition indicated all *Sidra* and *Haftorah* portions of the weekly synagogue service, provided all captions in German as well as Hebrew, and included the Apocrypha as a supplement, including the third book of Ezra and the third book of the Maccabees as translated by David Cassel. "And in this way," as Philippson concludes his preface, dated "Bonn, March 1874," "let the age-old, holy word reach those who love it, who have long avoided its sounds, teachings and admonitions, or who have studied it little or not at all. May the places it finds be many and welcoming, and in the spirit of pure insight into the divine, uprightness and piety of heart, love of humanity, of justice and of peace, offer its ancient blessings anew: 'illuminating the eye, and strengthening the spirit!'"

Salomon Herxheimer produced a biblical translation to a somewhat muted response, aimed at countering "the daily and increasing disregard, indifference, and fading of interest in Judaism, on the one hand, and the ossification of Jewish religious life on the other." His translation, which began to appear in 1842, was titled *Die 24 Bücher der Bibel in Hebräischem Texte, mit worttreuer Übersetzung, fortlaufender Erklärung und homiletisch benutzbaren Anmerkungen* (The 24 Books of the Bible in Hebrew Text, in Translation Faithful to the Text, Explanatory Material and Notes for Sermons). In the meantime, Jakob Auerbach had begun a new version of the Bible possible now that truly "faithful" translations were once again available, a work issued with, among others, "young female readers" in mind, paraphrasing the most difficult and scandalous passages. His overly modest title—*Kleine Schul- und Haus Bibel* (The Compact Bible for School and Home) was meant to "to warn with the utmost severity against any confusion [of this translation] with the Bible itself," as the foreword to the first edition of 1858 puts it.

Samson Raphael Hirsch's concern, by contrast, was with the Bible itself. His translation of the five books of Moses was in print from 1867 onward, and his rendering of the Psalms available since 1882. Both editions were distinguished by their copious, line-by-line commentary, and were the equal of what Mendelssohn and Zunz had achieved. But at the point where Buber and Rosenzweig achieved a decisive breakthrough to immediacy, with their revolutionary, innovative translation of the name of God, Hirsch, founder of the modern Orthodox movement, chose a different way out. Hirsch retained the Hebrew wording, or a Hebrew euphemism, or printed the name of God in spaced type, as "G o d," thus renouncing any desire to put his translation to the ultimate test. Mendelssohn, on the other hand, had been forced to use the term "the Eternal" as his stopgap solution to this problem, even though it was technically incorrect. In keeping with his own interpretation of Exodus 3:14, Mendelssohn was unable to find any common expression that would signify God's eternity, existential necessity, and providence in a single term. He settled for "eternity," a compromise formation that at least had the virtue of satisfying the broadest possible audience, and would be taken up by Zunz.

Two other complete translations would be produced in what was soon the twentieth century: Simon Bernfeld's *Die Heilige Schrift* (The Holy Scripture) of 1903 and Lazarus Goldschmidt's *Die Heiligen Bücher des alten Bundes* (The Holy Books of the Old Covenant) of 1921. Following these, two final, monumental works of biblical translation were undertaken, one completed after the reign of terror of 1933–45, and the other in face of those awful years, the work of Martin Buber and N. H. Tur-Sinai (Harry Torcyner) respectively, both of whom had in the meantime emigrated to Jerusalem. For the Jewish quest for a German Bible—whose fulfillment they embody—had not come to an end.

Tur-Sinai's *The Holy Scripture* owed a substantial debt to Zunz's translation, and as Tur-Sinai himself reminds us in Introductions of 1937 and 1954, follows in the footsteps of Zunz and Mendelssohn in particular by taking up the term "the Eternal" for the name of God. Produced at the request of the Berlin Jewish community, which needed a clear, accurate and complete German text for liturgical recitation in its liberal synagogue, the translation fulfills its task well. Many leading liberal and conservative rabbis and scholars lent their assistance to the project, including Elias Auerbach, Emil Bernhard Cohn, Max Dienemann, Julius Galliner, Sally Gans, Benno Jacob, Emil Levy, Ludwig Levy, Seligmann Pick, Georg Salzberger, Hermann Schreiber, Cäsar Seligmann, and Max Wiener. Leo Baeck was the chair of the Biblical Commission they served on from 1924 forward, given its charge by an earlier chief rabbi of Berlin, Siegmund Maybau, in 1907. The fourth and final volume of the final, newly edited edition appeared in 1959.

But the voice that speaks in the Buber and Rosenzweig translation would do so only for the Torah, Kings, the prophets, and Chronicles that together comprised the project of germanizing the Bible they undertook. Their technique was extremely innovative in several important respects. In an intentionally peculiar fashion, Buber and Rosenzweig use German in an attempt to mimic the acoustic patterns of the Hebrew, repeating every root sound as it reappears by using a German consonantal equivalent. The Bible's original language is thus reproduced for the reader through assonance, consonance, and the use of key words, giving the verbal qualities of the original Hebrew text a new attention and respect heretofore lacking in Jewish and Christian translations alike. The second innovative change of the Buber-Rosenzweig translation was its division of the biblical text into breathing units by the use of breathing-colons. For Rosenzweig believed that "the drawing of breath . . . is the natural segmenting of speech," and his translation tried to replicate the spoken quality of a text of rhythmically structured units once transmitted orally.[5] The third innovation was their accomplishment itself, which became more than simply a translation. Their work became a revolutionary approach to, and embodiment of, revelation itself.

Rosenzweig himself said as much: "The only justifiable translation [of God's name] is one that makes prominent not God's being eternal but his being present, his being present for and with you now and in time to come."[6] Hence there could be only a single fitting and suitable keyword capable of conveying all the nuances of meaning his text required. "In the rendering of the thus clarified name," Rosenzweig explains, "this fact can be condensed into the three dimensions of the personal pronoun: the speaker, the one spoken to, and the one spoken of. Only in the pronoun is the meaning of the One who is present in one of three ways, the One who is in one of three sorts of presence, concentrated into a single word."[7] Or in Buber's formulation:

> that is, [we chose not to] express God's being-with-me, being-with-you, being-with-us conceptually, according to the notion of the constant, Mendelssohn's 'the Eternal,' [but to find an equivalent that] would embody it in full presence. That is what is done in our translation by the pronouns: the I and MY when God is speaking; the YOU and YOUR when God is spoken to; the HE and HIS when God is spoken of.[8]

A case in point must here suffice. Moses confronts the difficult task of announcing to the sons of Israel that he has been called to lead them, and does it as follows: "When I come to the Israelites and say to them, 'The God of your fathers has sent me to you,' and they ask me, 'What is his name?' what shall I say to them?" (Exodus 3:13–15). Afterward, he receives the following answer:

> Gott sprach zu Mosche:
> Ich werde dasein, als der ich dasein werde.
> Und sprach:
> So sollst du zu den Söhnen Jißraels sprechen:
> ICH BIN DA schickt mich zu euch.
> Und weiter sprach Gott zu Mosche:
> So sollst du zu den Sohnen Jißraels sprechen:
> ER,
> der Gott eurer Väter,
> der Gott Abrahams, der Gott Jizchaks, der Gott Jaakobs,
> schickt mich zu euch.
> Das ist mein Name in Weltzeit,
> das mein Gedenken, Geschlecht für Geschlecht.

> And God said to Moses,
> 'Ehyeh- Asher-Ehyeh I AM WHO I AM.
> He continued,
> Thus shall you say to the Israelites,
> I AM sent me to you.'
> And God said further to Moses,
> 'Thus shall you speak to the Israelites:
> HE,
> The God of your fathers,
> The God of Abraham, Isaac, and Jacob,
> has sent me to you.
> This is my name forever,
> This my appellation for all eternity.[9]

HE, the I AM WHO I AM, is thus also someone who can be spoken to in person. He is not coincidentally therefore also someone who can once again be perceived and addressed, the YOU addressed by every member of the Jewish people as they become part of the biblical tradition and its transmission over time. In modern culture, of course, any assertion by God, or about God, has become questionable, treated as if an almost idolatrous attempt to represent that which is forbidden any representation whatsoever, an injunction based, moreover, on religious reverence rather than modern doubt (Exodus 20:4–5, Deuteronomy 5:8). And even in this world, the voice retains its power to take emotional hold of and inspire those who hear its call. Mendelssohn's restoration of the Jewish core of the Hebrew Bible, achieved by removing the christological accretions and the Germanic inflections clouding its surface, had already signified the new historical juncture at which German Jewry had arrived. Mendelssohn's translation regained that Jewish core, a process that reached completion only with the German version that Buber and Rosenzweig produced. Let these three different German versions of the third Psalm—a text that permits a range of different translations—stand as evidence of what the Jewish quest for a German Bible achieved. The Buber and Rosenzweig translation of the divine name directs our attention to clues in a biblical original that does not always give us a precise indication of who I, HE, and YOU should be. Mendelssohn's version is as follows:

> Ach Ewiger, wie sind der Feinde so viele!
> So viele, die sich setzen wider mich!
> So viele, die von mir frohlocken:
> 'Für ihn ist keine Hülf' bei Gott!'
> Du aber, Ewiger! bist ein Schild für mich,
> Setzest mich zu Ehren, hebst mein Haupt empor!
> Mit lauter Stimme ruf' ich an den Ewigen;
> Und von seinem heil'gen Berg' erhört er mich.
> Nun lieg' ich ruhig, schlafe,
> Erwache; denn mich hält der Ewige.
> Vor Myriaden Volks ist mir nicht bange,
> Umhergelagert wider mich.—
> Auf, Ewiger! Du rettest mich, mein Gott!
> Das Kinn zerschlägst du meinen Feinden,
> Zerschmetterst der Verruchten Zähne!
> Hülfe findet man
> Bei dem Ewigen.
> Deinen Segen über dein Volk!

The same Psalm is rendered by Samson Raphael Hirsch as follows:

> G o t t, wie viel sind meine Dränger,
> Viele, die wider mich aufstehen, Viele, die von meiner Seele sprechen: Hilfe ist
> für ihn doch nicht bei Gott, dem Richtenden, mehr—!
> Und du bleibst doch G o t t, Schild um mich, ja meine Ehre, und erhebst auch
> jetzt mein Haupt!

Weine ich, so rufe ich zu G o t t, und er hat mich bereits erhört von seines
  Heiligtums Berge—
Ich habe mich niedergelegt,—bin gleich eingeschlafen,—bin erwacht, weil
  G o t t mich stützen will!
Darum fürchte ich nicht vor zehntausenden Volkes, die ringsum sich wider mich
  gestellt.
Erhebe dich G o t t, hilf mir mein G o t t; denn du hast allen meinen Feinden
  den Wangenstreich gegeben, hast der Gesetzlosen Zähne gebrochen.
Doch bei G o t t steht die Hilfe; über dein Volk deinen Segen—.

Buber and Rosenzweig, however, write, or rather speak—in fact, they issue
a call to rejoice in the presence of He who is so vividly present to them,
rejoicing that He—the God of Abraham, Isaac, and Jacob—and his I AM
WHO I AM remain eternally present to their world. Having been addressed by his call, they assume their responsibility in the answer they
provide:

DU,
wie viel sind meine Bedränger geworden!
Viele stehen wider mich auf,
viele sprechen von meiner Seele:
'Keine Befreieung ist dem bei Gott.'
      Empor!
DU aber bist ein Schild um mich her,
meine Ehre und was hochträgt mein Haupt.

Meine Stimme zu IHM—ich rufe,
er antwortet mir von seinen Heiligtumsberg.
      Empor
Ich, hinlegte ich mich und entschlief,—
ich erwachte, denn ER hat mich gehalten.
Vor Volks Mengen fürchte ich mich nicht,
die ansetzen wider mich rings.

Steh auf, DU,
befreie mich, mein Gott!
schlugst ja alle meine Feinde aufs Kinn,
die Zähne der Frevler zerbrachst du.
DEIN ist die Befreiung:
über dein Volk deinen Segen!
      Empor!

YOU, my foes are so many!
Many are those who attack me;
>   many say of me,
>   'there is no deliverance for him through God.'
But YOU are a shield about me,
>   my glory, who holds my head high.

I cry aloud to HIM
>   and he answers me from his holy mountain.
I lie down and sleep and wake again,
>   for He sustains me.
I have no fear of the myriad forces
>   arrayed against me on every side.

Rise, YOU,
Deliver me, O my God!
For you slap all my enemies in the face;
>   You break the teeth of the wicked.
Deliverance is YOURS:
>   Your blessing be upon your people.
Selah.[10]

TWENTY-THREE

Judaism's Message of the Kingdom of God

German Jewry's contribution to modern Judaism's outer development was of momentous import, helping to bring about the founding of the Jewish state and the World Jewish Congress. But the work it accomplished in shaping Judaism's inner renewal was more important still. For while the destruction of Jewish life in Germany may have brought its civilization to an abrupt halt, it also raised their work to a new level of meaning. We will soon survey the incisive significance of that ending, the suffering of its victims, and the deeper significance conveyed by everything that managed to survive this forced conclusion to their world. The accomplishments of German Jewry constitute a rich and exemplary legacy bestowed upon the world's Jewish communities, and the nations of mankind as a whole, displaying the confident certainty of a Jewish cultural renaissance matching the greatest cultural achievements of Jewish antiquity and the Jewish Middle Ages. The era of German Jewry was once again able, like its predecessor, to establish and pursue a wealth of paths that led into the future.

This same sureness of purpose encompassed the spirit of Baeck's *The Essence of Judaism*, when facing up to the challenge of the utter contempt for Judaism expressed by *The Essence of Christianity*, brought Baeck to coin the term "world religion" in response. Judaism had once again been conceived of as active, living agent of history, a world religion that could never show disregard for what were once its "daughters" and were now its "sister religions," if only as a simple matter of self-respect. Baeck's book is permeated with this self-certainty, and it confronts the contemporary world of modernity and its future with confidence as it acknowledges the unchanging demands made by the Jewish past in full, a past that "envisions and awaits its own historical fulfillment only in the universal kingdom of God that contains all men." In his enlarged, second edition produced after the end of the First World War in 1922, Baeck reasserts the core message of his work of 1905, while transmitting Judaism's prophetic message of the kingdom of God anew:

> Of many peoples and communities it has been said that they had too great a past to expect a future. Even if this judgment be applicable to a religion, it can certainly not be legitimately applied to the Jewish religion, because in it arose a constant renewal of the central religious self—quite apart from the great idea of the future as it was propounded by Judaism. . . . Religious universalism is thus a fundamental part of the Jewish religion; it becomes the principle of an historical religious task. Israel is a world religion in that it sees the future of mankind as the goal of its pilgrimage. It could indeed be called the world religion because all religions which made universalism their goal sprang from Judaism . . . in the belief that commands obedience, which sees man as made in the image of God and the good as capable of realization, there resides the certainty both that the good will be achieved and that it has a *future*. . . . Creation stands as guarantor of the future. Man cannot believe in the beginning and doubt the end, not believe in the path without knowing its goal. . . . All moral and religious will is at bottom a form of respect, a belief, and at the same time a certainty in what will be. Whoever has received the commandment has also received its prophecy. The future's meaning is the meaning of life.[1]

This is not the future conceived of in the "pagan" world, with nature's immutable, eternal cycle of return: a new spring after every winter, before things die anew in the fall. Nor is this the "future" of the Greeks, a temporality based on reason, conceived of as a constant temporal movement that is at once pushing forward, changing, and standing still, as if an eternity outside of time, and a departure from temporality itself. Judaism breaks with such notions of cyclical time, seeing every transient moment as progressing toward a goal, the kingdom of God, which stands as both the end toward which history strives and a future goal beyond all historical striving whatsoever. Just as the covenant joined under Moses in the Sinai envisioned a mission that runs counter to all that had existed, this covenant's beginning conceives of both a path and the end toward which it led. That path runs counter to nature, to reason, and athwart all human "development," "progress," and "plans," but at the same time it enjoins humanity to work toward a redemption whose shape has been disclosed, and to rejoice by progressing toward the universal liberation of every living being and the world as a whole. Empty pagan temporality, and the mythological tales of the Greeks pale before history's progressive, all-encompassing responsibility, calling the earth toward its final goal.

How utterly beyond compare and unforgettable this turn to the kingdom of God truly was, a move contrary to both nature and reason! Mankind was enjoined to move forward, despite the repetition of natural cycle, to never turn back, despite the limits of reason reflected in temporality itself. Instead of transcending time, mankind was commanded instead—in the face of all natural obstacles, setbacks, and temporal limitations—to progress toward an ultimate fulfillment. The once and future legatees of the covenant as it was sworn were destined to push onward toward the "conquest of the beyond:" so that everything might elevate itself to the level of the divine image in which it was created.[2] Or in the words of Leo Baeck: "the beyond enters the here and now, eternity comes down to earth in order to point the way to the future, and to become it."

Another book independent of Baeck's that incorporated this conception clarified one of its most important consequences. While the message of the kingdom of God was an ancient one, this book made it clear that this message meant something utterly new in the era of modernity: an upheaval. Hadn't the first generations of the era of Jewish emancipation believed that they had lived to see this biblical promise of the kingdom of God fulfilled on earth? Hadn't Jewish liberals tried to eradicate all mention of the kingdom to come from the liturgy? Hadn't the Zionists hastened to realize the hope of the future kingdom that inspired them on the ground? And hadn't the Orthodox tried to view the "Messiah" as nothing but the outward sign of a redemption that would essentially have already been achieved? In 1921,

Franz Rosenzweig's *The Star of Redemption* reinvested the future with a value distinct from any such contemporary, anticipatory figurations. Rosenzweig's vision represented a striking new insight into the meaning of the future that raised it to the level of a redemptive promise: of the kingdom of God. But Rosenzweig—seized by the message of the kingdom while a student of philosophy—would at the same time deprive himself of some of the essential power of his insight, unable to make a clean break with philosophy and seize the future. Rosenzweig, to be sure, conceived of the promise of the kingdom of God as identical with the message of Judaism, as one of the necessary and constituent elements of Judaism's past and present significance. However, he approached the watchword of the kingdom of God and broke through to its biblical origin via the detour of German idealism. Rosenzweig thereby failed to grant the message of the kingdom the full weight of its productive, contemporary meaning, which its own biblical origin had inspired.

According to Schelling's *Philosophy of Revelation*, modernity stands at the threshold of the kingdom of God's fulfillment as part of the Johannine age of the holy spirit, a period bereft of pope, sermon, priesthood, sacrament, scriptural wisdom, and faith in the letter. Schelling takes his cue from the work of Joachim of Fiore, most likely through Johann August Neander, a convert from Judaism to Christianity and pioneer of ecclesiastical history. According to this conception, the traditional, apostolic succession of father and son sustained by Peter and Paul had been continued in the Roman Catholic and then the German Protestant Church. The new covenant, he argued, arose to fulfill Jeremiah's prophecy, and to create the age when "they shall teach no more every man his neighbour, and every man his brother, saying, Know the LORD: for they shall all know me, from the least of them unto the greatest of them" (Jeremiah 31:34, King James Version).

Joachim—whose possible Jewish origin has long been a subject of speculation—at least granted Judaism the distinction of representing the era of the father, if not the son. Schelling, by contrast, argued that redemptive history proper began only when Christianity came on the scene. Rosenzweig's system absorbed this inaccurate slight to the Jewish tradition without thinking it through, and his thought was never fully able to come to terms with the consequences. Hadn't events beyond the purview of the church, Rosenzweig argued, increased the scope of redemptive history from that point forward? Hadn't migration alone led first to the era of Roman

Catholic predominance, and then to the renaissance as its German Protestant fulfillment? Judaism's reemergence in the era of "Jewish emancipation," he argued, then began to challenge Christianity's previous monopoly on the power of the sacred, a challenge ushering in a whole new "era of John."

And even if a new Johannine epoch had in fact arrived, Rosenzweig knew that the same problem of Christian predominance would present itself in another guise. Multiple Christian denominations, different religions, in fact—with Roman Catholicism, German Protestantism, and the Russian Orthodox among them—offered competing visions of salvation, creating an unprecedented situation. Judaism, Rosenzweig concluded, bore primary responsibility for insisting that this plurality of different messengers of revelation be taken seriously. Its claim to existence as an independent tradition deserving of respect challenged the limits of the Christian framework, he asserted, no matter how wide they might be cast. Judaism's claim to existence, after all, compelled the acknowledgment that revelation has more than one messenger, and thus provided the impetus for a wide-ranging re-evaluation of the Christian position.

But how would Jewish self-certainty face the challenging modern fact that revelation now possessed a multiplicity of authentic messengers? Should Judaism remain faithful to its own mission in their midst, and if so, how? Does Judaism's mission make any sense after the Messiah has supposedly already arrived, as the Christian tradition has it, the redeemer who in any case was and remains the Messiah for all believing Christians? The answer that sounded powerfully forth was yes: Judaism's own message retains an enduring importance, even in the face of a Christianity that may claim a monopoly on religious fulfillment, but in which it plays a co-determining role.

Yes, Judaism's particular religious mission remains a fact, just as its people's enduring faith in that mission remains a fact. The martyrdom of Jewish innocence that took place between 1933 and 1945 has now been recognized as one of the defining events of the modern age, together with the Jewish people's all too obvious endurance as God's "suffering servants." Today, the fact that the particular religious mission of the Jewish people will endure can be doubted only by those as yet unmoved by the Bible's message, or by those who seek to fall away from it. That mission, and the particular faith that is Judaism, continue to assert their meaning and contemporary significance. For those concerned with the Christian Messiah, these events represent the so-called signs—like the "return to Zion" contemporary with the advent of modernity, or the "judgment" that was supposed to precede it. All such signs, however, refer us without exception to the future, where the kingdom of freedom and profound peace waits to be fulfilled. In the interim, confusion has reigned where the notion of the kingdom is concerned. The concept of a redemptive, meaningful history culminating in the kingdom of God as its ultimate goal has been falsely identified with actual historical progress leading *toward* the kingdom of God. Historical progress has been mistaken for historical redemption, when redemptive history remains possibility rather than fact. Jewish and Christian expectations, religious achievements, and disappointments, have already traveled a four-thousand-year road toward the kingdom of God, bringing it closer, but also laying premature and overly particular claims to its design by swamping it in false specifics. The challenge to us that modernity's renewal of the message of the kingdom represents asks us to move beyond such misleading and specific claims. The powerful advances made by nineteenth-century biblical criticism took important steps in this direction. This move forward, initiated by Protestant scholars, was at the time of assistance to Judaism, unable to keep with Spinoza's pathbreaking invention of modern biblical criticism that had emerged in its midst. Marxism's provocative notion of the kingdom of God contributed in its own way to this renewal, and the Christian rediscovery of the message of the kingdom soon began to find expression in the writings of figures as varied as Johannes Weiss, Albert Schweitzer, Johann Christoph Blumhardt, and Leonhard Ragaz.

The visible signs, as it were, that came to define the coming of the kingdom of God, conflating it with the presence of a personal harbinger—the "Messiah"—became predominant at a particular historical moment, it now had to be acknowledged. And other signs and portents regarded as infallible indicators of the coming of the kingdom had already come and gone. Christian scholarship on the Bible's origins marginalized and ignored Judaism's own traditions and insights. Scholars ignored the fact that the founder of Christianity had not dictated Judaism's shape and that the prevalence of Christian norms in European society had not prevented Judaism from leading a vital historical existence of its own. Research into the origins of Islam, and Marxism, whose eschatological visions borrow heavily from the notion of the kingdom of God, without rendering either Christianity or Judaism superfluous, reaffirms rather than questions the necessary mission of these two religions. "Biblical criticism," its "discoveries," as well as research into the origins of Christianity and its "excavations," have all led to the same single, core truth, valid here and everywhere. A truth that, despite all that has been derived from it and takes it as a point of departure for perennial laws, now as ever, still awaits its fulfillment.

That truth is the message of the kingdom of God first envisioned at Judaism's covenantal founding in the desert at Sinai. With it, the world received a message that proclaimed the existence of a future realm of freedom, profound peace, and happiness for all of creation and the universe entire. Biblical prophets from Amos through second Isaiah and on to the Psalms would reinterpret and deepen that vision, connecting the kingdom's hope with the first great disappointment that followed entry to "the promised land." The idea of the kingdom of God does not promise salvation from without, nor does it promise redemption to a "chosen" people while condemning other nations to utter havoc, as has so often been assumed. The kingdom of God is given to us as a task, as something to achieve, and the Jewish people, like all peoples, are to be judged by how close they come to realizing its dream. The suffering that quest demands—a suffering recognized, as well as affirmed, in biblical Jewish texts—permits us to determine the course of our future, and provides the measure by which that future will be judged. The kingdom of God's ultimate fulfillment is yet to come, and every sorrow suffered in service to God draws it a step closer. But the freedom, joy, and profound peace of the kingdom will only be fully realized when every individual shares its bounty in equal measure.

Let us now, however, return to the question with which we began. What does the fact that modernity contains numerous authentic bearers of the message of revelation mean for the self-certainty of the Jewish tradition? Should Judaism remain faithful to its own particular mission in the face of Christianity, and if so, how? And is talk of such a mission at all meaningful, given the existence of Islam, or of Marxist thought?

If Jews survive the indignation and pain inflicted by an endless history of persecution, merciless repression, and shameful humiliation, with one attack following closely on the heels of the next, leaving unhealed wounds in their wake, the fact of the existence of this plurality of movements stands as an enthusiastic legitimation of the Jewish tradition, indeed, one for which

Jews can be grateful. And what an extraordinary event it is, through the "religious division of labor," which for Rosenzweig remained limited to the mission of Judaism and Christianity (its only authentic messengers in his view), the message of the kingdom of God, originating in Judaism, has Catholicism, Protestantism, the Russian Orthodox Church, Islam, and Marxism as well.

"A division of labor is at work in redemptive history": this was the formulation and watchword for this phenomenon I suggested in the original edition of the current work, first published in 1957. The concept remains crucial if we are to understand the deep sense of satisfaction Jews feel, despite the extraordinary events that have carried the message of the kingdom of God throughout the world and multiplied the different groups who have become its messengers. The affirmation of Judaism's message and mission that this dissemination represents permits Jews to bear the bitter wounds that each of these groups have dealt the Jewish people in their turn. And this feeling of satisfaction is not restricted to the Jews alone. It can, should, and will be shared by all who carry the message of revelation, by everyone who, as part of the same biblical inheritance, seeks the same biblical ends—with none claiming any more certainty about their own truth than that its realization will lead to this same goal, which has not yet reached its fulfillment.

In the Middle Ages, truth carried by the other meant vexation. In the modern, dialogical era, the fact that one's neighbor holds a different but equally valid vision of the truth defends against the temptations that arise when one's own message falls short of its realization, and faith in one's own tradition begins to falter. Though we have reached a new juncture in the history of human development, with the earth's reaches fully explored, much work remains to be done, more than we ever believed would be needed to bring redemption to pass. The question is still—posed in a new form—one of how a variety of fundamentally different religious visions, many of them quite new, can find realization in a historical process that leads to the redemption of all. The tasks involved are differentiated and complex, making it impossible for one or even two traditions of religious revelation—whose truths do not, for this reason become any less valid—to fulfill them on their own.

What religious territory then belongs to Judaism, given the tasks it has relinquished to other faiths, or that it no longer performs now that other faiths carry the message of revelation as well? Are there certain tasks, or one in particular, that Judaism and no other tradition can perform, though so many faiths, drawing on the same biblical inheritance, are striving to reach the same goal? Why does the division of labor in redemptive history continue to require this particular people?

Judaism's enduring and particular significance, whose transmission remains the task of the Jewish people, makes them indispensably necessary to all present and future carriers of the message of the kingdom of God, and rests on the tripartite uniqueness of the Jewish role. First, the Jewish people remain our only actual witnesses to the beginnings so fundamental to the idea of the kingdom of God; Judaism thereby stands surety for it—the second unique aspect of its mission—and, as its only surviving guarantor, grounds its historical veracity and proclaims its historical significance. Third, Judaism, and the Jewish people Judaism set forth on their historical journey toward the kingdom of God, and toward it alone. That journey alone gives the world a living proof of the fact that although great strides have been made toward the kingdom, its fulfillment is yet to be achieved, for otherwise, this people would not still be underway.

The universal significance of the message of the kingdom of God the prophets announced from the start is apparent to us now, as modernity's panoply of authentic traditions of revelation passes before our eyes. That universality is just as apparent in the apostates who seek liberation from those very traditions, and in turn fashion ways of affirming that message anew. It is precisely the universality of the message of the kingdom that today requires the persistence of Judaism's particularity, and not for the last time, as it did in the past and will in the future. Because Jewish history alone bears witness to the historical origin of that message, and shows us that its future—of freedom and the profoundest peace—demands historical action if it is to come to pass. Because only a world and redemptive history that is accompanied by the testimony of a living Judaism will never come to an end so as long as the kingdom has not come—until the kingdom will have come!

PART FOUR

TWENTY-FOUR

The End

Modernity's break with the Middle Ages provided the point of departure for our earlier presentation, a break that affected Judaism as well. While Judaism kept pace with the most advanced developments in antiquity and throughout much of the Middle Ages, it was eventually unable to stay in step, a consequence of the hard blows that fate dealt it from without. It was not until Mendelssohn's *Jerusalem, or On Religious Power and Judaism* of 1783, and his German translation of the Five Books of Moses and the Psalms, published that same year, that an important turn occurred, a turn accompanied by the American Revolution of 1775 and its Declaration of Independence a year later, on one hand, and by the French Revolution on the other, whose far-reaching effects began to be felt after 1789.

Three centuries had already been squandered. The catastrophic expulsion of the Jews from Spain made it impossible for Judaism to build on its promising beginnings and enter modernity alongside the West's other leading nations. A full century and a half would elapse between the Inquisition and Spinoza's birth. The Jewish entry into the modern world that took place between 1492 and 1783 was more than jeopardized by a second "Spanish Catastrophe": the Cossacks' pogroms in the East prevented the Jews once again from achieving their modernity as a united people. On the other hand, the Baal Shem Tov's leadership of the Hasidic movement in the age of Mendelssohn would allow profound and powerful modernizing impulses to take hold in Eastern Europe. But their progressive force could not shatter the Jewish ghettoes throughout Poland and Russia, whose external grip and internal bars were far more forceful than in the West. Mendelssohn's achievement at the same time placed him at the forefront of German Jewry. From him, the German Jewish community received its first realistic, self-conscious sense of its own independence. His influence would draw the Jewish people as whole in its wake, and garner him worldwide acclaim. Mendelssohn raised the flag of Jewish emancipation not as a sectarian but a public act, inseparable from the boldest and most progressive movement of his era: the common struggle being waged by a united humanity for the freedom of mankind as a whole.

The crucial and determining role German Jewry came to play in the outer development and inner renewal of modern Jewish life resulted from the fact that German Jews were the first to achieve full civil enfranchisement, and a self-awareness that was no less encompassing. The fact that their achievement took place in a Germany rising to the heights of its European and indeed worldwide prominence also played no small role. After receiving the first volume of Buber and Rosenzweig's German translation of the Bible, Alfred Mombert wrote Buber on February 11, 1926. In complimenting their effort, Mombert singled out a translation, a unusual effort for an important writer to praise as a source of linguistic strength and creativity: "Our ancient, old-new Bible, having endowed the German language with its own sources of strength, is more than justified in expecting a revivification from the German language back in return. The language is mature enough today to be up to the task, as it has not been for a long time. For something of surpassing greatness stands close behind our German language today: German music."

Mombert was responding to a rare and lofty historical moment, when a process of mutual give and take promised to replace what had previously been a one-way street. The decades of Mendelssohn and after had seen

German literature and philosophy as well as German music carried to extraordinary creative heights by a German Jewry entering the modern world. German Jewish accomplishments in German literature, thought, and music kept Germany's world preeminence at a peak when the German cultural elite began to turn its energies elsewhere, to decline, or began to pursue blind alleys that would lead to the abyss. Located at center of a Western Europe that for a few short decades became the pace-setting cultural center of the world, the sum total of Judaism's creative energies joined the arc of that cultural ascent, and more. Spurred on by the opportunities afforded by Germany's ascendance, Jewish achievements soon became a force to be reckoned with in their own right, for the Jewish contribution drew on unique sources for its creative power. The disproportionately high number of Jewish achievers attained well-earned successes, as if making up for the lost time when Jewish creative energies had been dammed up and shut out, until they were finally able to find a full and active expression.

Accelerated by Germany's hour in the intellectual sun, German Jewry used its thousand-year roots in German soil to climb to new heights, growth that had been artificially confined for many long centuries and now exploded into bloom for a few short but especially fruitful decades. German Jews who moved ahead in the post-Mendelssohn era could look to a number of "privileged" or "court Jews" who had blazed the path, and to a widely dispersed, long-established Jewish population in the German villages. They could also turn to an intellectually gifted replacement force longing for opportunities to advance in the "eastern Jews." The Ostjuden, whose communities for the most part had originally migrated from Germany, spoke a Yiddish that preserved the structure of medieval German, and thus made the transition to modern German with quickness and ease.

Some German Jews, insecure about their status in the larger society and whose self-awareness and self-confidence had far to go, would indeed have excluded the "Ostjuden" from Germany. Hermann Cohen, however, took up their cause—to mention but one of the most German of all German Jews—and became a passionate advocate on their behalf in two powerful essays, "Polish Jewry," and "Closing Our Borders." Published during World War I and meant for the same audience as his *Deutschtum und Judentum* (German Culture and Judaism), both pieces stand up for Polish Jewry by characterizing the calamitous consequences of their exclusion:

It is a long life-experience that connects a German like myself, born in Anhalt, with these people from the East. I have honored many of these men as my Talmud teachers, and preserve grateful memories of almost each and every one of them deep in my heart. These men taught me what the qualities of dedicated scholarship, selfless endurance, pure intellectual idealism and morality truly mean. . . . And they unite this intellectual energy with an unflagging sense of religious commitment. . . . There can be no one who has not admired the spiritual distinction of a Polish Jew, which no friend of humanity among us will encounter in any more noble form. I find no kind of anti-Jewish prejudice more deeply disturbing than this, because none affronts pure humanity as deeply as the display that is made of despising these people, the cross-bearers of an accursed hatred of the Jews . . . This I must fight, both as a German and as a Jew.[1]

The confidence acquired by Judaism's inner renewal had once again carried the day, this time expressed in Cohen's conviction that a loyalty uttered in a single breath to the German fatherland, his own Jewish community, and the Jewish people in all its variety was fully consonant with a Jewish path. Cohen had expressed the Jewish certainty that the various roots of Jews and Jewish communities were also German roots, exemplary evidence of a more profound peace and mutual understanding destined to encompass humanity as a whole.

The larger import of Judaism's journey since the time of Mendelssohn was not of course limited to things German. But since the Jewish path to modernity was blazed through Germany, Jewish achievements brought fame and honor both to the Jews and their German homeland. Pride in those accomplishments kindled a strong love of the fatherland in German Jewish hearts. Sinister German feelings toward the Jews, of course, were developing at the same time. German Jews dismissed those attitudes for far too long, refused to take them seriously for even longer, and thus put up with anti-Jewish feelings for an unacceptably long period. Spectators of German Jewish history, or descendants of the German Jews themselves, rush to judgment on this fact. But it is too easy to overlook the fact that annihilation smashed down German Jewish doors at the very moment when German Jewish creativity was at its peak. It was natural for German Jews to feel that snatching a bit more time to secure the harvest of their most mature and valuable achievements was priority number one, before the deadly danger descended in full. In perfect hindsight, critics often find the German Jewish reaction impossible to understand: why did the German Jews fail to mount a unified and consistent opposition across the broadest public front? Even when the German government carried through on its long-threatened ban of all ties between Germans and Jews, its decree met with little more than annoyed indifference from German Jews, who discounted, minimized, and dismissed once more the significance of the act. This dismissal occurred despite the fact that the deadly dangers of the situation had been illuminated, as if by a bolt of lightning, when the boycott of Jewish business was declared on April 1, 1933. Despite the fact that Leo Baeck, president of the Reichsvertretung der deutschen Juden (Reich Association for German Jews) established in its wake, spoke the bitter truth that was incomprehensible before and even during the boycott, but which was now irrefutable fact. "The thousand-year history of Germany's Jews," Baeck declared, "has come to an end."

At an end: that common history already finished on April 1, 1933, because the fundamental basis of the German Jewish relationship had been destroyed. Baeck explained this break twelve years later upon his welcome in New York on December 4, 1945, after the martyrdom of Jewish innocence had become fact: "An historical epoch has come to a close for us as the Jews of Germany. Such an era comes to a close when the fundamental hope, belief, and trust on which a relationship rests must finally be consigned to its grave. Our belief was that the German and the Jewish spirit could meet on the same ground, and that their union would prove to be a blessing. This hope was an illusion—and the era of Jews in Germany has ended forevermore."[2]

The German Jewish history that had already come to an "end" in 1933 nevertheless continued to move forward until 1943, under the passionate leadership of no less a figure than Leo Baeck himself. Life went on despite the monstrous institution of the Nuremburg Laws of September 15, 1935, which effectively deprived German Jews of their citizenship, went on in the face of everything that had already taken place between April 1, 1933, and the entry of this "legislation" into force! Life would continue to go on despite the yawning abyss that opened on the night of November 9–10, 1939, descending in its ultimate form and unmasking the violence that was to come. The unimaginable but nonetheless quite calculated and actual unleashing of a murderous pogrom on German soil in the midst of the twentieth century had occurred, carefully planned and executed by culprits put up to the task. And the deed was neither contradicted nor opposed by the general populace as they carried out the frenzied and sacrilegious torching of every synagogue in Germany. In the face of this, Jewish life carried on, despite the mandatory elimination of the category of "German Jew" enjoined by the tenth clause of the Citizenship Statute, requiring the name of the Reich Association of German Jews to be changed to the Reich Association for Jews in Germany.

Jewish life went on in spite of everything. Indeed, the Jews did much more than that. They carried on in Germany and on behalf of Germany, struggled and succeeded in intensifying their efforts, went forward with creativity and inspiration surpassing all that had gone before in both breadth and depth. Stalwart in their vision, German Jewry continued to take pleasure in their existence as Jews. Schools, universities, houses of study, clubs, presses, newspapers, magazines, and theaters all flourished, either as continuations of older institutions or innovative new ones, realizations of the Jewish spirit that were exemplary in their own time and remain models for us today. No blow was fateful or dispiriting enough to bring social welfare efforts to an end, work that had once been largely devoted to assisting Jewish communities abroad. Every dark and precipitous turn for the worse was met with an unflinching effort in response. But April 1, 1933, and September 15, 1935, were followed by the night of November 9–10, 1938, and July 4, 1939, only to be succeeded by the night of February 12–13, 1940, when in Stettin, the first deportation to an unspeakably horrible death was announced one hour and carried out as a crime just as quickly the next. Thousands of Jewish men, women, and children and the residents of Jewish old-age homes were suddenly devoured.

Not a single inch of territory was willingly ceded. To the very end, the vast power of the German state constantly hobbled and hindered the organized Jewish efforts mounted in response, and finally did away with them entirely. The Berlin police closed the last offices of the Reich Association for Jews in Germany on July 10, 1943, two hundred years after Moses Mendelssohn's arrival in Berlin. The closing took place 160 years after the turning point of 1783 that Mendelssohn accomplished, just a few short months after the deportation of German Jewry's leading men and women, Leo Baeck among them, who had worked indefatigably to the very end.

What is the ultimate significance of this ending? And another question we shall return to later: to what extent should this ending be considered a final closing of the books? Should the greatness German Jewry displayed in this final chapter be understood as something closer to guilt, despite the clear-eyed recognition of the end, in whose wake stretched the long decade from 1933 to 1943? Do such considerations cast a pall on their otherwise shining accomplishments? Or does the brilliant light cast by German Jewry shine all the brighter as such apparent, or actual shadows begin to draw nigh?

The decision to carry on with Jewish life was not, to be sure, a carefully mounted decoy plan mounted on a grand scale by the German Jews to effect their escape. Their intent was clearly not to conduct a massive Jewish emigration behind a carefully constructed camouflage screen of normalcy. Recognizing this fact, we can still say that although emigration was not the hidden plan that justified a compliant stance toward the authorities, it was still an active program of its own that saved more than half of all German Jews, as a more detailed account will shortly show. What was at stake was nothing less than the inner development of modern Jewry, powerfully and creatively initiated at the turn of the century. In attempting to preserve the fruits of that development, German Jewry was granted a tranquil dignity and intrinsic satisfaction. And today's beneficiaries of that achievement, now taken for granted, have no conception of what was involved.

It still remains the case that German Jews were unacceptably submissive, staying put too long in order to ripen and reap the bounty of the hard-won progress their labors had produced. In accepting the abrogation of their equality under the law, they consented to the abolition of basic human rights that all men must protect and defend. Though ignored at the time, this point was made clear in H. G. Adler's 1955 book on Theresienstadt, a priceless historical document even more significant as a self-aware voice of Jewish self-critique. But this is only half the picture. Wasn't the whole world deceived about the nature of the terrifying threat emanating from Nazi Germany as well? Weren't the Jews of other nations also misled about Germany's ultimate intentions, until any chance to emigrate had long passed? Weren't other Jews forced into ghettoization, when the policy was extended to them, just as it had been imposed on German Jews in 1933? Hadn't these Jews also accepted the ghetto because it seemed to offer the chance to go on with their lives, when the imposition of the ghetto was to bring nothing but death?

Any desire to reflect upon the apparent blindness, thoughtlessness, and partial guilt German Jewry bears for its own destruction, will in the end stir more compassion than indignation in those who consider the meaning of "the legacy of German Jewry." Can anyone who lived through these events be wise enough, righteous or guiltless enough, to sit in judgment over what occurred? In this case more than almost any other, sins of omission and neglect were the shadow side of human gifts that had, until that point, expressed themselves as virtue and virtuosity, and in the German Jewish talent for rectitude and efficiency. Creative artists, fervently absorbed in their work, disdainfully disregarded every signal and warning sign that the ground beneath their feet was about to collapse. Support for the fatherland, and finally gratitude for the solidarity they had once shared with their fellow citizens, furthered this pattern of denial. The result was their absolutely unsuspecting attitude toward the abyss to come, an attitude supported, unfortunately, by what had been common norms of morality, truth, beauty, and justice.

Then there was their loyalty, which they expressed to the bitter end. The same loyalty German Jews had shown their own as well as other Jewish communities now refused to abandon the Germans, despite Nazi warnings and eventually the Nazi decree abrogating all ties between the two peoples forever. None of these ties could be "disproved" by the Nazis, or annulled as anti-Jewish accusations were transformed into outrageous criminal offenses by groundless and arbitrary acts of will. And the German Jews themselves—during that final decade, when their history had already "come to an end"—showed us just how much devotion, energy, and loyalty they invested in establishing their deep connection to German culture. What was actually being carried to its grave here, as Leo Baeck wrote, was hope, belief, and trust. Hence the long delay that elapsed before German Jewry could look the truth squarely in the eye.

In the end, this delay in facing the truth was not unreasonable given the circumstances. The facts must be recalled to general awareness again and again. German Jewry had sparked the inner renewal of modern Judaism: the impulse to hold fast to those achievements and preserve them as a kind of irreplaceable seed stock was a wholly understandable one. Given the varied levels of development that other Jewish communities in varied states and regions had then attained, no direct or immediate transplantation was possible. Every delay that helped assemble that material thus seemed more important than life itself, for the legacy of German Jewry pointed to a path that led beyond.

Could anyone have predicted that the unimaginably shameful persecution then underway and its regime would last ten, and finally twelve years, enough time to bring actual annihilation to pass? While threatening to envelop more than just the German Jews in its destruction, the criminals took them first, as the most vulnerable and exposed victims. Wasn't it possible that the murderous reign of terror would last a few short months, or years? Didn't the rest of the world have eyes in its head, with intelligence sources in Germany and without, and more crucially, weren't they armed—which the German Jews of course were not? And what about the Christian response, and what of the "good Germans?" To accuse those who persisted in their work of passivity, despite the world's resignation in the face of this threat, is almost always a way of evading self-scrutiny about our own degree of responsibility, a situation shared by all present and future citizens of the earth, when they face up to what man is capable of, and what he has done to his fellow man in the modern world.

One example selected from many will represent the kind of dignity and authentic grandeur German Jewry displayed as it bore up throughout the decade of 1933–43, its progressive spirit serving as a beacon for the future as it had before. The German Jews' response was always creative, never accepting their fate for a single instant, though much simply had to be taken in stride. New attacks that seemed to spell the "end" for the German Jews were never accepted as final; and whatever could not be fended off was transformed internally, when nothing could prevent new restrictions from being imposed—indeed, was transformed by the act of acceptance itself:

> I offered my back to the floggers,
> And my cheeks to those who tore out my hair.
> I did not hide my face
> From insult and spittle. (Isaiah 50:6)

It was Jewish New Year. The order had come down that the word "fatherland" had to be stricken from the synagogue service. Ellen Littmann, who was there when Leo Baeck stepped up to the pulpit, tried to hold her nervous anticipation in check. What was the right thing to do when uttering the New Year's blessings? Should the decree be flouted or obeyed? Should the prayer asking for God's intercession on behalf of the nation be omitted, an act that would cede ground to the enemy? Or should they stand fast? What was the proper course to take, now that their own fatherland had blocked their path?

The path continued for those who, under Leo Baeck's guidance, found a replacement for the fatherland taken from German Jews. They constructed a bridge leading them beyond Germany, and back to it in a deeper sense. Baeck replaced "fatherland" in the New Year's prayer with a new term, directing his words to a new addressee: to all men of good will.

TWENTY-FIVE

Sorrow

Between the end that descended upon German Jewry and the beginning of the long process of picking up the pieces and going on, undertaken by everyone who managed to escape, what I have called the martyrdom of Jewish innocence took place, true sorrow.[1]

For even if the inner renewal and outer development of German and modern Jewry could somehow be erased or forced to a premature close by the surrounding world—as in Germany, and in the threat that some Jewish communities still face today—the martyrdom of Jewish innocence could never be annulled. Those marched to their deaths ultimately triumphed over the end forced upon them, just like "Jacob, My servant, / Israel whom I have chosen!" (Isaiah 44:1). Words can be killed, deeds can always be outdone, and almost anything can be forgotten, but the dead of the biblical succession can never be ignored. For however little those surviving may wish to remember them, the dead remain firmly ensconced in their unconscious.

First, however, the fact that the biblical servant of God, in the image of Israel and the Jewish people, had once again become a contemporary reality, had to be recognized, though it still lacks wider acknowledgment:

He was despised, shunned by men,
A man of suffering, familiar with disease.
As one who hid his face from us,
He was despised, we held him of no account.
Yet it was our sickness he was bearing,
Our suffering that he endured.
We accounted him plagued,
Smitten and afflicted by God. (Isaiah 53:3–5)

Such recognition is an urgent task for all future Jewish generations, and for humanity as well. German Jewry's first step toward this milestone in its own inner development occurred when its own Jewish fate was reinterpreted as a version of the story of Job: when Margarete Susman in Zurich and Karl Wolfskehl in New Zealand established the deep connection between biblical truth and the contemporary reality they faced as German Jews.

We've all heard the objections to the idea of a special Jewish martyrdom countless times: haven't other nations mourned their own countless dead? Aren't the deaths of whole peoples still waiting to be properly mourned? Don't the millions of other dead of the Second World War top the figure of six million Jews? And haven't even worse, if not similar, things taken place since the beginning of recorded history?

The answer must be a resounding no: just as there are no martyrs outside the biblical succession, martyrdom in the proper Jewish and Catholic meaning of the term that begins with the Maccabean uprising, the first martyrs who died for their beliefs, setting a new measure for a martyrdom that in deed and truth signified their ultimate victory, and just as there are no "suffering servants of God" beyond the biblical message, other than as messengers of God, in which God's servant carries that message by suffering a "representative sorrow," as in the first Babylonian exile, so there has been no death like that of modernity's "martyrdom of Jewish innocence."

This is not to scant the significance of the Second World War's other victims, the dead of previous wars, or those who died in the bloody and fratricidal struggles that have so often marred the calm of otherwise peaceful eras. Their losses are no less precious than the Jewish dead. We intend no slight whatsoever toward any of this endless host of innocent victims, no disregard toward those who suffered as bitterly as any Jew. Our aim is simply to answer in the name of the one to two million Jewish children under fourteen who perished, and for the millions of women and the aged whose innocence was immediately and obviously apparent to the enemy, though the men murdered alongside them were just as innocent because they were killed simply for being Jews. Memory in this case means answering in the name of those killed for simply being Jews. The Jewish people itself must stand up for the suffering of these Jewish victims—and for their death—in the manner of the message its people carries, just as the victims themselves met their martyrdom with its message in hand.

"The rampart heaped with millions of innocent murder victims," as Margarete Susman wrote in her groundbreaking interpretation of *Job*, "has created a bond of fate infinitely stronger and much harder to shatter than any denominational creed."[2] Rather than confront its force, Jews may try to escape from their dead and from their people's continuing mission, tempted from without or led astray by their own devices. But the rampart covered with millions of innocent victims of murder is a new burden in their destiny. A bond infinitely stronger and harder to shatter than any denominational creed "unites this people with a fearful sense of the common destiny they share. From its radical dispersedness, a new inner unity is being established in a manner unknown to previous generations, who had ceased to grasp such unity as their task: a unity that leads this haunted people home to itself, regardless of the changes it might undergo."[3]

"Can any Jewish person," Susman writes, "think it was a coincidence to be born a Jew at this hour, to find himself confronting a Jewish destiny? Hasn't God made use of Satan to tell the Jewish individual what is expected of him? A people heeding the natural drive for self-preservation would certainly have crumbled given the momentum generated by Satan's attack. The power to combat this temptation to have done with Jewish existence can spring only from the deepest source of its origin, nourishing the people as a whole and allowing them to stand against nature's course. That kind of energy can only have come from the clear conviction"—first expressed in the Book of Job in pathbreaking manner—"that self-dissolution would represent the consummate affirmation of Satan's power, and a failure to appreciate the hand hidden behind him . . . the source of the Jewish people's refusal to surrender rests on a secret that has well nigh become unspeakable:

that the dark destiny God has imposed on his people is nothing other than the burden and pledge of his love." Even Jesus, the Christian Christ, Susman declares, "were he to encounter a Jew of today, and appreciate the deep difficulty this decisive experience involves: Jesus himself would not direct the Jew toward the light emanating from the open door of the Church, but toward the darkness, where his people were bleeding from a thousand wounds."[4]

A similar affirmation of the same truth can be found in the sentiment expressed by a representative of Russian Jewry, a branch of the Jewish people separated from the Jewish people as a whole for decades. Ilya Ehrenburg made that declaration at his seventieth birthday celebration held in Moscow in early 1961, recalling the unforgettable plea for help entitled "We Polish Jews," which the poet Julian Tuvim had transmitted in 1944. "The blood coursing through our veins," Ehrenberg said of Tuvin, "and the blood we bleed, not 'Jewish blood,' but the blood of Jews shed in gushing rivers and broad streams, makes me feel as if I had been baptized in this new Jordan, confirmed in the bond of deepest brotherhood sealed by the blood of Jewish martyrs."

But once the biblical Job was grasped as the paradigm for the travails suffered and witnessed from 1933 to 1945, the paralyzing sting of the end that crashed down—eliminating the Jews of Germany, along with the majority of Europe's other Jewish communities—had been removed. Other ages had expressed an intimate affinity for figures such as Abraham, Moses, or David, and in his middle and later years, Karl Wolfskehl voiced the deep affinity he felt for Saul. "I have forever felt an uncanny, special affinity for this most singular figure in the whole of our ancient history," he confesses in a letter of 1939.[5] But another letter of the same year already interprets things differently: "I feel more and more that the figure of Job and his suffering are the most authentic representations of the Jewish destiny."[6] Wolfskehl expressed similar sentiments in 1944 when referring to the new work he had begun in New Zealand; the all but finished book would "stand under the sign of Job," he remarked.[7] As Wolfskehl put it in 1946, "Otherwise I receive all kinds of things from Switzerland that closely concerns me, including a book that runs remarkably parallel to my own experience by Margarete Susman, a friend of old."[8]

The book that "ran remarkably parallel" to Wolfskehl's own experience was published in Zurich in 1946 as Susman's *The Book of Job and the Fate of the Jewish People*. Wolfskehl's poetic work did not appear until 1950 as *Job, or the Four Mirrors*. Just as the Book of Job gave Susman a framework for reflecting on Jewish history over the ages, including its beginnings, the question of Jewish "guilt" and persecution and Zionism as well, so Wolfskehl's *Four Mirrors* adds up to something more than another piece of biblical exegesis. Wolfskehl's Job becomes the figure for Judaism's suffering, message, and mission. Representing the full historic sweep of Judaism itself, Job embodies its existence as Israel, the Samson in its character, as well as Judaism's prophetic stance. All this, and tidings of the kingdom of God, find expression in the messianic figure of Job:

> You, the Call, hark! This concerns you, you whom he strikes:
> Are you not the seal, are you not the founder?
> From the start and forever after, are you not one?
> Each one a not-I, each one part of your being, Yours,
> Each one: a thread of the halyard. One: as warp and woof,
> All mere droplets of wine at God's banquet.
> And Abram, isn't that you crossing the Euphrates?
> And you, Moses, aren't you broadcasting the Torah's seed?
> And David, is that you drawing nigh to your kingly deed?
> Or the Gaon, mediating the council with a voice that is clear?
> Aren't you the Baal Shem Tov dancing to bring the Shekhinah near?
> Always Job, received into the lap of need that is dire,
> Always Job, chosen to squat in the mire,
> Always Job, circled by the flame of the voice![9]

Always the same Job, recalling the hallowed beginning, "when God watched over me, / When His lamp shone over my head, / When I walked in the dark by its light. / When I was in my prime, / When God's company graced my tent / When the mighty one was still with me" (Job 29:2–4). This salutary understanding shapes the beginning of Judaism just as much as Abraham's setting forth for the future as he crossed the Euphrates, toward the desert and the covenant to be joined at Sinai. In the words of the prophet Hosea, "I fell in love with Israel / When he was still a child; / And I have called [him] My son / Ever since Egypt" (11:1). But disappointment soon ensued, bringing blow after sorrowful blow—only the beginning of bitter blows yet to come—until the core beliefs anchoring Jewish existence were besieged. A suffering Judaism was led into temptation wherever it turned, whether seduced into seeing a false significance in its suffering or tempted to take the wrong way out. This was Job's dilemma, as expressed in the jeer of his wife: "His wife said to him, 'You still keep your integrity! Blaspheme God and die!'" (Job 2:9). Job, however, who had already pronounced his immortal words after the first fateful blow—"the LORD has given, and the LORD has taken away; blessed be the name of the LORD" (1:21)—still gives her the following answer: "You talk as any shameless woman might talk! Should we accept only good from God and not accept evil?" (2:10).

Job righteously asserts the human need for acceptance and for devotion. But his advice is soon trumped by the all too human quest for the ultimate cause, or the various causes, of suffering. The possibility that Satan might be the origin of all sorrow—the "hinderer," in Buber's translation—at first seems to promise a deeper explanation. With Satan in charge, suffering no longer seems arbitrary. But in a deeper sense, Satan is simply a distraction from the depths of suffering that are to be measured. More instructive than the fact that Job and the Jewish tradition grant the Satanic explanation a provisional validity is the fact that both give "the hinderer" only a fleeting attention at best. Goethe's Faust struggles to the bitter end with the devil, who gets the better of him. But the messianic Job-Israel-Samson-prophet figure does not struggle with Satan, to whom he never surrenders for even one instant, but with Him who, according to the Jewish tradition, rules all without exception, even Satan. For if such a figure does exist, he is one of the "sons of God," as the text emphasizes (1:6, 2:1). But whether "hinderer" exists or not, the stipulated limit with regard to actual power and ultimate vacuity from the start is that he is powerless to take Job's life as such, though everything else that belongs to Job is placed in Satan's hands (2:6).

At this point Job's three so-called friends enter the picture, and the surrounding political and social world begins to pry—from the Jewish people's Jobian perspective—into the inner struggle of the suffering servant. In the end, their meddling will be judged severely, though this aspect of Job's story has rarely been noticed, and given even less serious attention by Judaism's postbiblical neighbors up until and including our own day. Yet the unsurpassed insight the Book of Job offers us into Job's friends emerges with piercing clarity from the story's denouement. Satan and Job's fourth "friend" reap the harvest of disregard they have so richly earned and are simply ignored. Other companions, meanwhile, are dispensed with differently: "The LORD said to Elifaz the Temanite, I am incensed at you and your two friends, for you have not spoken the truth about Me as did My servant Job" (42:7). Everything these "friends" suggested about the sufferer and his sorrow was wrong. All their would-be advice on the way to achieving salvation was false, and everything the sufferer, as Job and Judaism as a whole, observed about the surrounding world rang true. In the end, the question of whether God will unleash his wrath and punish these "friends" is therefore left wholly to Job's discretion, and intercession: "Go to My servant Job . . . and let Job, My servant, pray for you; for to him I will show favor and not treat you vilely, since you have not spoken the truth about Me as did My servant Job" (42:8).

Job's three friends, however, are not brought into play for nothing: despite their errors—or rather precisely on account of those errors and the challenge they provide—these false supporters motivate a crucial step forward in the tale. For the unimpeachable "righteousness" that allows Job to bear up under his initial temptations, and the excuse that Satan is the cause of his suffering—the Book of Job's fallback position—do not offer answers that will stand the test of time. "Think now," Elifaz the Temanite declares at the beginning of his first speech, "what innocent man ever perished? / Where have the upright been destroyed? As I have seen, those who plow evil / And sow mischief reap them" (4:7–8). Neither virtuous acquiescence to suffering nor the idea that some external cause thwarts our well-being and happiness adequately explain the magnitude of what is at stake, for "Evil does not grow out of the soil, / Nor does mischief spring from the ground; / For man is born to [do] mischief, / Just as sparks fly upward" (5:6–7). Suffering calls for responsibility, and one that puts humanity squarely in charge. To rely on endurance alone, or to assume some deeper and unknown "reason" for our suffering, and thus to go on ascribing our guilt to superhuman powers simply will not do. But to take this insight into human responsibility—a notion deepened throughout Job's confrontation with his friends—to mean that wherever we find suffering, its cause is human guilt and, moreover, a guilt belonging to the sufferer alone, fails once more to grasp the truth that has almost become obvious at this point in Job's travails.

Bystanders have always tried to blame the victims for their sufferings. Vile self-righteousness tries to slough off responsibility and the obligation of compassion with accusations that try the victim instead. This trap has often been laid for the Jewish people, and Jews have been forced to bear it to an astonishing degree. Some have even internalized the charge, whether they have already entered sorrow's straits or are about to, regardless of whether suffering has cut them down with its punishing blows. The only explanation for such persistent and frightful persecution must be that the Jews must have brought it on themselves—or so this line of thought goes. The only way to put an end to this suffering is for the sufferer to confess his culpability and agree to change his ways. Simply stop being a Jew, and become a Christian, a Muslim, or a Marxist instead: the world has always exonerated itself by offering this kind of "solace" as "friendly advice," washing its hands of guilt after the fashion of Pilate (Matthew 27:24). Remain Jews, and you'll have no one to blame but yourselves when you've been crushed.

But the advice of Job's friends, notwithstanding its injustice in other respects, still points us toward a crucial insight. Job's suffering and his ability to endure it all, going on despite every kind of misery and threat, are intimately bound up with his specific character, the Jewish individual Job truly is. The question, of course, is whether such Jobian, or Jewish "guilt" offers an adequate explanation for his sorrows: does this really explain the responsibilities of victim and bystander in full? And don't we face the same ethical incongruity that seems so inescapable when all is said and done: the yawning chasm between Job's individual guilt and the amount of suffering he is called on to bear? Even if Job, or Judaism were somehow guilty, and thus responsible for the sorrow afflicting them, why have others far more guilty not been forced to suffer at all? When will they have to harvest the accumulated malice they planted and produced themselves? "Why do the wicked live on, / Prosper and grow wealthy? / . . . Their homes are secure, without fear; / They do not feel the rod of God. / . . . They spend their days in happiness / . . . They say to God, 'Leave us alone, / We do not want to learn your ways'" (21:7 ff.)

Job is even willing to confess his guilt, since "Man cannot win a suit against God" (9:2), or, as Elifaz the Temanite puts it, "What is man that he can be cleared of guilt, / One born of woman, that he be in the right? (15:14). But what can this or any conceivable admission of guilt made under such circumstances really mean? Job has been subjected to every terror, stripped of children, home, fortune, and reputation, and given "friends" who make an already unbearable situation worse by blaming Job for the suffering he has been forced to bear. Those friends even blame him for the pain his neighbors have had to endure. The massive suffering that rains down and teaches those in ever wider circles beyond him does not originate in any guilt of Job. Having been tested by everything sorrow can throw against him, Job cannot cease proclaiming his innocence, protesting against those "friends" who seek the guilt that must have earned him the depths of his sorrows: "Far be it from me to say you are right; / Until I die I will maintain my integrity. / I persist in my righteousness and will not yield; / I shall be free of reproach as long as I live" (27:5–6).

Instead, Job presses forward, leaving behind all his friends and bystanders. Their search for the meaning of suffering remains fixated on the sufferer himself. They disdain any question or comment pointing to their own responsibility for suffering by shifting it onto the victim, while latching on to the sufferer in their fixation ever more tightly. Through it all, Job presses closer to Him, in whose "hand is every living soul / And the breath of all mankind. / With him are wisdom and courage; / His are counsel and understanding" (12:10,13,16), and manages to counter with the following reproach:

> How many are my iniquities and sins?
> Advise me of my transgression and sin.
> Why do You hide Your face,
> And treat me like an enemy . . . ?
> Let me know what you charge me with,
> That You seek out my iniquity
> And search out my sin?
> You know that I am not guilty . . . (13:23–4,10:2,6,7)

The question of the meaning of suffering has never been stated more crassly, for nobody's sorrows are greater than the sorrows of an innocent man. Job's answer retains an unsurpassed significance for modernity and our understanding of its "martyrdom of Jewish innocence." But before the Book of Job divulges it—with an ending that unveils a new perspective that gives the story a crucially different twist—the same answer is presented in a distorted fashion. By presenting that answer in an absolutely false manner, the Book of Job first warns us against anyone who tries to make use of it in a similarly facile way. Elihu, a member of the tribe of Ram, cannot prevent himself from sticking his nose where it doesn't belong, and delivers a long and bombastic oration. Everyone is forced to listen, to be sure, though no one really hears. The speech is never mentioned again and is destined for oblivion, like the superfluous Satan himself. "See, God is beyond reach in His power," Elihu declares, "Who governs like Him? "God," Elihu says, "is greater than any man," and even possibly greater than his creation (33:12) / Who ever reproached Him for His conduct?" (36:22–23). Such vacant verbiage, like all empty theological pronouncements, sounded the same in Job's day as they do in our own. There's always some theologian at hand ready to cite "the word of God" accurately, but who gives us nothing but his own limited human perspective, and like much of the counsel he receives, Job has the good sense to reject it: "But I, like you, have a mind, / And am not less than you" (12:3). Words no longer provide sufficient answer. The hour of revelation is at hand.

"Job receives no answer," writes Margarete Susman, "to the questions he has posed at the very brink of his ability to endure," never receives the kind of substantial response a man of his intellectual caliber should command. "Something else befalls him: a truth that seems incomprehensible suddenly envelops him within its gigantic wave, answerless."[10] Job suddenly discovers himself face-to-face with HIM, the God in whom he had never ceased believing, and confronts him in the most literal, immediate, vital way imaginable. The face to face encounter with God Job had almost given up hoping for is suddenly granted him, long after his friends had already given up trying to convince him that the only way someone like him—a suffering man, endlessly protesting his innocence—could meet God face to face was to break down and confess his guilt. The biblical "I AM THAT I AM" instead "suddenly envelops him like a gigantic wave." Rather than give Job an answer, God places Job himself on the spot, interrogating the man who sought to place HIM in question, until Job goes dumb: "See, I am of small worth; what can I answer You? / I clap my hand to my mouth. / I have spoken once, and will not reply; / Twice, and will do so no more" (40:4–5). But the "answer" to be found in the answerless, overwhelming, and omniscient revelation gripping Job does not offer itself to be understood in this fashion. Job must set forth, as Judaism has been setting forth ever since the time of Abraham, and answer to HIM. "And Job said in reply to the LORD,

> I had heard You with my ears,
> But now I see You with my eyes.
> Therefore, I recant and relent,
> Being but dust and ashes. (42:5–6)

What is Job repudiating here, and what does he now repent? That he reached the brink of despair only because the faith that so obviously gave him the strength to endure his suffering trials was his through hearsay alone. Job's single weakness—indeed his only errant moments during his innocent travails—occurred at that brink of despair: "But now I see You with my eyes." And while Job behaved righteously while suffering his trials, he would have been more righteous still had he endured them less unerringly than he did. Just as it is never justifiable to hurt others, so it is never justifiable to flee our responsibility in the face of suffering by refusing to combat it to the greatest extent possible, whether by alleviating or ameliorating its sorrow. Suffering is always an evil, an affliction. But to be afflicted is not an expression of evil, but its result. The sufferer who endures without losing faith—who withstands, in other words, all the miseries and threats that could lead him astray—makes it clear to the rest of us in exemplary fashion that good can indeed triumph, and that an all-encompassing and redemptive meaning stands behind life as well as death. Provided, of course, that one stipulation has been fulfilled: that the man of sorrow has neither sought nor desired his trials, nor succumbed to them, without a fight, out of weakness. For suffering is never a necessary evil, never a fate that simply has to be.

Then and only then can one subjected to suffering rise above it in steadfast endurance—when his resistance cannot forestall his suffering—whose endurance confirms the revelatory truth previously known through hearsay alone: "But now I see You with my eyes." The Book of Job does not identify with dust and ashes—Job condemns himself to these only in hindsight—but with the project of overcoming their humiliating power: "My Lord GOD will wipe the tears away / From all faces / And will put an end to the reproach of His people / Over all the earth" (Isaiah 25:8). This prophetic vision of Isaiah, later taken up by John (Revelations 7:17, 21:4) informs the Book of Job as well. The promise that all sorrows will be healed, the man who remained steadfast in suffering, his neighbors, and all mankind will be redeemed and brought to the kingdom of God, also finds moving expression in Wolfskehl's final Jobian reflections. Entitled "Messianic Job," the poem includes the Hebrew prayer "*Baruch-hu*" ("Praised be He"), the equivalent German expression, "*Gelobt sei Er*," and the "Shema," the watchword of the Jewish faith: "*Shema Yisrael*" ("Hear O Israel, the Lord Our God, the Lord is One").

> Rising from all, the Yes of the One Hallelu.
> Joining the spheres as one in the Baruch-Hu.
> Heaven and Earth unite in the Shema,

As it was in the beginning, forever on.
You're there too: Yes, it is you.
For now you are He, and He is you.
You, Job, You: the Messiah . . .[10]

The Book of Job proclaims this prophecy as its conclusion: "The LORD restored Job's fortunes when he prayed on behalf of his friends." These "friends," spared damnation through Job's intercession alone—which precedes the redemption about to ensue—are included in its new dispensation. The cleansing of the humiliation still clinging to Job follows soon after: "Thus the LORD blessed the latter years of Job's life more than the former" (42:10). The Book of Job will give us a precise catalog of Job's new fortune in the end, detailing the number of sheep, camels, cattle, and asses he receives. We learn of the seven new sons borne him and the three beauteous daughters with which he is once again blessed. But none of this signifies a fall, or any backsliding into a new obsession with the empty things of this world: "The first he named Jemima [Dove], the second Keziah [Cinnamon], and the third Keren-happuch [Horn of eye-shadow]. Nowhere in the land were women as beautiful as Job's daughters to be found" (42:14–15). The same hard and brutal "dust of the earth" where Job suffered, and where modernity's martyrdom of Jewish innocence was led to its death, becomes the setting where every tear—finally—is wiped away. Here, on the brutal dust of the earth, those victims blamed by those ultimately more guilty for the very suffering they endured will have their humiliation wiped away as well. The Book of Job ends in fitting fashion by invoking "a new heaven and a new earth." Following out the allusion to Isaiah (65:17), Job's final verses invoke a new world, to be created beneath the firmament of the earth on which we live, where those who have suffered in innocence will not have suffered in vain.

TWENTY-SIX

Continuity

After the end that descended on German Jewry, and after the guiltless suffering of its victims—after Auschwitz, an "event of world-historic significance," dwarfing "all that had gone before, defining the boundary between the present and a bygone era"—those elements of German Jewry that managed to survive deserve a full accounting.[1] But how can Auschwitz be the defining break marking the end, if such a continuing Jewish presence in fact exists? To put the question somewhat differently: what does it mean—if anything at all—that some carry on after the end that, in all its brute facticity, has come crashing down?

Three modes of continuity can be discerned after the respective turning points of 1933, 1943, and 1945. These ways of carrying on with Jewish life in Germany need to be carefully distinguished from what has in fact come to an end. What has been concluded is German Jewry's existence as a vibrant part of the German population, rooted in the fatherland for millennia: a community sharing equally in the common future and destiny of the

German state. The history of German Jewry has continued, but beyond the borders of Germany itself, and through what the children of Germany's Jews have been able to salvage on their own. In the meantime, Jewish life in their old German homeland has been carried on in a different, no less impressive manner by a new group: the Jews of Germany. Nor has the inheritance of German Jewry—as an independent phenomenon—been cast aside. A third and incomparably powerful, future-oriented expression of German Jewish continuity is represented by the legacy of German Jewry itself. Its creative spiritual force transcends both its creators and those who follow in its footsteps, calling upon Jews and indeed men and women everywhere to take up its work. The legacy of German Jewry discloses the substance of their future in all its essential dimensions, and offers them a source of mutual assurance and support.

We will shortly give a brief history of the German Jews after the war, though most of them turned away from the legacy they produced. We will also give a detailed appraisal of the situation of the Jews in Germany today. Their new life cannot divest itself of the legacy of German Jewry, whether they assume the role of successor consciously or implicitly, or whether they carry on joy or sorrow. But it is first incumbent upon us to recall the staunch and loyal persistence German Jews displayed before German Jewry as an entity had been struck down. Numbers, as we know, never tell the whole story. Statistics never give material strength and human numbers the decisive edge in human affairs. Heart, soul, and spirit do. That truth has never been exemplified in a more inspiring and vivid fashion than it was in the case of the German Jews.

At the start of the 1930s, Jews comprised a little less than 1 percent of the German population. This number had been slightly higher in the preceding era, but had been on the decline in percentage terms as the rate of increase in the population as a whole grew at a far greater rate. The Jewish community originally distributed throughout the country had, of course, concentrated itself in regional pockets. But the Jewish population of Berlin—after Warsaw, Lodz, Budapest, and Vienna, the fifth-largest Jewish center in Europe—still amounted in 1860 to a mere 3.5 percent of the city as a whole. That number had reached as high as 5 percent in 1890, declining steadily thereafter to 4.9 percent in 1900, and 4.3 percent in 1925. In 1939, after six years of persecution, and after two-thirds of all remaining German

Jews had been concentrated in Berlin, Jews made up only 1.07 percent of the city's population.

These figures raise another question: what percentage of the world's Jewish population did German Jewry comprise? A surprisingly small amount, as it turns out. According to Arthur Ruppin's figures, German Jews accounted for 3.5 percent of the world's Jewish population by 1930. The total number of Jews living in German-speaking regions as a whole amounted to 861,000, that is, 5.4 percent, making German-speaking Jews one-twentieth of world Jewry as a whole.

What became of this Jewish community after 1933? A survey of self-declared Jews conducted in Germany in June 1933, after roughly 50,000 Jews had already been forced to flee, placed their number at 499,682. A census of 1939 added 19,717 to that number through natural increase, and listed 52,005 other Jewish residents of Germany with two Jewish grandparents and 32,669 with at least one Jewish grandparent. What happened next? According to Bruno Blau's estimate, the number of "full Jews," as they were called, decreased in the six years following 1933 by more than half, or 57.4 percent, through 34,000 more deaths than births and conversions that totaled roughly 3,500, with approximately 250,0000 of almost 500,000 lost to emigration. Another 65,000 Jews managed to emigrate after that point, 135,000 were deported, and 68,000 died a more or less natural death. Only about 20,000 escaped persecution or annihilation in Germany itself, whether by going into hiding secretly or in the open, sometimes after returning from deportation: in other words, only 3.5 percent of the Jewish population of 1933.

And a final question: what became of the German Jewish emigrants? The bitter truth for many was that they suffered the same fate as those who stayed behind: in Europe, fleeing Jews often fell into the hands of the German authorities and were deported and murdered in the end. Roughly 537,000 refugees through the year 1942—360,000 from Germany, 147,000 from Austria, and 30,000 from Czechoslovakia—had by 1955 been resettled as follows, according to the Association of Jewish Refugees in Great Britain: 180,000–200,000 in the United States; 60,000–90,000 in Israel, taking only Jewish refugees from Germany into account; 45,000–50,000 in England; 40,000 in Argentina; 10,000–20,000 each in Brazil, Chile, Australia, South Africa, and France; 2,200–2,600 in Uruguay, Belgium, Sweden, and Columbia; and fewer than 1,700 in Switzerland and Bolivia.

The end that crashed down on German Jewry, and the martyrdom of Jewish innocence that occurred, signaled finality, but a strong and evident will to continuity as well: more than half of the German Jews managed to escape. Wherever the numbers of those rescued reached the tens of thousands—in the United States, Israel, South America, and England—survivors banded together and sought to rebuild new centers to sustain their way of life. In this show of fealty to German culture, German Jews acted just as countless other Jewish communities had done, showing more loyalty to the nations that had left an indelible mark upon them than those nations had shown them. Many factors played a role in preventing German Jewry from reestablishing itself as a living entity overseas. The monstrous German crime, beggaring comparison with any previous persecution, robbed the immigrants of any pride the immigrants might have taken in their German origins. And the dark side of those characteristic traits German Jews shared with other Germans also played a fateful role. These included a desire to go it alone, party-line behavior, too much intellectuality, a proclivity to self-hatred, and a deficit of civic commitment and political courage. Finally, a grievously difficult economic situation pushed cultural life to the margins for far too long, even though sustaining cultural ties is absolutely crucial if community life is to thrive. In the end, no regrouping of what was once German Jewry was ever successfully achieved.

The "second generation" of the survivor generation soon discovered that Jews in other countries do not shrink from identifying as Jews while successfully undertaking every sort of Jewish and non-Jewish enterprise, and now reproaches its parents for unnecessarily denying its German Jewish heritage, or its angst-ridden efforts to preserve it. But the chance for self-assertion, once it has been squandered, never returns. Today, the hope remains that the enduring richness of the German Jewish legacy will be bestowed upon the future generations of successors of German Jews, inspiring them with fresh encouragement. Judaism has supported the possibility of renewal time and time again throughout the ages, endowing its people in every era with a love of life that looks to the future. But the actual work of carrying that inheritance forward cannot yet be built on, only hoped for. The revival of Jewish life in Germany of unexpected proportions and significance does not represent an easing of the situation, or at least not an easing alone, but a challenge with problems of its own. Without its own vital force in the present, its future task would simply be to bring the memory of a past that had almost reached its full end to fruition. But the present poses challenges all its own that will undoubtedly co-determine the final shape of the legacy of German Jewry.

"Jews are living in Germany once more. This fact needs to be faced squarely, and more: it needs to be recognized and affirmed."[2] The "German Jews" who sustain only a piecemeal continuity—outside of Germany—with the past have been joined by the "Jews in Germany," whose link with the past is likewise partial at best, but who are also carrying the tradition forward. It is therefore no longer acceptable to limit today's incarnation of German Jewry to the community that existed until 1933, or until 1943, or to lump it together with whatever desirable or undesirable historical actions undertaken by "German Jews" now dispersed throughout the world. The desirable or undesirable effects of having Jews once again living in Germany carry just as much weight. The history of this new community established in 1945 already comprises four quite distinct periods. Their unique situation must be kept in mind when considering the history of German Jewry, for Jews in the Germany of today have been shaped by the German Jewish legacy and in turn have begun to shape it into something all their own.

The history of the "Jews in Germany" opens with an upswing that lasted from 1945 to 1948. A period of sharp decline soon followed that was not brought to a halt until roughly 1952. A new push forward begins in 1953, and was succeeded by a fourth period of a gradually slowing upswing around 1959. This despite the fact that to the outside world, this period looked like a continuous and even splendid revival of Jewish life in Germany. Who are these "Jews in Germany"? In part they comprise those remaining German Jews, survivors numbering roughly 15,000, who reestablished their communities after 1945. An umbrella organization was founded on July 19, 1950, the Central Council of Jews in Germany, both to further Jewish affairs and to advance Jewish demands for better protection, public support, and reparations. Another segment of the population is made up by a different group of survivors, Jews from the East or the so-called displaced persons: the remnants of those millions hounded to their deaths, and who numbered roughly 200,000. As World War II came to a close, these Jews left their hideouts and fled the death camps, and found themselves in Germany, together with the mournful 15,000 German Jews who remained. These survivors represented a mere fraction of their own, original Jewish population, though they amounted to a significant number of people. For the sake of these Jewish survivors who remained, it was simply impossible for Jews who managed to emigrate or settled abroad to call for a "complete break between the Jewish and German peoples," a position that would have otherwise been necessary given what had occurred. For those Jews who remained in Germany were at the time justified in all their demands for aid and their demand for recognition as Jews, and in fact saw to both of these tasks with all the passion of those who had just tasted all the torments of hell.

For three years, the Central Committee of Liberated Jews of Germany, founded in Munich, undertook bold efforts on behalf of the displaced; this period, in fact, still awaits its historian. The founding of the State of Israel on May 14, 1948, then enabled the logjam to be broken, and the immediate mass emigration of the vast majority of Eastern European Jewish survivors soon ensued. For most of the refugees had regarded Germany as a mere way station. By 1952, the Jewish population of Germany was back down to a mere 17,427 Jews. By then, however, the *Wirtschaftswunder*, or "economic miracle," had already taken hold. The fortunes of Germany's Jews rose with the economy as a whole. The signing of the German-Israeli reparations agreement on September 10, 1952, sparked a surge in the number of returning survivors to Germany. These thousands and thousands of returning emigrants were extraordinarily important to the few Jews then in Germany, increasing their number by a third, as a good number returned with relatively large families in tow. By roughly 1961 returning refugees made up almost half of the 25,000 members of all Jewish communities in Germany. This wave of returning refugees—63 percent came from Israel—comes to a standstill in 1959. This halt in returning emigrants was due to many factors. The fact that the successfully executed program of mass extermination had almost deprived German Jewry of its entire next generation played its role. That catastrophe and its unparalleled dimensions remain no easier to grasp today than they were then, and thus are often dismissed as a factor all too quickly. The truth is that the catastrophe has in no way been compensated for by the so-called process of reconstruction.

A few additional figures, along with the more detailed account offered in Harry Maor's foundational work of 1961, *On the Reconstruction of Jewish Communities in Germany*, will serve to make this point clear.[3] What is the "significance" of Jews in Germany today? They comprise .05 percent of the population as a whole, or one Jew for every two thousand German citizens, while in 1871—with a Jewish population of 1.05 percent—there was one

Jew for every ninety-five Germans.[4] The only European countries in which Jews make up a smaller percentage of the population than in the Germany of today are Yugoslavia and Finland (.03 per cent), Norway and Albania (.02 per cent), and Spain and Portugal (.01 percent). To elaborate the damage in other terms: the number of Jewish men today exceeds the number of Jewish women to an unusual extent due to their "selection" in the concentration camps. In 1956, there were 301 Jewish women for every 1,000 Jewish men of marriageable age born between 1909 and 1927, while for the population as a whole the ratio stood at 53 women for every 47 men of similar age. And yet another bitter disproportion is to be found in the cohort of those aged forty and above: in the likewise no longer wholly "natural" distribution before 1933, this group made up just 37 percent of the Jewish population as a whole, while today, it amounts to 66 percent.

The period from 1951 to 1958 saw only 2,478 Jewish men and 899 Jewish women marry, with a mixed marriage rate of 72.5 percent for the men and 23.6 percent for the women. The corresponding figures for German Jews between 1901 and 1930 were 19.6 and 12.2 percent respectively, also astoundingly high figures, but negligible in comparison with the 350 percent increase for men and the twofold increase for the women. According to official German statistics, the period between 1955 and 1958 saw 496 children born to Jewish couples, and 516 from mixed marriages; in this same period, Jewish communities themselves reported only 222 births. According to Maor, the unavoidable explanation of the difference is that "the majority of the children of mixed marriages and a considerable number of those born to wholly Jewish couples kept their distance from the Jewish communities." The result? "The current status and future outlook for the Jewish population of Germany have all too clearly reached a point that makes their disappearance as an independent group in little more than a generation a certainty, though a lower birth rate in a given social group does not necessarily signify its incapacity to remain a vital part of the society."

Maor's examination of the reconstruction of Jewish communities is also instructive. He concludes that they no longer sustain the full range of Jewish activities needed to give members of the Jewish community a feeling of strength and pride. More than two thousand years ago, Simon the Just taught his people that the world rests on three foundations: Torah (learning), religious observance, and charitable works. Of these, only the third pillar still stands for the Jews of Germany today. The amount spent by the

Jewish communities on welfare and administration comprises no less than 77 percent of their entire budget. It is therefore no surprise that the Federal Republic of Germany suffers from "an almost total absence of intellectually active Jews of any stature. . . . There are a few Jewish actors, a few Jewish directors and editors of publishing houses, but scarcely any journalists of note and not a single Jewish editor of any of the large West German newspapers. . . . Of the three Jewish members of the Bundestag, one has renounced Judaism. By the middle of 1959, Cologne, Berlin, Düsseldorf, and Fürth had each but a single Jewish city council member. In the political parties and their organizations, Jews play no role whatsoever." Maor offers a final point not without its own humor, despite its bitter and painful truth: "If we judge by the 'success rate' of Jewish fund drives, the 'top 10,000' Jews of Germany in fact consists of a mere 2,000."

Today's German Jewish community, therefore,

is, in its current shape, largely determined by those who came on the scene after 1945. . . . Continuity between today's population and those who once comprised the organized Jewish communities can be found, if at all, only in traces. . . . The dynamic of these new communities owes far more to the modern principle of looking after the common interests of those who had been harmed. . . . Jews in Germany survive chiefly through business and from pensions. They fulfill no economic function whatsoever. . . . The amalgamation of chiefly business occupations with the role of community functionary must be seen as a pernicious development, since Jewish civic offices necessarily appear as degraded and those who fulfill them on behalf of the community hardly enjoy anything approaching status, nor do they represent a stabilizing factor or an objective authority. . . . Since the continuing existence of the Jewish community, when not wholly fictional—not infrequently the case—must be guaranteed, if need be, in the absence of any communal structure, this has led in Germany to the existence of salaried senior officials, who alone assure the continued operation of given communities. . . . [As a result,] the attempt to sustain the social cohesion of these communities (for *these* communities) is bound to fail, creating a truly tragic state of affairs for the many Jews arriving in Germany without friends, family or connections, and especially tragic for the elderly. The possibility that the Jews of Germany will fail the final task assigned to them by the Jewish world beyond Germany, which still views them in hostile terms—to care for the aged, and to provide for homeless refugees upon their return—must be considered a great danger indeed.

One chance remains, and opportunity is contingent on today's "Jews in Germany," who might carry on with the legacy of German Jewry, sharing the same regard for its meaning held by those outside Germany proper. The hope is that the enduring richness of that legacy will inspire its legatees to take up the work already begun, and to pursue it with increasing ardor and self-awareness. With the help of that legacy the Jews in Germany can transform themselves into a Jewish community with its own distinctive stamp. Inspiration, of course, can always falter. This would certainly be the case if the Jews in Germany—or the German Jews outside of Germany fall prey to the same temptations—were to regard the future potential contained in the legacy of German Jewry, already a support, as a guarantee that their future rests assured: a future that shares with the future of German Jewry only the current quest for continuity. In the end, the German Jews owe that future to their ancestors, and the Jews in Germany to their predecessors, not themselves. Surety for the future of today's Jews in Germany, however, will be gained only when these heirs to the German Jewish legacy stand up to their own challenge and conquer the future themselves.

TWENTY-SEVEN

The Legacy of German Jewry

The third way in which German Jewry carries on is as the legacy German Jews took with them as they escaped, and in the spirit of today's Jews in Germany, a legacy that remains part of both groups yet is also something independent as well. German Jewry's moment still shines as a beacon for modernity as a whole, and the trailblazing significance and influence their accomplishments continue to exert depend on neither its creators nor their inheritors. For when all is said and done, German Jewry's legacy calls on Jews and all mankind to share in an inheritance that comprehends, reaffirms, and ensures all that is crucial to their common future.

German Jewry proved itself to be one of the most deeply characteristic and in every important respect fundamental representatives of the West, proving its mettle as partner in its two-thousand-year struggle for the ideals the West holds dear. In the end, the judgment we form of the German Jewish legacy will apply to the present and future prospects of the West as a whole. Despite their universal dissemination and de facto acceptance in every part of the world without exception, modern Europe's unparalleled cultural achievements have still not achieved full recognition, and remain vulnerable to new losses and oblivion. Like the legacy of German Jewry that both transforms and complements them, Europe's achievements are before all else an irreplaceable seed stock to be carefully collected, tended, and preserved, and even more thoughtfully handed down to future generations. These are the seeds of a Western preeminence that has been doubly super-seded at the century's end. First, because Europe frittered away its decisive role once and for all in the two world wars it waged, and second, because as far as modernity is concerned, the kind of single world center we have known since the Middle Ages no longer exists.

In compiling, preserving, and transmitting this preciously fertile trove in all its potential, the legacy of German Jewry represents not the sense of an ending, but a signpost that points us toward the future. That legacy asks us to seriously consider the fact that the end of a crucial epoch in the world history of the Jewish people is at hand, along with the end—in every sense—of Western hegemony. "We alone are not concerned," writes Leo Baeck in just this sense, "when we become a matter of concern." Baeck came upon his insight when looking back on Judaism as such, in the last paragraph of his *The Essence of Judaism*: "Our claims are the claims of con-science, of the commandment. We do not desire to be honored, but rather that truth and justice be honored."

Based on several telling examples, and on Baeck, whom we have just quoted, as the most salient one, the following conclusion can be drawn. The battle Jews waged to the bitter end for an authentic dialogue between Juda-ism and Christianity, while carried out for Judaism's benefit, also fought for fundamental truths and rights that Christianity and all peoples share. Ger-man Jewry's battle for equality enabled it to scale heights of human experi-ence that all humanity may be inspired to enrich. Yet in this regard, their achievement lives on as a legacy and nothing more. Even the innovative consequences of the I-Thou reconception of the relation between Judaism and Christianity, with its worldwide influence in many fields, must be bracketed for the time being, because its acceptance is still nothing more than a hope. If this insistence that Judaism was Christianity's full equal was a victory, what is the significance of a victory recognized by the home team alone, a victory whose example was supposed to stand as a beacon to the world? Has what Baeck fought Harnack to achieve really been accomplished: a recognition and stature for Judaism fully consonant with what Christianity enjoys? Has this situation, and all its consequences, been realized or carried out in practice to the extent hoped for when the first edition of this work conceptualized this idea of religious equality as a "division of labor in redemptive history" that, without erasing any doctrinal distinctions or mutually defining differences, envisioned it as the path toward meaningful religious coexistence? Have we reached the point where the aspiration for such religious equality can ground itself not in the past, but in a vision of a judgment encompassing the present, while pointing out the future's path?

And has what Franz Rosenzweig called the "ecclesiastical-political point" of equal stature for Judaism and Christianity, which he fought to achieve, become unequivocally clear to the Christian neighbor: that an organized "mission to the Jews" is no longer acceptable? Certainly, a "mission to the pagans" and as a new task, an "inner mission" may be acceptable as part of tradition of religious revelation that presses one to serve as its messenger. "Neither missionary work as such, nor consciousness of one's mission, and the obligation to testify to it, nor its pronouncement" ought to be abandoned. "None of the world religions can withdraw from the world, to whose entirety they bring the good tidings that everything, can, should and will be redeemed. But as world religions, Judaism and Christianity can and must disavow the obligation of trying to convert one another. . . . No act other than relinquishing this program altogether will be the proofstone of their contemporary and future encounter. This act is not just a concession but a conquest as well: in the most literal meaning of the term, the future-laden conquest of Jewish, and Christian modernity."[1]

But has the Jewish party to this issue already done as much when German Jewry, at the high noon of its achievement, argued for Judaism's consistent equality with Christianity by conceiving of a division of labor in redemptive history? The organized Jewish "mission to the Christians" must be abandoned as well. Rosenzweig would never have imagined any such possibility. In the meantime, however, the first steps toward it have already been taken, and non-Jewish circles were not the last ones to demand this in surprising, even dismaying numbers. In the Germany of the 1960s, for example, an astounding and even disturbing number of Germans wanted to convert to

Judaism and become members of its people. Is this living up to the proposition that Jews should remain Jewish, and become the best Jews they can, Christians should stay Christian and do the same, allowing both groups to realize their existence as equally legitimate and necessary representatives of the Bible's truth? When will the acknowledgment sought by Judaism's Christian neighbor be granted to Judaism as well? And when will Christianity's covenant, now an accepted part of redemptive history, like the Jewish covenant itself, gain the recognition and acceptance of Jews? That acceptance could find a basis in a modern Jewish outlook that is vital if the I-Thou encounter is to succeed, or could spring from the inescapable recognition that Christianity, like other traditions, gives authentic and prophetic witness to the singular revelation of the message of the kingdom. But have Judaism and Christianity conceded that both of their traditions attest to that message with the same authority and legitimacy, and that each tradition displays deficiencies as well as genius, as it were, in its prophetic stance?

Where has the contribution represented by *Philosophy Out of the Sources of Judaism* received the serious treatment it deserves? Who has understood what it meant when Hermann Cohen, one of the "purest" philosophical minds of the century, and its leading neo-Kantian, on the verge of shedding the last trace of his Jewish particularity, instead became the inheritor of the philosophic tradition of Philo, Maimonides, and Spinoza, suddenly stumbling on the universal meaning and legitimacy his Jewish tradition held? Who has grasped the full significance and what ensued when Cohen, overwhelmed by the truth of that message, began to bear stammering witness to its enduring meaning for our present and future as well? And where has "dialogics" been given its due as a tradition that can be traced back to the young Hegelians, then rediscovered by Cohen, Rosenzweig, Buber, and other German Jewish thinkers in their turn, who understood dialogue as the redemptive turn in the philosophic quest: a perspective that sees contraries not as an affront to truth, but instead as their modern intensification, the profound and productive form in which they find voice? The dialogic idea has consequences for philosophy proper, interfaith relations, and the encounter between religion and philosophy as well. Its insight tells us that the unique totality of the equally unique universe in which we live can only find expression through two opposed viewpoints that argue contradictory truths, both of which are nonetheless correct. When the historical moment of dialogics has arrived, it is only this multiplicity of truths, whose contradictions had previously failed the test of totality, that can, through those very contradictions, open up the totality of the future.

And where has the world-historic significance of the Jewish people been adequately integrated into historiography? Where is that world-historic meaning seen as wholly compatible with its own content, requiring no minimization of the specific character of its material, crystallizing narrative, history, and redemptive history into one? For the meaning of Jewish history is that the Jewish path to redemption and the road traveled by humanity are never truly separate, but one and the same, and that Judaism's presence in history has been a presence shared with all peoples who have made history, and continue its course.

Or has the way Judaism inspires science, through its biblical conviction—that freedom, joy, and peace can and shall represent the universal future—where has this contribution become part of modern awareness, as Judaism's constant loyalty to its mission might lead us to assume? When will this biblical inspiration be recognized, an insight that in no way diminishes science's necessary commitment to science for the sake of science alone? Where has the recognition finally taken hold that only the scholar who accepts who he or she is—origins which can then become an explicit part of the research itself, or excluded altogether, whichever is more productive—can give scholarship all that it deserves? And what of the task of pursuing all knowledge from a Jewish point of view, that is, with a universal freedom to voice Jewish concerns? German Jewry was the trailblazer in this regard, fighting all external barriers to its pursuit of knowledge, as well as internal forms of suppression, down to its unmasking and exposure of Jewish self-hatred? These achievements have hardly penetrated the general awareness, and how little recognition they have gained, not as some exclusively "Jewish" achievement, but as part of the fundamental struggle for basic human rights! Only that Jew who accepts his or her Judaism—and the same goes for every ethnic group, gender or racial grouping, and everyone who accepts their particularity, whatever form it takes—can give his or her best to scholarship in any of its fields, and never be thwarted by what is best within, but instead always furthered by it.

And where has the watchword of the modern Jewish Lehrhaus been taken up and carried on—and where has modern Jewish literature, having passed the test of its experimental period with flying colors, acquired the respect and recognition it has earned? Where has this art been welcomed as a continuation of the *Haggadah*, in the Talmud's thousand-year-old tradition, and the work in the Lehrhaus as an equally creative continuation of "*halakhic*" learning? And who has noticed that the modern movement for adult education was not merely echoed in Jewish circles, but was easily fused with age-old Jewish practice and techniques? And who recognizes the turning of the tables that ensued when the Jewish Lehrhaus was taken as a model by Protestant as well as Catholic institutions, who learned just as much from their Jewish neighbors as the Jews themselves had received? Who is aware of any of this, or discusses these developments with conviction when they are proclaimed?

Whether in historiography, which not only needs to devote extensive resources to the exploration of Jewish contexts, but also owes its notion of a single human history to Judaism, or whether in the history of world philosophy, or intellectual history, the history of mysticism, or literary history, or in linguistics, which relies on Jewish languages that have absorbed elements of other languages and survived them: Jewish sources are indispensable to all areas of intellectual inquiry today. Judaism remains a crucial body of evidence in studying the transition from antiquity to the Middle Ages, from the early to the high Middle Ages and to the foundational movements of modernity as well. These connections remain vital if we are to grasp the full significance of the fact that the future's origins still rest on a biblical concept of history that the unbroken, living continuity of the Jewish people have affirmed time and time again. All these intellectual venues—and more—make Jewish research, and research into Judaism itself an imperative.

The discipline of Judaic studies promises to fill in some of these gaps, finally picking up where the Wissenschaft des Judentums left off, albeit at a limited number of universities, chiefly in the United States. Judaic studies has been a piecemeal affair, an utter failure in responding to these scholarly lacunae, and in the process ultimately failing to grasp Judaism, nowhere more so than in Germany. This, another bitter truth, cannot be passed over in the conclusion and prospect we offer here. The fact is that the legacy of German Jewry could have become productive more richly and rapidly in Germany than anywhere else, given the multitude of connections waiting to be established between Jewish culture and Germany's own path, and still could be, if the powers that be would only take hold of the vast potential waiting to be mined in its own history, and bring it to light. The fact that one of the motivating factors behind the beginnings of Judaic studies in the first place was Christian efforts to convert the Jews is not without its own advantages, after all. Just as modern Islamic studies emerged from the efforts of medieval missionaries but led to serious scholarly investigation and research in time, wholly detached from the project of conversion, a shift from "the mission to the Jews" to Judaic studies is now taking shape. But old prejudices die hard, and far too much of the old arrogance continues to make itself felt. In addition, an inability or unwillingness to address new difficulties that research into Judaism faces, a consequence of momentous changes in the Jewish situation, poses a formidable obstacle as well. Those changes, results of the monstrous crimes of 1933 to 1945, have left the Jewish people shaken, deeply wounded, and fundamentally transformed.

Many such factors contribute to the sad and unseemly state of Judaic studies in the academy today. Judaic studies are compromised without the vital support of the surrounding, non-Jewish community, when that community does not take Judaism seriously as an object of study and rejects Jews as a witnesses to their own truth, or unconsciously suppresses Jewish concerns while praising the Jewish past. That sort of praise requires no real personal commitment, raving about the Jewish future in a way that pits it against the interests of the contemporary Jewish community. That community itself is often ignored, since research might expose a past for which the non-Jewish community bears responsibility. Such a Judaic studies can, as today's German version of it has amply demonstrated, "miss the actuality of Judaism's present and future entirely, just as missionaries to the Jews did, despite their constant and active preoccupation with Judaism. . . . Where in Germany, in the decade and a half that has elapsed since the turning point of 1945, has even a single chair of Jewish studies been established, a chair that would empower Judaism's past, present and future to articulate itself with full authority, in all its living richness and variegated unity, in a voice of its own?"[2] Nowhere!

A final "Where?" concerns the summit of the German Jewish accomplishment: the enduring attestation its legacy offers to the modern meaning of the Bible, and the powerful rearticulation of biblical truths it achieved. In this connection, we could discuss the Jewish quest for a German Bible, the new form German Jews gave to Judaism's message of the kingdom, and the sufferings of a people who became one of the historical successors to the suffering servant and to Job. Where has this people's enduring testament and modern recasting of the biblical tradition been acknowledged as carrying on the message of freedom, joy, and peace? Where has their cultural testimony been greeted and continued with the thorough care and honesty it deserves, and which its usefulness to later generations in fact demands? The message of freedom and peace—that the aims of progress and a united humanity are indeed one—can only be sustained as long as its biblical roots remain firm. Without them, the doubt that inevitably follows the ever-present pain and dissatisfactions of everyday existence, and historical existence as such, cannot be held at bay for long. Wave after wave of disappointments would soon put an end to our will to endure once and for all. The fact that biblical truth has once again become a historically forceful presence in the midst of the twentieth century serves as an inspiration to Judaism and mankind as a whole: good tidings not just for the "staffs of Jacob," the tribes of Israel who make up the Jewish people, but also—thanks to their embassy—a message to all the earth's peoples, a light to the "tribes of the earth":

> It is too little that you should be My servant
> In that I raise up the tribes of Jacob
> And restore the survivors of Israel:
> I will also make you a light of nations,
> That My salvation may reach the ends of the earth. (Isaiah 49:6)

Who knows it, and who that knows it disseminates what the prophetic legacy of German Jewry proclaims? That it is possible to participate in the project of modernity with unstinting engagement and complete devotion, while remaining grounded in the biblical truth. German Jewry is the proof. The Jewish community of Germany kept faith with its people's four-thousand-year-long world and redemptive history by meeting the challenge of its contemporary world: harkening to the call of modernity, they heeded Judaism's call as well.

As they did so, no role fell to the German Jews other than one that which had to be theirs. Having all but completed the path toward human fulfillment and achievement that challenges all mankind with its promise, German Jewry reached its summit of intellectual and spiritual development in the midst of a Europe that by and large refused to treat them as equals. As a result, their accomplishments—like Europe's—can be understood as a past that remains incomplete, or to put it more precisely, as a past whose meaning can only work itself as a legacy, the future task left for a united humanity to understand and fulfill.

For just as referring to German Jewry always meant speaking of Judaism in its entirety, a Judaism the German Jews never lost sight of, so it is that when we speak of Judaism, we also refer to humanity as a whole, whose future, seen from the vantage point of Judaism's biblical exodus and awakening, has become a certainty as well as a task. That task is one in which more and more, and one day all men and women will take part, every people and every nation, in the manner that best befits it, a task in which Judaism has always joined and at which it continues to labor, so that Judaism, this people, and its covenant shall endure, and endure forevermore.

"My 1933"
Hermann Levin Goldschmidt

Inroduction

Written four decades after the publication of the first edition of *The Legacy of German Jewry*, *My 1933* is also the last text Hermann Levin Goldschmidt wrote. A diagnosis of a terminal illness made it clear that only a few months were left. During these last months, Goldschmidt began to compose a collection of texts that would offer his own version of "1933," as he became increasingly disappointed and frustrated with a growing wave of memoirs that seemed to catch up with that past. In part, Goldschmidt wrote his own 1933 to reclaim his own version of those events. His own narrative has little sympathy for memoirs that combine accident and destiny in a teleological sleight of hand, leaving German-Jewish culture behind as an historical relic. Instead, Goldschmidt takes the implicit and explicit voices of critique leveled at German Jews in postwar culture, and makes it part of an inner debate. Referring to himself as both "he" and "you," Goldschmidt rejects the

model of survival as synthesis, or "integration" as he calls it. "My 1933"—
the central text of this collection—represents a different kind of self-assertion achieved through a searing act of self-examination. In the form of an
inner dialogue, Goldschmidt addresses to himself the challenging questions
faced by his generation of survivors. Just as *The Legacy of German Jewry* and
Goldschmidt's thought as a whole argued for a dialogue that could imagine
the future by opening up the hidden potential of the past, Goldschmidt's
last text offers a post-contemporary vision. Goldschmidt's stocktaking in
this way becomes more than a review of his writings and thought. The
critical edge of his text makes itself felt in a style that is unsparing in its
self-examination: precisely those qualities his critics often claimed had been
forgotten, ignored, or suppressed. Written against the grain of the postwar
fashion of judging the past, "My 1933" instead reminds us that the past's
ethical and dialogic demand on us—to discover its meaning for the present
and future—remains unfulfilled.

—Willi Goetschel and David Suchoff

"Concerning ourselves, we remain silent: *de nobis ipsis silemus*. Philosophy
represents its engagement in the court of wisdom with the resolve of this
formula for self-effacement that originates with Bacon (1620) that Kant will
use as his motto for the second edition of the *Critique of Pure Reason* (1787).
De re autem quae agitur petimus, as Bacon modifies the saying, which Kant
would repeat. It is not a matter of keeping silent about ourselves—which
would merely be the objectivity of an illusory, value-neutral position—but
rather means . . . that kind of for/bearance, and self-conscious ab/dication,
which contrasts that which is worth saying from that which we can say about
ourselves, but is not."

—H. L. Goldschmidt, *Book of Wholeness /
Sefer Ha'Schlemut*, Zürich 1993, no. 30

At least today the question that cannot be put off any longer is being asked:
What really happened back then—in 1933? What were its consequences:
those that were addressed? Disputed? Silenced? Repressed? Not to mention:
How did you yourself act back then? These questions are accompanied by
the nagging—and from a personal point of view—hardest question of all:

How were you able to experience what you did and—when confronted
with the evil you experienced back then, in all its stupidity, its unspeakable
stupidity: how is it you were able to survive such evil?

How were you able—and you showed yourself to be quite adept at this task—to somehow find a way to survive that reality, which you experienced first-hand in a location granted you entirely by chance? And how were you able to survive that experience—thanks to the option that remained open to you—in your own original, German linguistic territory on the soil of Zürich, from February 15, 1938, forward? How did you survive in sur- roundings where, for one thing, there were no bystanders who could set themselves up as judge and jury over your actions? In a Zürich where you also—and at the very same time!—wanted to remain loyal and succeeded in doing so to those who shamefully betrayed you: betrayed you in the most disgraceful way? Undeterred in your joyous desire to follow in the footsteps of that intellectual spirit? A spirit whose successors—both men and women—have not ceased to demonize your existence and that of the entire Jewish people? While you eventually came to stand side by side with the representatives of your new Zürich homeland—men and women both?

The unremitting question still digs at you: whether the survivor did nothing more than live through the horror that threatened him with mur- der from 1933 forward. Far from an idle threat, this horror was eventually realized in the practice of what was no idle threat, but unimaginably realized in the practice of its own terrible malpractice. Were you who survived it simply a coward, and anything but brave? As an all too eager hindsight would have it, did that survivor really continue his own intellectual develop- ment through it all—or, to put it more accurately—right through the shadow of Auschwitz? Did he then continue that creative development over decades: for sixty-five years?

In fact, did his intellectual development succeed thanks to the affirmative message of Judaism—a message utterly cast down and besieged, only to discover that affirmation—secretly—as it passed through that very storm, despite or on account of the "sacrifice of Jewish innocents" (in the image of Job)? Did that affirmation correspond to his own development, thanks to the continuing legacy of German Jewry? (He was the last of the German Jews, or so the rumor went.) Did his development succeed in yet another fashion—by contesting the undermining and eventual loss of every signifi- cant aspect of Europe's meaning and dignity: by carrying the legacy of Ger- man Jewry into the future, by exploring its connections with Western philosophy?

Some may deny this account, and others may concede its general thrust—hesitantly, and with reservations. But who do we have to thank for the notion of "dialogical correspondence?" To whom do we owe the idea of *Setting Contradiction Free?* To what tradition do we owe a title like *Thanks to Switzerland: Philosophy from Rousseau to Turel*, or *Pestalozzi's Unfinished Revolution.* Or *Self-Development as Self-Analysis*, and the infelicitously masculinized title that was *How Man Becomes Who He Is, And What He Can Do For Himself*, as well as *A Jewish Affirmation of the World's Future* (along with its subtitle, *A Documentation of Swiss Cooperation Since 1938*)? Or finally, a work completed sixty-four years after 1933, *Stoics Today?*—an expression of deepened confidence in the modern world of globalization, on the foundations of Greek thought that developed thanks to Judaism's sources of certainty?!

Add to all that the questions that assail this soon to be eighty-four year old man himself, as he faces his imminent and not entirely unwelcome departure at this unavoidably retrospective hour. And these questions that assail him arise from within. Some of them ask him to justify himself and his actions, but a desire for self-clarification can be heard in them as well. What really happened to you then—what really happened to you, and for you—back in 1933?

The contemporary witnesses are gone: first, because the extended family circle and all the rest of his social network and school friends were scattered after that date. Later, insofar as they were Jews and unable to escape, they were killed. And you—there's no use denying it—never accepted the exclusion that began when you were given your walking papers by the German publisher Ullstein on March 1, 1934 (when you became "unemployed," a status you kept for the rest of your life, including in Switzerland). You never accepted your exclusion as a kind of personal negation, but as something that liberated you instead. You therefore received those acts that meant to exclude you—which pushed you to the margins your whole life long—as confirmation of your steady progress—literally steps forward!—that permitted your more joyous approach to Judaism and a more exultant mode of practicing philosophy to emerge. Though rejected as a Jew wherever you turned and barred from your original home by stupidity, viciousness, disloyalty, and envy, your exclusion enabled you to take your first steps on a path whose spiritual and intellectual stirrings had long been felt within. The only difference now was that the challenges you faced had become far less avoidable, and so they have remained.

He made, it must be admitted, many attempts—especially in Switzerland—to secure his financial situation by finding a permanent appointment (or at least an academic affiliation) that would get him enough academic recognition to pay the bills. The steady intellectual progress, however, that was inseparable from his willingness to be integrated at the same time kept him from ever fully achieving that aim. In the process, he learned that it was the concept of integration itself that was becoming increasingly obsolete—not him. Premature solutions proved to be too narrow as they offered themselves to him one after the other (while teaching, for example, for 71 semesters at the colleges of continuing education in Zürich and Basel), except the philosophical approach that relates to the whole. The unusual drive to synthesis this experience fostered within him—under the abiding sign of contradiction he sustained—finally led beyond each of these attempts at achieving an integration the world would have been all too glad to see him accept. All the ensuing unrest he experienced became the dark side of his ability to perceive the whole with serenity: the wholeness of a knowledge and certainty that can be grasped only through their opposition to one another! With one another! For one another!

What Switzerland might bring (as it subjected him to its own kind of denial, in the dismissive nonacceptance it showed him after 1938, following his rejection by Germany) was not yet on the horizon in 1933. Like the five acts of a drama, the events of 1933 descended on a still largely unprepared, foolish, and dewy-eyed youth in that decisive year. There would be more such occurrences in the future. Soon, he would need a deeper grasp of their actual character, along with much greater clarity about what they meant (aside from the single and singularly most fearful event he would confront a decade later, and in undeniable detail: Auschwitz).

INTRODUCTION

1. Gershom Scholem, "At the Completion of Buber's Translation of the Bible," in *The Messianic Idea in Judaism and Other Essays on Jewish Spirituality* (New York: Schocken, 1971), 318.

2. See Gershom Scholem, "Jews and Germans," in *On Jews and Judaism in Crisis: Selected Essays* (New York: Schocken Books, 1976), 71–92.

3. For a fascinating account of Scholem's continuation of the "German" norms of the Wissenschaft des Judentums in Jerusalem, see David N. Meyers, "Gershom Scholem: Between 'Pure Science" and 'Religious Anarchy,'" in *Reinventing the Jewish Past: European Jewish Intellectuals and the Zionist Return to History* (New York: Oxford University Press, 1995), 171–176. The interplay between German and Jewish culture in Scholem's work is also explored in a special issue of *The Germanic Review* 72, no. 1 (1997), edited by Willi Goetschel and Nils Roemer.

4. *Der Nihilismus im Licht einer kritischen Philosophie*, reprinted in Hermann Levin Goldschmidt, *Philosophie als Dialogik, Werke* 1 (Vienna: Passagen, 1993).

5. For a discussion of the historical context of Goldschmidt's work, see Willi Goetschel, "1957 Hermann Levin Goldschmidt receives the first Leo Baeck Prize for *Das Vermächtnis des deutschen Judentums*," *Yale Companion to Jewish Writing and Thought in German Culture, 1096–1996*, ed. Sander Gilman and Jack Zipes (New Haven: Yale University Press, 1997), 704–709.

6. See Jürgen Habermas, *The Post-National Constellation: Political Essays*, trans. and ed. Max Pensky (Cambridge, Mass.: MIT Press, 2001).

7. See Goldschmidt's *Philosophie als Dialogik* (1948) and his *Hermann Cohen und Martin Buber. Ein Jahrhundert Jüdisches Ringen um Wirklichkeit* (1946), both in *Werke* 1.

8. Goldschmidt's essays on literature are now collected in volume 4 of his collected works, *"Der Rest bleibt": Aufsätze zum Judentum* (Vienna: Passagen, 1997). See also Willi Goetschel, "A Jewish Critic from Germany: Hermann

Levin Goldschmidt," in *German Literature, Jewish Critics: The Brandeis Symposium*, ed. Steve Dowden and Meike Werner (Rochester, N.Y.: Camden House, 2002), 149–165.

9. Hermann Levin Goldschmidt, "The Key to Kafka," *Commentary* 8, no. 2 (August 1949).

10. See Willi Goetschel, "'Gibt es eine jüdische Philosophie?' Zur Problematik eines Topos," *Perspektiven der Dialogik: Zürcher Kolloquium zu Ehren H. L. Goldschmidts*, ed. Willi Goetschel (Vienna: Passagen, 1994), 89–109.

11. See David Suchoff, "Widersprüchliche Identität: Judentum und Postmoderne im Werk Hermann Levin Goldschmidts," in ibid., 111–123.

12. The mission statements and program of the Freies Jüdisches Lehrhaus in Zürich are reprinted in Hermann Levin Goldschmidt, *Die Botschaft des Judentums, Werke* 3 (Vienna: Passagen 1994), a book that also contains an important discussion of Rosenzweig's Lehrhaus.

13. See Leo Baeck, *The Essence of Judaism*, trans. Irving Howe (New York: Schocken Books, 1948).

14. Theodor Adorno, *Negative Dialectics*, trans. E. B. Ashton (New York: Continuum, 1973), 3.

15. See Michael Brenner, *The Renaissance of Jewish Culture in Weimar Germany* (New Haven: Yale University Press, 1996).

16. Margarete Susman, *Das Buch Hiob und das Schicksal des Jüdischen Volkes* (Frankfurt am Main: Jüdischer Verlag, 1996).

17. Hermann Levin Goldschmidt, "Von der Weltschöpfung zur Weltvollendung—12 Thesen," in *"Der Rest bleibt, Werke IV*: 19.

18. For a suggestive discussion of the contemporary transnational significance of German Jewish thought, see Steven E. Aschheim, *Beyond the Border: The German Jewish Legacy Abroad* (Princeton, N.J.: Princeton University Press, 2007).

CHAPTER 1: ORIGINS OF THE MODERN

1. For background and sources, see Michael E. Stone, ed., *Jewish Writings of the Second Temple Period: Apocrypha, Pseudepigrapha, Qumran Sectarian Writings, Philo, Josephus* (Philadelphia: Fortress Press, 1984), 29.

2. Benedict Spinoza, *Theologico-Political Treatise*, trans. Martin D. Yaffe (Newburyport, Mass.: Focus, 2004), 42.

CHAPTER 5: EQUAL RIGHTS, NOT ASSIMILATION

1. Moses Mendelssohn, *Jerusalem or On Religious Power and Judaism*, trans. by Allan Arkush (Hanover and London: UP of New England, 1983), 84f.

CHAPTER 8: EMANCIPATION'S GREATEST FOE

1. "Only on the ground of modernity do we begin to see this arrogant attempt to step backwards toward a totality that has clearly been superseded: the

'totalitarianism' that ensues is criminality and absolutely nothing more." Hermann Levin Goldschmidt, *Dialogik: Philosophie auf dem Boden der Neuzeit* (Frankfurt: Europäische Verlagsanstalt, 1964), 17.

CHAPTER 9: THE FINAL STEP TO EMANCIPATION

1. Moses Hess, *The Revival of Israel: Rome and Jerusalem, the Last Nationalist Question*, trans. Meyer Waxman (Lincoln: University of Nebraska Press, 1995), 43.

CHAPTER 10: A FEW FIGURES

1. Cf. Isaiah 43:21: "This people which I formed for Myself, That they might tell of my praise."

CHAPTER 11: THE DUAL LEGACY OF THEODOR HERZL

1. Leo Baeck, *This People: The Meaning of Jewish Existence*, trans. Albert H. Friedländer (New York: Holt Rinehart & Winston, 1964), 380.

CHAPTER 12: THE LIFEWORK OF MARTIN BUBER

1. Martin Buber to Theodor Herzl, 26 May 1903, Buber, *Briefwechsel aus sieben Jahrzehnten Band I: 1897–1918*, ed. Ernst Simon (Heidelberg: Verlag Lambert Schneider, 1972), 199.
2. Martin Buber, "Aus einer philosophischen Rechenschaft", in *Werke*, vol. 1 (Munich and Heidelberg: Kösel and Lambert Schneider, 1962), 1109–22, here 1114.
3. Martin Buber, "Drei Stationen", in *Der Jude und sein Judentum. Gesammelte Aufsätze und Reden* (Cologne: Melzer, 1963), 751.

CHAPTER 14: THE ESSENCE OF JUDAISM

1. Leo Baeck, *The Essence of Judaism*, trans. Irving Howe (New York: Schocken Books, 1948), 173–75, translation modified.
2. Martin Buber, "Jewish Religiosity," in *On Judaism*, ed. Nahum Glatzer (New York: Schocken Books, 1967), 80, 93, translation modified.
3. Leo Baeck, "Preface to Book Two," *This People Israel* (New York: Holt, Rinehart, and Winston, 1965), 148.
4. Ibid., 403.

CHAPTER 15: PHILOSOPHY OUT OF THE SOURCES OF JUDAISM

1. Hermann Levin Goldschmidt, *Die Botschaft des Judentums*, *Werke* (Vienna: Passagen, 1994), 3:65–68.

2. See Hermann Levin Goldschmidt, *Philosophie als Dialogik: Frühe Schriften, Werke* (Vienna: Passagen, 1992), 1:163–282 and the lecture of the same title delivered in 1944.

CHAPTER 16: WORLD HISTORY OF THE JEWISH PEOPLE

1. Simon Dubnow, *Weltgeschichte des jüdischen Volkes*, trans. A. Steinberg (Berlin: Jüdischer Verlag, 1925–1929), vol. 1, XXIX. For a more extensive discussion of the significance of Dubnow's *World History of the Jewish People*, see H. L. Goldschmidt, "Simon Dubnow's Darstellung des Judentums," in *Simon Dubnov, l'homme et son oeuvre*, ed. Aaron Steinberg (Paris: Section Française du Congrés Juif Mondial , 1963) 204–18.

2. Leo Baeck, "Volksreligion und Weltreligion" in Leo Baeck, *Wege im Judentum. Aufsätze und Reden, Leo Baeck Werke* (Gütersloh: Gütersloher Verlagshaus, 1997), vol. 3, ed. Werner Licharz, 154–66, quote: 158.

3. Ibid., 159.

4. Dubnow, ibid., vol. 5, 227f.

5. Dubnow, ibid., vol. 10, 543f.

CHAPTER 17: SCIENCE FROM A JEWISH PERSPECTIVE

1. Hermann Levin Goldschmidt, *Die Botschaft des Judentums, Werke* (Vienna: Passagen, 1994), 3:64.

CHAPTER 18: EDUCATION WITHOUT END

1. Franz Rosenzweig to Martin Buber, 19 August 1922, Buber, *Briefwechsel aus sieben Jahrzehnten Band II: 1918–1938*, ed. Ernst Simon (Heidelberg: Verlag Lambert Schneider, 1972), 114.

2. Franz Rosenzweig, *On Jewish Learning*, ed. Nahum Glatzer (Madison: University of Wisconsin Press, 1955), 99. Translation modified.

3. Ibid.

4. Franz Rosenzweig, *Kleinere Schriften* (Berlin: Schocken Verlag, 1937), 82.

5. Ibid., 91.

6. Ibid., 89.

CHAPTER 19: JEWISH LITERATURE

1. Gustav Karpeles, *Geschichte der jüdischen Literatur* (Berlin: M. Poppelauer, 1920; rpt. Graz: Akademische Druck- und Verlagsanstalt, 1963), vol 1:iii.

2. Ibid.

3. Karpeles, ibid., vol 2: 429.

4. Ibid., 419f.

5. Ibid., 420.

6. Franz Rosenzweig, Letter to Gertrude Oppenheim, May 25, 1927, *Briefe*, ed. Ernst Simon and Edith Rosenzweig (Berlin: Schocken, 1935), 596.

7. Alfred Wolfenstein, "Das neue Dichtertum des Juden," in Gustav Krojanker, *Juden in der deutschen Literatur. Essays über zeitgenössische Schriftsteller* (Berlin: Welt-Verlg, 1922), 333–59, quote p. 359.

1. *Das leere Haus. Prosa jüdischer Dichter*, ed. Karl Otten (Stuttgart: Cotta, 1959), 621.

2. Ibid., 603.

3. *Schofar. Lieder und Legenden jüdischer Dichter*, ed. Karl Otten (Neuwied am Rhein and Berlin-Spandau, 1962), 6.

4. Ibid., 25.

5. Ibid., 14 and 24.

6. Ibid., 16 and 19.

1. Theodor Lessing, *Der jüdische Selbsthass* (Berlin: Jüdischer Verlag, 1930, rpt. Munich: Matthes & Seitz, 1984), 38.

2. Hermann Levin Goldschmidt, *Die Botschaft des Judentums*, *Werke* (Vienna: Passagen, 1994), 3:58.

1. Martin Buber, "People Today and the Jewish Bible," in *Scripture and Translation: Martin Buber and Franz Rosenzweig*, trans. Lawrence Rosenwald and Everett Fox (Bloomington: Indiana University Press, 1994), 21.

2. Buber and Rosenzweig, "The Bible in German," ibid., 159.

3. Karl Wolfskehl, *Zehn Jahre Exil. Briefe aus Neuseeland 1938–1948*, ed. Margot Ruben (Heidelberg/Darmstadt: Lambert Schneider, 1959), 157f.

4. Moses Mendelssohn, *Gesammelte Schriften: Jubiläumsausgabe*, ed. Ismar Elbogen, Julius Guttmann, Eugen Mittwoch in association with Fritz Bamberger, Haim Borodianksi, Simon Rawidowicz, Bruno Strauß, and Leo Strauß, continued by Alexander Altmann in association with Haim Bar-Dayan, Eva J. Engel, Leo Strauß, Werner Weinberg. 19 vols. (1929–32; Berlin: Akademie Verlag; Stuttgart-Bad Cannstatt: F. Frommann, 1971ff), vol. 9.1:56.

5. Rosenzweig, "Scripture and Word," ibid., 43.

6. Rosenzweig, "'The Eternal': Mendelssohn and the Name of God," ibid., 105.

7. Ibid.

8. Buber, "On Word Choice in Translating the Bible," ibid., 88, translation modified.

9. *The Jewish Bible*, JPS, modified.

10. Jewish Publication Society translation, modified.

CHAPTER 23: JUDAISM'S MESSAGE OF THE KINGDOM OF GOD

1. Leo Baeck, *The Essence of Judaism*, trans. Irving Howe (New York: Schocken Books, 1948), 30, 68 ff., translation modified.

2. Cf. Hermann Levin Goldschmidt, *Die Botschaft des Judentums, Werke* (Vienna: Passagen, 1994), 3:95.

CHAPTER 24: THE END

1. Herman Cohen, "Grenzsperre", in *Jüdische Schriften*, (Berlin: Schwetschke & Sohn, 1924), vol. 2, 378–380, quote 379f.

2. See Arnold Paucker, "Responses of German Jewry to Nazi Persecution 1933–1945," *The German-Jewish Dielmma from the Enlightenment to the Shoa*, ed. Edward Timms and Andrea Hammel (Lewiston, Queenston, Lampeter: Edwin Mellen, 1999), 211–27, see esp. 211–13.

CHAPTER 25: SORROW

1. See "Toward the Kingdom of God," *Die Botschaft des Judentums, Werke* (Vienna: Passagen, 1994), 3:91 ff.; "Seite an Seite mit dem Evangelium: Die Gottesknechtlieder," ibid., 3:141 ff., and, most important, "Das Jüdische Verhältnis zu Deutschland," ibid., 3:255 ff., which contains the first use of the phrase "the martyrdom of Jewish innocence"; H. L. Goldschmidt, "Juden vor dem Problem der Christenfrage: Jüdisch-Christliches Gegenüber seit 1945," in *Christen und Juden: Ihr Gegenüber vom Apostelkonzil bis Heute*, edited by Wolf-Dieter Marsch and Karl Thieme (Mainz, 1961).

2. Margarete Susman, *Das Buch Hiob und das Schicksal des jüdischen Volkes*, (Zurich: Steinberg, 2nd ed. 1948), 162; the Suhrkamp 1996 edition follows the first edition of 1946 and lacks the important preface dated May 1948 and responding to the foundation of the State of Israel. Suhrkamp, 129.

3. Ibid., Suhrkamp 132.

4. Ibid., Surhkamp, 131.

5. Karl Wolfskehl, *Zehn Jahre Exil. Briefe aus Neuseeland 1938–1948*, ed. Margot Ruben (Heidelberg/Darmstadt: Lambert Schneider, 1959), 52.

6. Ibid., 45.

7. Ibid., 179.

8. Ibid., 301. Two letters by Wolfskehl to Margarete Susman, which appeared for the first time only in 1972 in the journal *Castrum Peregrini*, prove conclusively that the "parallels" Wolfskehl emphasizes in 1946 between his own Job and Susman's can be traced back ten years earlier, to the Job interpretation he shared with his spiritual and intellectual "sister." Wolfskehl wrote from Recco, near Genoa, on July 12, 1936: "The Job book! With it you undertake

quite an imposing project. Splendid, splendid, splendid! And where is the essay it originated from? Don't send it to me . . . and I ask you as urgently as possible: write me again, and send me exactly what I asked for." And from New Zealand, on September 5, 1938, or 1939: "and as I discovered myself, I found the age-old and ever-present meaning of Job, my sister—you who explained Job to me for the first time." "Karl Wolfskehl und Margarete Susman: Briefe," *Castrum Peregrini* CII–CIII (Amsterdam 1972), 20–72, 57f and 62.

9. Karl Wolfskehl, "Der Vierte Spiegel: Hiob Maschiach," *Hiob oder die vier Spiegel* (Hamburg: Claassen Verlag, 1950), 21.

10. *Das Buch Hiob,* Suhrkamp, 136.

11. Wolfskehl, "Der vierte Spiegel," 26.

CHAPTER 26: CONTINUITY

1. Hermann Levin Goldschmidt, *Die Botschaft des Judentums, Werke* (Vienna: Passagen, 1994), 3:257.

2. Ibid., 3:260.

3. Harry Maor, *Über den Wiederaufbau der jüdischen Gemeinden in Deutschland seit 1945,* diss. (Mainz 1961).

CHAPTER 27: THE LEGACY OF GERMAN JEWRY

1. Hermann Levin Goldschmidt, *Die Botschaft des Judentums, Werke* (Vienna: Passagen, 1994), III:128–29.

2. H. L. Goldschmidt, "Juden vor dem Problem der Christen: Jüdisch-Christliches Gegenüber seit 1945," in *Christen und Juden: Ihr Gegenüber von Apostelkonzil bis heute,* ed. Wolf-Dieter Marsch and Karl Thieme (Mainz: Matthias-Grünewald-Verlag, 1961), 248. Compare with the more detailed discussion of German and Christian work in Judaic studies of the present.